Fundamentals of Investment

An Irish Perspective

Second Edition

GW00673629

Fundamentals of Investment

An Irish Perspective

Second Edition

**Brian O'Loughlin
and Frank O'Brien**

g GILL EDUCATION

Gill Education
Hume Avenue
Park West
Dublin 12
www.gilleducation.ie

Gill Education is an imprint of M.H. Gill & Co.

© 2011 Brian O'Loughlin and Frank O'Brien

978 0 7171 4978 0

Index compiled by Cover to Cover.
Print origination by Carrigboy Typesetting Services.
Printed and bound by CPI Group (UK) Ltd, Croydon, CR0 4YY.

*The paper used in this book is made from the wood pulp of managed forests.
For every tree felled, at least one is planted, thereby renewing natural resources.*

A catalogue record is available for this book from the British Library.

To Belinda and Geraldine for their encouragement and support

Support Material for
Fundamentals of Investment, An Irish Perspective
by Brian O'Loughlin and Frank O'Brien

Dynamic and easy-to-use online support material for this book is available on our website.

*Provides **lecturers** with*:
- PowerPoint slides
- Web links to financial sites and data
- Self-assessment problems
- Multiple choice questions.

To access lecturer support material on our secure site:
1) Go to *www.gilleducation.ie*
2) Log on using your username and password. If you don't have a password, register online and we will email your password to you.

*Provides **students** with*:
- Web links to financial sites and data
- Self-assessment problems
- Multiple choice questions.

To access student support material:
1) Go to *www.gilleducation.ie*
2) Search for *Fundamentals of Investment* and click on the link in the right-hand column.

Contents

Chapter one

Introduction

The financial services industry worldwide and in Ireland was booming when the first edition of this book was published in 2006. In the previous two decades the Irish financial sector had grown and evolved into an important part of the domestic economy. The success of the Irish Financial Services Centre (IFSC) added a strong international dimension to the industry.

In the intervening years the global financial system has gone from boom to bust at breathtaking speed. The Irish financial sector and the Irish economy were hit harder than most by the near collapse of the global financial system in 2008. It will be some years yet before the Irish financial system fully adjusts to the new realities. What is clear is that the domestic banking sector will become much smaller than it was at its peak. The international sector, based in the IFSC, held its own during the crisis and it can continue to increase in terms of employment and assets over the medium term.

REGULATORY CHANGES

The Financial Regulator was formally established on 1 May 2003 as the single regulator for virtually all financial services in Ireland, with the passing of the Central Bank and Financial Services Authority of Ireland Act 2003. Changes made in the aftermath of the 2008 financial crash have brought the Central Bank back to centre stage in the regulation of the Irish financial sector. The Central Bank Reform Act 2010, which commenced on 1 October 2010, created a new single unitary body – the Central Bank of Ireland – responsible for both central banking and financial regulation. This new structure replaced the previous related entities: the Central Bank and the Financial Services Authority of Ireland (Financial Regulator). Of even greater significance is the shift from a light touch regulatory regime to an intrusive and assertive regulatory regime.

IRISH FINANCIAL SERVICES INDUSTRY

Although the domestic banking sector will contract in the coming years, the Irish financial sector will continue to be a large employer. The statistics below show the scale of the industry at end-2009:

- The total assets of domestic credit institutions stood at €798,244.
- Employment in the banking sector alone stood at 37,178.
- Total assets under administration in Ireland amounted to €1,878bn (end-2010).
- The market capitalisation of the Irish Stock Exchange stood at approximately €48bn (end-2010).

(Sources: *Central Bank of Ireland; Irish Funds Industry Association.*)

The international financial sector is a significant contributor to the Irish economy, with employment being in the region of 24,000 at end-2010. In addition, there is significant employment in ancillary services such as legal, accounting, etc.

What has become clear through the turmoil of the financial crash and its aftermath is the vital role played by a modern economy's financial system. A malfunctioning or broken system can have devastating consequences for the real economy. In the early part of the 2000s we would have described the Irish banking system as malfunctioning. It fed and encouraged the creation of a property asset price bubble that resulted in a major dislocation of the Irish economy. In tandem with this price bubble was a huge build-up in private sector indebtedness to wholly unsustainable levels. The scale of the excess has only crystallised in the aftermath of the global financial crisis, and indeed it will be many years before the total cost of the debacle to the Irish economy is known.

Rebuilding and re-engineering a robust and vibrant banking sector that is fit for purpose is one of the most important challenges facing the Irish economy. Ensuring that all those working in the industry – from directors and senior managers to bank branch financial advisers – possess the requisite skills and knowledge is a vital aspect of this process.

Staff education and training is critical to the continued development of the Irish financial services industry. In most sectors of the industry employees must now attain relevant professional qualifications and industry qualifications from bodies such as the Institute of Bankers, the Life Industry Association, the Insurance Institute and others. This textbook has been written with the needs of this group to the forefront. The book will also benefit third-level students who are studying investments for the first time as it provides an

Irish perspective that usefully supplements the many excellent international introductory textbooks.

IMPACT OF THE FINANCIAL CRISIS ON INVESTMENT THEORY AND PRACTICE

It will be many years before the full impact of the seismic events of 2008 work their way through the world's financial markets and regulatory systems. Without timely and massive government and central bank intervention, the global system would have gone into meltdown, which would almost certainly have led to a global depression. This did not happen and the global economy and financial system recovered in 2009/10.

The fundamentals of investing have not changed, yet the financial crash has led to some awkward questions regarding aspects of investment theory and practice. For example, a core underpinning of passive fund management is that financial markets are by and large efficient. Trillions of euros of assets are managed on a passive basis throughout the world. Yet the financial crisis highlighted the inefficiency of many financial markets and showed that many financial securities were priced at levels that bore little relation to their true 'value' and risk level. Although some of the assumptions and conclusions of modern portfolio theory are being critically re-examined, the crisis has re-instilled interest in the tried and tested techniques of valuing securities based on their capacity to generate cash flows into the future.

If there is one lesson that the crisis has emphasised, it is that the fundamental value of an asset eventually manifests itself. Therefore, many of the concepts and techniques underlying the valuation of securities in the first edition of this book are being re-embraced by serious investors. The core principles underlying the theory and practice of investment management have not changed. Sensible diversification across asset categories and a clear understanding of the implications of financial leverage remain at the core of managing investment risk and return. Our view is that much of what went wrong over the past decade in financial markets was because too many participants across the financial system lost sight of these core principles of investment. Excessive use of leverage and the belief that financial engineering could somehow spirit away investment risk have been shown up for what they are: fool's gold.

ORGANISATION OF THE BOOK

This book introduces the basic building blocks of investment and reviews the operations of the industry from a variety of perspectives. These include the retail investor, the pension fund investor and also the professional fund manager. The approach adopted is to introduce investment concepts and issues in a discursive manner. As far as practicable examples and illustrations are presented in the Irish setting.

Chapter 2 focuses on the mainstream investment assets: fixed interest, equities, property and cash. The key characteristics of each asset are outlined and basic valuation concepts such as dividend yield, price earnings ratio and gross redemption yield are introduced. The methods by which securities markets are organised and securities are issued and sold to investors are set out. The distinction between primary markets and secondary markets is explained and the mechanism by which an initial public offering is brought to the market is described. This chapter concludes with an outline of how securities are issued and traded on the Irish Stock Exchange.

Chapter 3 builds on Chapter 2 to provide a fuller analysis of bonds, including the valuation of bonds and the calculation of the flat yield and the gross redemption yield or yield to maturity. This chapter will help the reader to develop an understanding of how to value a bond by applying the time value of money concept. The nature of the inverse relationship between changes in interest rates and bond prices is examined and the important concept of duration is explained. The term structure of interest rates and its various applications are discussed. A new section on bonds as an asset class outlines the issues involved in managing bond portfolios. Corporate bonds and emerging market bonds are defined and examined. Finally index-linked bonds are described and compared with conventional fixed-interest bonds.

In Chapter 4 we examine ways of analysing and assessing the investment merits of a company's shares. What is the fair price for a share and how can we calculate it? What are the key financial ratios relevant to an analysis of the investment prospects of a company? What yardsticks should be employed to compare one share with another? Are there ways to establish the investment value of an equity market? How can equity markets in different countries be compared with one another? This chapter shows how discounted cash-flow techniques can be used to estimate the fair price of a share. The chapter then goes on to describe the most commonly used relative valuation techniques such as the price earnings ratio and the dividend yield.

Chapter 5 is a catch-all chapter that brings together the key quantitative yardsticks and financial ratios commonly used by investment practitioners. A brief description is provided for each concept together with illustrative examples where appropriate. Readers will find it useful to refer to this chapter when they wish to clarify the meaning of financial and valuation ratios that crop up regularly in any discussion of investments.

Chapter 6 introduces the key concept of risk and starts by distinguishing between the investor, the gambler and the speculator. It examines the relationship between risk and return and sets out the different sources of investment return. It explores the subjective nature of risk and what risk means to different investors. The quantitative concept of risk as defined and measured by Markowitz is examined. The insights of the Markowitz approach are extended to the implications for portfolio construction.

Chapter 7 develops further the important concept of Markowitz diversification. This chapter shows how a concept such as the correlation coefficient can be used to construct portfolios. The concept of the efficient frontier is discussed and the impact on the efficient frontier of introducing a risk-free asset is explored. The separation theorem is also discussed. Markowitz portfolio theory is normative in the sense that it describes how investors should go about the task of selecting portfolios of risky securities. Capital market theory tries to explain how security prices would behave under idealised conditions. The most widely known model is the capital asset pricing model (CAPM). The CAPM is attractive as an equilibrium model because it can be applied to the job of portfolio construction relatively easily. It does have a number of weaknesses and alternative theories have been developed, the most important of which is arbitrage pricing theory.

Chapter 8 analyses derivative contracts, which now form an intrinsic part of the global financial fabric. Derivatives first emerged in a significant way in agricultural commodities markets in Chicago in the mid-nineteenth century. Although financial derivatives made their appearance quite early in the history of stock markets, they have really only come to prominence since the early 1980s. Today financial derivatives play a central role in all developed financial markets. This chapter focuses on describing basic futures and options contracts and analysing how they can be used either to manage risk or to speculate on the price movements of underlying securities.

Alternative assets are defined and their characteristics listed in Chapter 9. Interest in alternatives has grown exponentially over the past decade as investors have striven to find ways to deal with the volatility and risks associated with investing in stock markets. Private equity, hedge funds and commodities are three of the more important categories of alternative asset, and each of these is analysed in this chapter.

Chapter 10 discusses the alternative of indirect investing used by many investors. With indirect investing the investor pools his or her assets with those of others to create a single pool of money that is then managed by professional investment managers in accordance with a well-defined investment strategy. A key feature of indirect investing is that, while not directly responsible for the asset, the investor is exposed to the same market risk as if he or she did hold the asset directly, and also reaps whatever investment return the asset generates (less management fees and expenses). In Ireland the unit-linked funds offered by life assurance companies form the backbone of the industry. The emergence of mutual funds – called open-ended investment companies or OEICs – has occurred as a result of EU Investment Services Directives. Once an OEIC is regulated in one EU country it can be sold throughout the EU. The basics of how these collective investment schemes are priced is discussed in this chapter. The role of investment advice and ensuring that individual investors are sold investment funds appropriate to their particular circumstances is a key issue that is addressed.

Chapter 11 introduces pension schemes and the legal and regulatory framework within which they operate. The role and responsibilities of pension fund trustees are outlined, particularly with regard to the fund's investments. The particular risks attaching to pension fund investment are described and investment objectives outlined. The central role of the trustees in determining investment strategy is discussed.

Chapter 12 examines the fund management industry, its scope, recent development, role and organisational structure. The key elements of investment management firms are introduced – philosophy, process, people and performance – and investment styles and skill sets are explored. The industry's investment decision-making processes and risk-control frameworks are outlined.

In Chapter 13 the central importance of growth and inflation is identified in determining asset prices and in driving both the real economy and the financial markets. The relevance of the economic cycle in influencing the asset allocation decision is discussed. Periods of speculative excess are examined to isolate their common denominators and to identify the insight that there is a difference between price and value.

Chapter 14 deals with the measurement of investment returns. The calculation methodologies most commonly used are described and their suitability for comparing returns across managers is discussed. Risk-adjusted return methodologies are also covered. The attribution of performance over the various sources of return is briefly outlined. The Chartered Financial Analyst Institute's Global Investment Performance Standards for the calculation and presentation of investment returns are described. The chapter concludes by discussing investment style analysis and manager selection.

In Chapter 15 we present an analysis of long-term historical investment returns. The decade ending in 2010 is examined in detail as it stands out due to the very low returns earned by equity and property investors compared with the long-run norms. A model for evaluating prospective investment returns is developed and shows that prospective returns are likely to continue to be lower than those achieved in the 1980s and 1990s. The implications of this for pension funds in particular is explored. This chapter concludes with a summary of what we believe will be some of the key structural changes that are likely to become a feature of the financial services industry in Ireland over the next decade.

GUIDE TO USING THE BOOK

The book is organised to facilitate those students who are working full time in the industry and it is suitable for most financial industry qualifications where investments form part of the curriculum. For those studying for the Qualified Financial Adviser (QFA) exam, this book is a useful supplement to the various teaching manuals published by the professional bodies. Those studying for the QFA or a similar level qualification can be selective in their choice of chapters. The following chapters will cover what is required for many modules:

Chapter 1   Introduction
Chapter 2   Securities Markets and the Investment Assets
Chapter 5   Investment Arithmetic
Chapter 6   Investment, Investors and Risk
Chapter 10   The Retail Investor's Choices
Chapter 11   Pension Fund Investment
Chapter 12   Fund Management
Chapter 13   The Real Economy and the Markets
Chapter 15   Investment Returns: History and Prospects

Those studying for the Graduate Diploma in Financial Planning and other similar level qualifications should cover the entire book.

Learning objectives are outlined at the beginning of each chapter and there is a summary at the end of each chapter. Multiple choice questions, self-assessment tests and case study discussion topics are included in many chapters and provide readers with opportunities to check their comprehension as they work their way through the material. Above all, our objective is to provide readers with a good understanding of investments and at the same time to stimulate further their interest in the subject.

Chapter two

Securities Markets and the Investment Assets

In this chapter the focus is on the mainstream investment assets – fixed interest, equities, property and cash. The key characteristics of each asset are outlined and basic valuation concepts such as dividend yield, price earnings ratio (PER) and gross redemption yield are introduced. How securities markets are organised and the methods by which securities are issued and sold to investors are set out. The distinction between primary markets and secondary markets is explained and the mechanism by which an initial public offering is brought to the market is described. This chapter concludes with an outline of how securities are issued and traded on the Irish Stock Exchange.

Learning Objectives

After completing this chapter you should:
- Have an understanding of the mainstream investment assets and the key characteristics of each security type
- Be able to distinguish between the primary and secondary markets for securities and be aware of the key players involved in the markets
- Be knowledgeable about the structure of the Irish Stock Exchange and how the market is organised.

SECURITY TYPES

In this section the focus is on the mainstream investment assets – bonds, both fixed-interest securities and index-linked securities, equities, property and cash. The term 'bonds' is often used to refer to fixed-interest securities only, even though fixed-interest securities are just one type of bond. The characteristics of other types of bond are also described in this chapter.

However, we will follow the market convention and the discussion on bonds refers to fixed-interest securities, unless specifically stated otherwise.

Bonds (Fixed-Interest Securities)

Fixed-interest securities or bonds are loans raised by borrowers from investors at fixed rates of interest for fixed periods of time. The borrower may be a government, a government agency, a state or a corporation. The lender or investor may be an insurance company, a bank, a pension fund or a private individual.

Typically the borrower, or issuer of the bond, undertakes to pay the investors a fixed rate of interest each year for the fixed period (or fixed term) and to repay principal, i.e. the capital amount originally borrowed, when the loan becomes due (or matures) at the end of the period. Essentially bonds are loans with pre-specified terms and conditions; they have been used by borrowers and lenders for centuries and provide returns in the form of income and repayment at maturity. The early bonds were issued by governments, often for the purpose of funding wars or colonial escapades. The UK was a leader in this regard and by the nineteenth century there was an active market in British government securities.

Bonds issued by the UK Government are often referred to as Gilt Edged Securities or Gilts. The term 'gilt edged' has its origins in the gilt embossing on the certificates, which denoted ownership of the bonds. In time, however, it came to signify the high levels of quality and security attaching to bonds issued by the UK Government. Historically, the Irish bond market was closely linked to the British market, and in fact historically the Irish Stock Exchange was a constituent part of the London Stock Exchange. The Irish Stock Exchange is now an independent exchange that is governed by the Stock Exchange Act 1995. The fact that the Irish £ exchange rate was fixed at parity to sterling up to 1979 cemented this link even further. Now, as a founding participant in the euro, the Irish Government bond market effectively forms part of the Eurozone bond market.

Bonds are divisible and are typically denominated in nominal units of €100 for bonds issued by Eurozone borrowers. The fixed rate of interest refers to the rate payable annually per €100 nominal and normally on maturity bonds are repayable at par, i.e. at €100 per €100 nominal.

Listings of bonds appear frequently in the financial press and in lists prepared by investment houses and stockbrokers. A bond is identified by its fixed rate of interest (or coupon), its issuer and its redemption date. For example, an Irish Government bond (or stock) is described below:

Government Stock

4.5% Treasury 18.4.2020

The coupon on this bond is 4.5% and this means that the issuer, the Irish Government, will make an annual interest payment of €4.50 to the holder of each €100 nominal of the bond up to and including the maturity date. On the maturity date (18.4.2020) the issuer will pay the holder €100 per €100 nominal of the bond. It is useful to visualise these payments in the form of a 'timeline' as illustrated in Figure 2.1.

Figure 2.1 Timeline – 4.5% Treasury 2020

If we imagine that today is 18.04.2011, we can see that the cash flows that will be generated by this bond can be set out with certainty. Starting in April 2012 an interest payment of €4.50 will be made annually per €100 of stock. At the maturity or redemption date a final interest payment of €4.50 is made, plus €100 (the nominal value of the bond).

Bonds issued by governments are usually quoted on a stock exchange and therefore trade freely on the open market. Bond prices are quoted per €100 nominal. Between the issue of a bond and its final repayment (or redemption) its market price will fluctuate around €100 depending on the investment environment, most particularly interest rate levels, and the interaction of buyers and sellers. Therefore, it is more often the case that investors purchase bonds at a price that is different from their nominal or par value. Referring to our timeline, the par value of €100 establishes only the cash amount that will be repaid to the investor on the maturity date. Assume that for the bond identified in the previous paragraph we find that today this bond is priced at €95 per €100 nominal. It will therefore appear as follows in listings of bonds:

Government Stock	Price
4.50% Treasury 18.4.2020	95.00

From this information the returns available to an investor who is willing to hold the stock to redemption may be calculated. The investor receives two returns.

Annual Yield or Running Yield

This is the annual cash payment (investment income) of €4.50 for each €100 nominal of stock purchased. As the investor paid €95 for each

€100, he receives a cash income yield each year between now and 2020 of:

$$\frac{4.50 \times 100}{95} = 4.7\%$$

In addition, the investor must take into account the movement from the purchase price of €95 to the €100 at which the bond will finally be redeemed on 18.4.2020. Because the price of the bond is trading below the par value, this is a positive amount of €100 − €95 = + €5 over the period of some nine years.

Again it is useful to visualise what is going to happen in terms of the timeline depicted in Figure 2.2. The line AB shows that the bond price will gradually rise towards €100 and on the maturity date the price of the bond will be exactly €100.

Figure 2.2 Projected Capital Gain when Bond is Purchased below Par Value

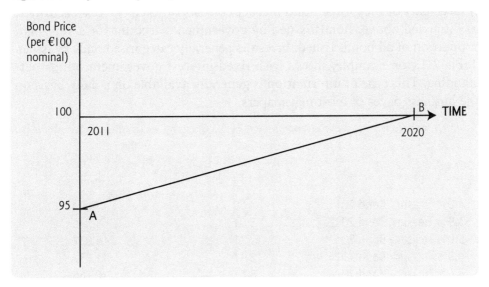

Gross Redemption Yield (GRY) or Yield to Maturity (YTM)

The Annual Yield discussed above does not take this amount into account. A second yield calculation – the Gross Redemption Yield (GRY) or Yield to Maturity (YTM) – takes into account both the annual income and the gain (or loss, if the bond price is below par) from the current price of €95 to the value on redemption of €100. In the case of the bond discussed above, because the current price of €95 is below (at a discount to) €100, the GRY will be higher than the Annual Yield.

Conversely, a bond which is priced above (at a premium to) its par value will have a GRY that is below its Annual Yield.

Incorporating this information on returns into our bond listing extends its identification as follows:

Government Stock	Price	Annual Yield	Gross Redemption Yield
4.50% Treasury 18.4.2020	95.00	4.7%	5.2%

Strictly speaking, the GRY is the interest rate at which the bond's price equals the discounted present value of all future payments (in our example €4.50 each year until 2020 and €100 on 18.4.2020).

Investment decisions in the fixed-interest sector – which stocks to buy or sell – are normally made on the basis of Gross Redemption Yield. The GRY is discussed in more detail in Chapter 3.

The Bond Market

A large part of the global bond market consists of fixed-interest securities, as discussed above. Bonds issued by governments account for a very high proportion of all bonds issued. Investors generally categorise bonds by issuer. Table 2.1, for example, shows Irish fixed-interest government bonds outstanding. This type of information is generally available on a daily basis on the business pages of most newspapers.

Table 2.1 Irish Government Euro-Denominated Bonds Outstanding Friday 26 November 2010

Bond	Gross Redemption Yield (%)	Amount Outstanding (€ million)
4.0% Treasury Bond 2011	4.59	4,604
3.9% Treasury Bond 2012	5.91	5,595
5.0% Treasury Bond 2013	7.31	6,037
4.0% Treasury Bond 2014	8.17	11,857
4.6% Treasury Bond 2016	8.57	10,168
4.5% Treasury Bond 2018	8.91	9,256
4.4% Treasury Bond 2019	9.02	7,700
5.9% Treasury Bond 2019	9.08	6,767
4.5% Treasury Bond 2020	9.07	11,852
5.0% Treasury Bond 2020	9.13	7,715
5.4% Treasury Bond 2025	9.11	8,284
8.75% Cap Stock 2012*	6.38	18
8.25% Treasury Bond 2015*	6.31	7

Note: Bonds marked * are currently designated as Non-Benchmark Bonds.
Source: Irish Stock Exchange.

The terms 'bond market' and 'fixed interest market' are used interchangeably, because most investors think of bonds as offering a fixed stream of income into the future. However, the term 'fixed interest' is not fully appropriate as there are many types of bond that offer something other than a fixed income stream. Other bond types include:

- Floating-rate bonds: Rather than being fixed, the coupon on the bond is variable and is usually determined with reference to money market interest rates. Usually, such bonds have a par value of 100 and have a fixed maturity date when they will be redeemed at par value.
- Zero-coupon bonds: These bonds have no coupon (pay no interest), but are sold at a deep discount to their par value (usually 100). They have a fixed maturity date.
- Index-linked bonds: Coupon payment and the final redemption payment are linked to the inflation rate. Each year the coupon paid increases by the relevant rate of inflation and the redemption value also increases in line with the rate of inflation.
- Convertible bonds: Coupon payments are fixed for a period of time, but on redemption the holder will have the right to convert into some other security.

Index-Linked Securities

The key risk that investors face from fixed-interest bonds is unexpected inflation. Annual interest payments and eventual repayment of capital on the redemption date are fixed and will not change, regardless of changes in the inflationary background. Inflation erodes the purchasing power of the annual interest payments and the final capital repayment, as investors in fixed interest discovered to their heavy cost in the high-inflation period of the 1970s and early 1980s.

In response to the need of investors for a degree of protection against inflation, and to facilitate continued funding of government borrowing, the UK authorities in 1981 issued index-linked securities. Over subsequent years a relatively small number of governments have followed suit – the US, Australia, Canada, France and Sweden. Because of the open-ended nature of the promise to compensate investors for inflation, index-linked securities are almost entirely the preserve of government or government-backed issuers.

The first-known inflation-indexed bond was issued by the Massachusetts Bay Company in 1780. The modern market is dominated by the UK, US and France. Approximately one-quarter of all UK outstanding government debt is accounted for by index-linked bonds. The largest market is the US market, where index-linked bonds are called Treasury Inflation-Protected Securities

(TIPS). The total global value of outstanding inflation-protected securities amounts to approximately $2 trillion.

Index-linked securities protect the investor against the impact of inflation by linking both interest payments and the eventual payment on redemption to an index of retail or consumer prices.

Therefore, when an investor buys an index-linked stock he receives a return that will rise with inflation, but that will be constant in real terms, i.e. in terms of purchasing power.

The conventions for denominating and describing fixed-interest securities apply also to index-linked securities:

Index-Linked Bonds	Price	Real Yield
UK 2.5% Index-Linked 2024	273.5	1.0%
US 3.625% Index-Linked 2028	129.5	1.7%

A UK investor, therefore, buying the UK Government 2.5% Index-Linked 2024 receives over the remaining life of the stock a real yield of 1.0%, i.e. in excess of inflation. If UK inflation in the period to 2024 is 3% p.a., his return in nominal (cash) terms will be 4.0% per annum; if inflation rises to 5% his return will be 6.0% p.a. nominal. The UK Government has undertaken to compensate the investor for whatever level of inflation occurs in the period to 2024. Real rates of return available on index-linked securities are important in their own right for bond selection within the index-linked sector, but also as a government-guaranteed benchmark for evaluating returns on the other investment assets.

Index-linked bonds have very different investment characteristics from those of conventional bonds (see Table 2.2), and should be considered as a separate asset class.

Table 2.2 Index-Linked versus Conventional Fixed-Interest Bonds

	Fixed-Interest Bonds	Index-Linked Bonds
Inflation Risk	Extremely high	Fully protected
Income	Nominal income flows known	Uncertainty regarding nominal flows
Price Volatility	Bond price fluctuation driven by change in nominal yield	Bond price fluctuation driven by change in real yield

Calculating the Real Rate of Interest

The real rate of interest (or return) is given by the expression:

$$R_r = (1 + R_n)/(1 + i) - 1$$

where: R_r = real rate of interest

R_n = nominal rate of interest

i = inflation rate.

Therefore, if inflation is 3% and the gross redemption yield on long-term, fixed-interest bonds is 5%, the real rate of interest is:

$$R_r = (1 + .05)/(1 + .03) - 1 = .0194, \text{ i.e. } 1.94\% \text{ p.a.}$$

Note that simply subtracting the rate of inflation from the nominal yield gives a close approximation.

Case Study: Eurozone Sovereign Debt Crisis

Bonds issued by governments are often referred to as sovereign issues. Bonds issued by countries such as the US, Germany, France and the UK are generally considered to be the safest (i.e. investors are highly confident that the issuer will meet all its obligations). Prior to the financial crisis that emerged in 2007/8, bonds issued by most developed-world governments were considered to be very safe. Hence the yield that, say, the Irish Government had to pay on its bonds was just a little higher, but very close to, the yield being paid by the German Government. In contrast, bonds issued by emerging countries were viewed as carrying a significant risk of default, and hence investors required a much higher yield before they would consider investing in such bonds.

On joining the euro, countries such as Ireland, Portugal and Greece initially enjoyed lower bond yields as investors began to assign a similar credit rating to all countries that adopted the euro. Hence all members of the Eurozone were able to fund their borrowing requirements at yields that were just a little higher than the yield on German bonds. For example, in 2008 the Irish ten-year bond was trading on a GRY of 4.6% compared with the German ten-year yield of 4.2%. The 'spread' between Irish and German Bunds was 40 basis points (0.4%). However, in August 2010 the Irish ten-year bond was trading at a GRY of 5.4%, compared with the German ten-year yield of 2.3% – a spread of 310 basis points (3.1%).

In early 2010 investors began to worry about those countries that were running very high fiscal deficits and that had been hit hardest by the credit crisis. Greece was perceived to be in a very weak position and yields on Greek bonds rose very sharply in the first half of 2010. Investors believed that there was a very high probability that

➡

the Greek Government would default on its obligations. The spread on Greek bonds went out to the unprecedented level of 860 basis points (8.6%). A joint IMF/Eurozone bail-out for Greece was put in place. By late 2010 similar concerns were developing over Irish, Portuguese and Spanish bonds. As the perceived weakest link, Ireland was forced to seek a bail-out and an €85 billion package was agreed in November 2010. Investors, governments and monetary authorities were expecting further difficulties to emerge during 2011 and beyond.

Yields on Benchmark Government Bonds			
	August 2008	August 2010	November 2010
Germany	4.2%	2.3%	2.7%
Ireland	4.6%	5.4%	9.4%
Portugal	4.7%	5.3%	7.2%
Spain	4.5%	4.1%	5.2%
Greece	4.9%	10.9%	11.9%

Corporate Bonds

Just like governments, corporations issue debt securities to fund their long-term financial requirements and these are generally referred to as corporate bonds. They are a major source of capital for many businesses, along with equity and bank loans/lines of credit. Usually companies that issue corporate bonds are relatively large and have a high public profile and/or their shares are listed on recognised stock exchanges.

The US has the largest and most varied corporate bond market, although the advent of the euro has meant that the euro corporate bond market is now also very large. Fixed-interest corporate bonds have identical features to fixed-interest government bonds: they are issued with a par value and a fixed coupon that is calculated on this par value; they usually have a fixed maturity date when the investor receives the par value. In the US, corporate bonds are issued with a par value of $1,000, and almost all have a standard coupon payment structure.

Corporate bonds offer a higher yield compared with most government bonds as investors are exposed to the risk that the corporate issuer will default on its debt obligations. Many investors in corporate bonds rely on the credit ratings agencies to assess the risk of issuers of corporate bonds. These ratings agencies also assign credit ratings to bonds issued by governments.

Assessing Credit Risk – The Credit Ratings Agencies

Credit ratings published by Moody's, Standard & Poor's and Fitch IBCA are meant to capture and categorise credit risk. However, many institutional investors in corporate bonds supplement these agency ratings with their own credit analysis. The financial crisis brought heavy criticism of the ratings agencies for not properly assessing the credit risks of many securities.

The categories used by the major ratings agencies are shown in Table 2.3. Taking the Standard & Poor's (S&P) categorisations, the highest quality issuers are assigned the AAA rating. Very few issuers are assigned this high rating. Only bonds issued by the strongest countries such as the US, Germany, France and Japan enjoy the highest rating. Since the advent of the financial crisis many countries, including Ireland, have been downgraded by these agencies.

Table 2.3 Credit Ratings

Description	Moody's	Standard & Poor's	Fitch Ratings
High quality – 'investment grade'			
Fundamentally strong issues with minimal risk of default; commonly referred to as 'gilt-edged'	Aaa	AAA	AAA
High-quality issues, which differ only slightly from the highest rated issues due to some factor causing perceived long-term risk	Aa1￼ Aa2￼ Aa3	AA+￼ AA￼ AA-	AA+￼ AA￼ AA-
Good ability to meet repayment obligation, but more likely to be affected by changes in economic climate than higher rated issues	A1￼ A2￼ A3	A+￼ A￼ A-	A+￼ A￼ A-
Medium-grade issues with reasonable protection, as conditions remain stable over the long term	Baa1￼ Baa2￼ Baa3	BBB+￼ BBB￼ BBB-	BBB+￼ BBB￼ BBB-
Lower quality – below 'investment grade'			
Possess speculative as well as investment characteristics, with ongoing uncertainties relating to the financial environment, and only fair protection	Ba1￼ Ba2￼ Ba3	BB+￼ BB￼ BB-	BB+￼ BB￼ BB-
Issuer could currently meet obligations, but protection of principal and interest over the long term is small, and changes in circumstances may lead to default	B1￼ B2￼ ￼ B3	B+￼ B￼ ￼ B-	B+￼ B￼ ￼ B-

Investment Grade and Non-Investment Grade

A crucial cut-off point in terms of credit rating is whether an issuer is considered to be 'investment grade' or 'non-investment grade'. On the S&P system, BBB is the lowest rung of investment grade. If an issuer's bonds fall below investment grade, then the yield tends to rise quite sharply as many institutional investors have policies that forbid investing in below investment grade issues.

Equities

An equity investment is an investment in the ordinary shares (or share capital) of a limited company. The equity investor is a part-owner of the company and this part-ownership is represented by a share certificate which sets out the number of shares owned. The proportion of the company owned by the investor is determined by the relationship between the number of shares owned, as defined by the share certificate, and the total number of shares in existence (in issue). This is illustrated in the table below:

Company	Total No of Shares in Issue	No of Shares Owned by Investor A	% of Company Owned by A
Company X	1,000	10	1%
Company Y	1,000	1,000	100%
Company Z	1,000,000	50,000	5%

Note: In most markets paper share certificates have been 'dematerialised', with title to shares held on a custody platform.

Where the investor invests in the securities discussed earlier, fixed-interest and index-linked, he has a contractual relationship with the issuer to receive the interest payments and final redemption payment as set out in the terms of issue. He is entitled only to these returns; there is no entitlement to any further participation.

The position of the equity investor is dramatically different. His share certificate identifies his co-ownership of the company: of its lands, buildings, plant and machinery; its stocks, work in progress and finished goods; its products, market shares and brand names; its client lists and customer goodwill; the strategic expertise of its management team and the operational skills of its workforce.

Within the legal framework of the company these assets and attributes combine to generate a stream of profits into the future. The equity investor, as co-owner, participates pro rata to his shareholding in this stream of future profits or earnings.

On the one hand, where the company is successful and enjoys powerful growth in profits, the equity investor may enjoy very large returns. After the company has paid its workforce, its various suppliers, its bank for any interest charges arising and its taxes, all the remaining surplus, no matter how large, belongs (is attributable) to the ordinary shareholders.

On the other hand, if the company is unsuccessful and plunges into bankruptcy, all those with a legitimate claim on its assets must be satisfied before any repayment is due to shareholders. Typically, when a company fails there is little or nothing left for shareholders. Shareholders, of course, enjoy the benefit of limited liability; they have the rather small comfort of knowing that they cannot lose more than 100% of their investment!

The equity investor typically may expect to receive two types of return from an investment in a company:

i)   An income return, based on the annual dividend (or distribution to shareholders) paid out of profits earned each year.
ii)   A capital return, based on the increase in the share price as it rises to reflect a rising stream of profits into the future.

The income return – the dividend – is relatively stable and typically will rise, reflecting higher dividends as profits increase. However, in periods of difficult trading dividend payments may be reduced (or cut) or suspended altogether.

The capital return is uncertain and volatile, especially in the short term. It is subject to fluctuations in the company's own profitability and to external fluctuations in interest rates and in the stock market. In the long run the generality of share prices may be expected to rise, since they reflect higher profits as the economy grows. At any particular point in time, however, the share price in the stock market is determined by the interaction of buyers and sellers, i.e. it is subject to the laws of supply and demand.

Calculating Earnings Per Share (EPS) and Dividends Per Share (DPS)

Shareholders and investment analysts normally assess the investment merits of a company with reference to a variety of valuation metrics that are usually calculated on a per-share basis. The two most commonly used ratios are earnings per share (EPS) and dividends per share (DPS). The numerical example here illustrates how these important ratios are calculated:

➡

ABC plc

Excerpts from ABC's Profit & Loss Account (€ millions)
Profit After Tax   €120 m
Dividends Paid   €40 m
Retained Earnings   €80 m

Current Share Information:
Number of Shares in Issue 1,000 million
Share Price   €2 per share
Market Capitalisation = shares in issue x share price

$$1,000 \text{ million} \times €2 = €2,000 \text{ m}$$

Earnings Per Share = Profit After Tax/No. of shares in issue

$$€120 \text{ m} / 1,000 \text{ m} = 12.0 \text{ cent}$$

Dividends Per Share = Dividends Paid/No. of shares in issue

$$€40 \text{ m} / 1,000 \text{ m} = 4.0 \text{ cent}$$

The income return – which is based on a tangible, cash dividend – is measurable and is normally expressed as a dividend yield, calculated as follows:

$$\frac{\text{Dividend per share (cents)} \times 100}{\text{Share price (cents)}}$$

Therefore, for ABC plc with its share price standing at 200c, and assuming it has just paid an annual dividend of 4c per share:

$$\text{Dividend Yield} \quad \frac{4c \times 100}{200c} = 2\%$$

Normally the shareholders will expect the dividend to rise over time as, hopefully, the profits of the company increase. The capital return is uncertain and therefore cannot be quantified in advance.

The Price Earnings Ratio (PER)

The most commonly used convention for measuring and comparing company valuations is the Price Earnings Ratio or PER.

A company may be expected to generate a stream of profits into the future. The shareholder is a part-owner of that stream of profits.

➡

Earnings per share is a measure of the amount of profit after tax earned in a financial year, which is attributable to each share issued by the company.

The PER is a profit-based measure of the company's perceived worth, relating share price to earnings per share.

With ABC plc's share price at 200c and earnings per share (EPS) of 12c in its most recent financial year:

Price Earnings Ratio:

$$\frac{200c}{12c}$$

$$= 16.7 \text{ times}$$

The higher the PER, the greater the expectation for future growth in earnings.

See Chapter 4 for a full analysis of the yardsticks employed to value equities.

Property

A property investment is an investment in bricks and mortar. Property investment may embrace both residential and commercial properties. In Ireland, on the one hand the private investor is heavily involved in the residential property market (houses, apartments, holiday homes). On the other hand, institutional involvement by pension funds and life companies in residential property is relatively low, both in Ireland and the UK. This is in contrast to the US and Continental Europe, where institutional investors are significant players in the residential property market. Commercial property investments typically include offices, retail shops and industrial buildings (factories, warehouses). Development opportunities include factory outlets (out-of-town retail shopping malls) and leisure centres. Property, especially commercial property, is a 'big ticket' activity. Involvement in the direct property market, i.e. where the investor owns the building, requires large resources – potentially very large. For this reason the market in commercial property is dominated by institutional investors and very high net worth individuals and families.

A variety of investment vehicles have been developed to enable smaller investors to indirectly access commercial property investment, including Real Estate Investment Trusts (REITs); property unit trusts, e.g. IPUT in Ireland; and property unit-linked funds promoted by the life assurance industry.

In Ireland unit-linked property funds sold by life assurance companies are a popular vehicle for property investment. Overseas, REITs have become popular. A REIT is in fact a company structure that has particular tax advantages to enable it to distribute most of its income without paying tax.

The income distributed to a shareholder only becomes taxable in the hands of the shareholder.

Like equities, property returns are not guaranteed. The returns enjoyed by the property investor depend on the success of the building in attracting tenants who, over time, will be willing to pay rising rents. Location is the critical factor in determining the long-term success of a property investment.

A particularly attractive feature of the Irish and UK office property markets from an investment perspective is the convention of the long leases incorporating upward-only rent reviews, normally after 5–7 years. This provides high visibility of rental returns. However, the law is being changed and it is likely that leases with upward-only rent reviews will become a thing of the past.

A key investment attraction of property is that it offers the prospects for a relatively high income that grows over time.

This income return is measured by the Rental Yield as follows:

$$\frac{\text{Current Rent Receivable}}{\text{Property Value}} \times 100\%$$

Assume that Investor A, owner of an office building valued at €10m, let the building three years ago at a rental of €0.5m per annum.

Rental Yield: $\dfrac{€0.5 \text{ m}}{€10.0 \text{ m}} \times 100 = 5\%$

A second yield calculation, with applications in property valuation and in comparing different properties, is the Equivalent Yield. The Equivalent Yield allows for an uplift in the existing rent to current rental values.

Assume in the example above that the building could currently be let at €0.75m per annum, compared to the €0.5m agreed three years ago.

Equivalent Yield: $\dfrac{€0.75 \text{ m}}{€10.0 \text{ m}} \times 100 = 7.5\%$

Investors in property may also benefit from capital appreciation, as capital values rise to reflect rising rents. Just like equities, such capital appreciation is uncertain and will depend on how well a particular property performs in terms of rental income growth. Capital appreciation will also be a function of overall trends in the economy; in particular, movements in interest rates and bond yields exert a large influence.

Of course, like equities, property involves substantial risks. If rents fall and the economy weakens, property values will fall and investors will experience reduced capital values.

Cash or Bank Deposits

Cash is normally regarded as a short-term investment and not usually as a suitable investment vehicle for long-term investors. In fact, cash plays three roles in investors' strategies.

i)   It may be held to meet short-term obligations or liabilities, e.g. to meet payments to current pensioners.
ii)   It may be a temporary home for funds as the investor awaits more attractive opportunities than those currently available.
iii) It may be an investment vehicle in its own right and held for longer periods if the investment environment is adverse. Holding cash will cushion the investor from the impact of falling values in the other investment assets and, importantly, will provide the wherewithal to buy the other assets when they have fallen into low ground. In other words, cash can play an important role as a diversifier of investment risk.

Cash returns, i.e. interest on deposits – no matter how low – always look attractive if the other assets are generating negative returns.

A critical consideration for the investor is to determine the appropriate term (or duration) of the deposit. Cash may be placed on deposit from periods ranging from one day (or overnight) out to one year, or even longer in the case of more sophisticated money-market instruments. Key considerations in determining the deposit term include:

• the investor's view of the outlook for interest rates;
• the investor's requirement to access the deposit to take advantage of market opportunities as they emerge;
• the availability of other sources of finance, including cash flows.

Perhaps even more critical is the creditworthiness of the deposit-taking institution. The marginal improvement in deposit rates that might be achievable by moving a deposit from a strong bank to a weaker bank will rarely compensate the investor for the loss of the deposit if the weaker bank should fail.

Uniquely among the investment assets, cash generates only one stream of return. The nominal value of the deposit is always fixed in absolute terms. An investor who puts €100 on deposit will always receive €100 on maturity of the deposit. Capital value is fixed; there is no capital return, positive or negative.

The investor receives an income return only. The interest rate will be fixed for the duration of the deposit, and if the deposit is renewed or rolled over the interest rate for the succeeding period will be set at the levels then prevailing.

Cash therefore provides certainty of income return only for relatively short periods. Because of fluctuations in interest rates there is no certainty of long-term income return, either in absolute (nominal) or real (after inflation) terms.

Cash or Money Market Instruments

Deposit or savings accounts held at banks, building societies and credit unions, and savings bonds and certificates issued by the Post Office, may be classified as non-marketable financial assets. Marketable money market instruments fall into a number of broad categories:

- Treasury Bills (US); Exchequer Bills (Ireland): This is the premier money market instrument, a fully guaranteed, very liquid IOU from the issuing government. Treasury bills are sold every week by auction at a discount to face value. Therefore, the discount determines the yield. Effectively, they are a zero-coupon bond with a short maturity, usually three, six or nine months. Outstanding (already issued) bills can be purchased and sold in the secondary market, which is an extremely efficient market where dealers in government securities stand ready to buy and sell these securities.
- Commercial Paper: A short-term, unsecured promissory note issued by large, well-known and financially strong corporations. Commercial paper is usually sold at a discount. Although issues can trade on a secondary market, most issues are held by the buyer to maturity.

Interbank Market

This is the marketplace where banks come together to borrow or lend from one another. As well as borrowing and lending amongst themselves banks can also lend money to and borrow money from the relevant central bank. While there is no physical location where transactions occur, properly functioning interbank markets are vital for the efficient functioning of financial systems.

Investment Assets and Alternative Investments

Our discussion has concentrated on the traditional investment assets of bonds, equities, property and cash. The vast bulk of funds invested resides within these asset categories either directly, or indirectly through financial products.

There is much debate about so-called alternative investment categories such as commodities and hedge funds. It is arguable whether these are alternative asset classes, or are merely different forms of trading strategies. These are reviewed in detail in Chapter 9. In this introductory chapter we confine ourselves to the traditional asset classes, and the table below sets out the key characteristics of each major asset class.

Asset	Type of Return	Advantages	Disadvantages
Cash	Interest income only	Capital is secure	Rate of return lower than other assets
Bonds (Fixed Interest)	Income return is known in advance; prospect of capital appreciation if bond is traded	Bonds issued by the large developed-world governments considered to be risk free (credit risk); cash flows are definite	Returns are not protected against inflation; long-term returns are likely to be lower than property or equities
Bonds (Index-linked)	Income return starts low but rises in line with inflation; principal amount at maturity rises in line with cumulative inflation over the life of the bond	Provides automatic protection against inflation by raising the coupon payments and the principal sum to be paid at maturity in line with the relevant inflation index	Likely to under-perform in a low-inflation environment
Property	Income in the form of rents which can be expected to grow over time; prospects for capital appreciation	Total returns will reflect the performance of the relevant local economy	Transaction costs are very high and property investments are generally very illiquid
Equities	Income in the form of dividends which can be expected to grow over time; prospects for capital appreciation	Total returns will reflect the performance of individual companies	Asset class that experiences the highest volatility of returns

HOW SECURITIES ARE ISSUED

Companies issue and sell securities to investors in order to finance their operations, as well as to expand their businesses. Usually companies issue equity and long-term corporate bonds to fund their long-term capital needs. Governments issue bonds to fund borrowing needs that may include a deficit on day-to-day spending and spending on capital projects such as building a new roads infrastructure.

A market where a company or a government issues new securities for cash is referred to as a primary market. New sales of Irish government bonds, sales of new shares by, for example, CRH all occur on the primary markets. The issuers of these securities – the Irish government, CRH – receive cash from buyers of the new securities, who in turn receive new financial claims on the issuers. Where the issuer is selling securities for the first time, the issue is referred to as an initial public offering (IPO). One of the most high-profile and controversial IPOs on the Irish market was the sale of Eircom shares by the Irish Government in 1999. At the time equity markets had been rising for several years and telecom stocks had become the darlings of the market. The owner of Telecom Éireann (name later changed to Eircom) was the Irish government, which saw the flotation of Eircom as the first step in a process of bringing share ownership to a wide range of ordinary individuals. The government embarked on a major publicity campaign to market the shares to the ordinary public, most of whom had never invested directly in the stock market before. The process of setting the sale price and deciding on the marketing campaign was highly complicated.

The subsequent collapse in the share prices of technology and telecom companies in 2001/2 resulted in capital losses for most Eircom investors. Lessons were learnt when it came to the Aer Lingus IPO, which came to the market in 2006 with much less hype.

The key players in the sale of new securities, either an IPO or the sale of new securities by an already-listed company, are:

i)   The issuer.
ii)   The originating investment bank.
iii) The underwriting syndicate – usually the originating investment banker will put together a syndicate of banks that will agree to underwrite the issue. This ensures that if investors back off from purchasing the new securities at the last minute, the syndicate will buy the securities from the issuer at a pre-agreed issue price.
iv)   The selling group of investment bankers and stockbrokers – this will usually comprise the underwriting syndicate (or the stockbroking arms of the syndicate members), possibly plus selected domestic and overseas brokerage houses.
v)   Investors – these will include pension funds, insurance funds and unit trusts, as well as private investors.

Investment bankers act as intermediaries between issuers and investors. The issuer sells its securities to investment bankers, who in turn sell the securities to investors. As well as acting as an intermediary, the investment banker is normally the key adviser to the company throughout the entire planning process that precedes a new issue. This advice covers topics such as the type of securities to be sold, the likely appetite amongst investing institutions for each different type of security, the price and the timing of the sale.

Underwriting New Issues: Often investment bankers will underwrite the newly issued securities. In other words they commit to purchasing the new securities at the placement price irrespective of market conditions. This is a very valuable service from the point of view of the issuers – it gives them certainty that they will receive cash for the newly issued securities. There is, of course, a price in high underwriting fees and/or a spread for the investment bank through purchasing the shares at a discount to the placement price. The lead investment bank will typically form a syndicate of investment banks to spread the risk. In turn these investment banks may further sub-underwrite the risks with the potential end-buyers of the securities – pension funds and investment funds. Although the investment bank or syndicate of banks buys the new securities from the issuer, their intention is to sell on the securities immediately to investors. In successful new issues the investment bankers quickly place the new shares with long-term institutional investors and retail investors.

After the IPO

Once securities are listed on a stock exchange, further issues can be made through a variety of routes. Any new securities issued will be exactly the same as the existing securities in terms of par value, rights to dividends, voting rights, etc. Companies whose shares are listed on an exchange can issue and sell new shares to existing and new shareholders through either a Placing or a Rights Issue.

In a Placing, new shares are issued by a company and sold to investors, who may already be existing shareholders but would normally include new investors. The sale of the shares will normally be organised by an investment bank (or a syndicate of banks for a large issue) appointed by the company. Usually the price of new shares will be pitched at a level that is close to the most recently traded price of the existing shares.

In a Rights Issue, new shares are offered only to existing shareholders. Usually the price of the new shares will be pitched at a significant discount to the most recently traded price of the existing shares. Companies will usually take the rights issue route when the amount of new capital being raised is large relative to its current market capitalisation. Rights issues are normally underwritten (for an underwriting fee) by the company's stockbroker or investment bank. From the company's perspective this guarantees that it will raise the targeted new capital.

From the perspective of the current shareholders in a company, a rights issue is attractive in that they have the option to retain their existing percentage stake in the company. An example illustrating the mechanics of a rights issue shows why this is so.

Rights Issue

A company has 1m shares in issue with a current market price of 40c. It has just announced a rights issue of 1 new share for every 3 shares held at a price of 30c per new share. The rights offer will be open for 21 days and during that period share-holders will be able to trade the nil-paid rights as well as the existing shares. Prior to the announcement of the rights issue a shareholder with 3 shares had an investment valued at:

$$3 \times 40c \text{ (original market value)} = €1.20$$

If this shareholder takes up his rights on the closing date of the offer, he will then have the following:

$$
\begin{array}{ll}
3 \text{ shares @ 40c} & = €1.20 \\
1 \text{ new share (cost 30c)} & = €0.30 \\
\hline
4 \text{ shares valued at} & \quad €1.50
\end{array}
$$

Therefore: each share is valued at €1.50/4 = €0.375

Each share now has a theoretical value of 37.5c and this is known as the theoretical x-rights price.

During the offer period a shareholder can trade in the rights or what is known as the nil-paid shares, which will have a theoretical value of:

$$
\begin{array}{llll}
\text{Ex-Rights price} & - & \text{Subscription price} & = \text{Nil-Paid price} \\
37.5c & - & 30c & = 7.5c
\end{array}
$$

A shareholder who does not wish to take up his rights can sell the nil-paid shares in the market. In this way shareholders who choose not to take up the rights offer are not disadvantaged compared with those shareholders who subscribe for the new shares.

A shareholder who decides to subscribe for the new shares will of course increase his monetary stake in the company. However, his percentage stake will remain exactly the same pre and post the rights issue. This is because the mechanism of a rights issue ensures that a subscribing shareholder with (say) 1% of the company will take up 1% of the new issue. Shareholders who do not subscribe will see their percentage stake in the company decline, i.e. they will suffer some dilution. This does not involve any loss in value, since the shareholder has not invested any further funds in the company. Furthermore, the nil-paid shares can be sold in the market so that non-subscribing shareholders do not suffer any loss if the new shares are priced at a discount to the 'old' shares. In some cases non-subscribing shareholders may use the proceeds of the sale of their nil-paid rights to subscribe for a fraction of their rights entitlement.

From the perspective of shareholders, and particularly small shareholders, the rights issue mechanism of selling additional shares is attractive and equitable. There are, however, some drawbacks from the company's perspective, namely:

- There is usually a significant time gap between the announcement of a rights issue and the subscription date. Shareholders must be provided with full and detailed information regarding the issue to ensure that they are fully informed about the prospects for the business. All relevant available information concerning the business must be made available to shareholders so that they can make an informed investment decision. During the offer period the market in the company's shares will be subject to normal market volatility. Clearly, adverse market developments outside anyone's control could severely jeopardise the eventual success of the issue. Because of this risk most companies will pay investment banks an underwriting fee to underwrite the issue if shareholders shun the issue for whatever reason. This clearly adds to the cost of selling new shares.
- Because of the onerous rules regarding a rights issue and the time involved, companies generally use this capital-raising mechanism sparingly. Therefore, rights issues will normally be resorted to only for major corporate events, such as a take-over, a major expansion or a major capital reconstruction.
- In times of distress, rights issues may be the only way for publicly traded companies to raise capital. They can do this by issuing new shares at a very large discount. This acts as an effective inducement to the existing shareholders to subscribe, since they would suffer substantial dilution in their percentage shareholding if they did not subscribe.

While a rights issue has some disadvantages in terms of cost and management time, it is the favoured mechanism in Europe for raising substantial additional capital. Where the number of new shares being sold is less than 10% of the outstanding issued share capital a company has the option of using a Placing to sell the new shares. Stock exchanges usually have rules regarding such placings to ensure that existing shareholders are equitably treated. In Ireland the price of the new shares must be at a discount of no more than 5% to the most recently traded price and the amount of shares issued cannot exceed 10% of the issued share capital. Placings have the advantage of much more rapid execution than a rights issue and the associated transactions costs are significantly lower.

From the perspective of company treasurers the availability of the rights issue alternative is a critical benefit of having a stock market listing. In a scenario where a company is going through a very difficult time, most sources of long-term finance tend to dry up. Banks are reluctant to extend finance to weak companies and bond investors are likely to shun issues of corporate bonds from distressed companies. Also, in times of overall market weakness even strong companies can find it difficult to raise finance at an acceptable cost. In such circumstances a company that requires long-term finance has the option of bringing a rights issue to the market. The price at which the shares are pitched may be low, implying a high cost of equity to the company. However, if the company requires extra finance for survival this is the price that it must pay. The key point is that for quoted companies access to the capital market virtually never dries up. This became very apparent in the aftermath of the financial crisis when many companies, in particular banks, raised vital new capital through the rights issue route.

STOCK EXCHANGES

A stock exchange will normally prescribe criteria for listing in terms of the history of the company, its profits and capital, the integrity of management, and other factors relevant to potential investors in the business. The Irish Stock Exchange (www.ise.ie) was originally part of the London Stock Exchange, but it is now an independent exchange. The Markets in Financial Instruments Directive (MiFID), implemented in November 2007, is the relevant legislation governing the Irish Stock Exchange (ISE) and its markets.

The Irish Stock Exchange Limited ('the company') is an Irish private company limited by guarantee. This legal structure was adopted in 1995 by the then founding member firms of the ISE, who formed the guarantors of the company.

Listing of Securities

The ISE is the designated competent authority for the listing of securities in Ireland. Any company that wishes to be admitted to the Official List is expected to comply with the basic conditions set out in the 'Listing Rules'. Some of the key provisions are set out below:

- The company must be validly organised under the laws of its country and must be operating in conformity with its articles of association.
- The securities must be freely transferable and at least 25% of any class of shares must be in the hands of the public. A percentage lower than 25%

may be acceptable to the ISE if the market will operate properly with a lower percentage.

- All fundraising exercises require a full prospectus to be prepared.

Continuing Obligations of Listed Companies

All applicants to the Official List automatically agree to comply with the conditions set out in the 'Continuing Obligations'. Some of the key requirements are set out below:

- A company must notify the ISE of any price-sensitive information.
- Directors' dealings must be announced and restricted to specified time periods.
- Explanatory circulars must be sent to shareholders regarding major acquisitions or disposals of assets.
- The company must have permission from shareholders to repurchase its own shares.
- A company must issue a half-yearly report within four months of the period end and a preliminary statement of annual results within four months of its year-end. Annual accounts must be produced within six months of the company's financial year-end.
- Issues of equity securities must be offered to existing shareholders in proportion to their shareholding (i.e. by way of a rights issue). This protection is meant to avoid the shareholders' interests being diluted. However, shareholders can vote to disapply these pre-emption rights and most listed companies have such shareholder approval. Normally, such approvals are capped at a predetermined percentage of a company's issued share capital, usually 10%.

The objective of these various listing requirements and continuing obligations is to ensure that a fair and orderly market is maintained in the company's listed securities at all times.

Dealing on the Irish Stock Exchange

The ISE operates one regulated market as defined by MiFID: the Main Securities Market (MSM), which is the market that most people are familiar with. The MSM is the principal market for Irish and overseas companies. It admits a wide range of security types such as shares, bonds and funds to listing and trading.

The ISE also operates the Enterprise Securities Market (ESM) and the Global Exchange Market (GEM), which are exchange-regulated markets and multilateral trading facilities (MTFs) as defined under MiFID Regulations.

The ESM is an equity market designed for growth companies. The GEM is a specialist debt market for professional investors.

Securities admitted to trading on the MSM and GEM are considered to be admitted to the Official List of the ISE.

The ISE operates a different dealing system for Irish government bonds and for equity and other quoted securities.

Irish Government Bonds

The Irish government bond market revolves around the primary dealers who are recognised by the National Treasury Management Agency (NTMA) and who apply for registration by the ISE as a primary dealer for Irish government bonds. The primary dealers are responsible for quoting continuous two-way prices in Irish government bonds. Primary dealers therefore commit their own capital as they act as principals when dealing in Irish bonds. As a recognised primary dealer a firm takes on certain obligations, which include quoting firm, two-way prices in those bonds specifically notified by NTMA, subject to minimum sizes and maximum bid–offer spreads. The existence of a continuous market in Irish government bonds enables stockbrokers to efficiently execute client orders in government bonds.

Primary dealers are granted certain privileges in return for making bid and offer prices. These include:

- Exclusive access to funding by NTMA through auctions of bonds.
- Access to NTMA for the purposes of borrowing and lending stock.

Irish Equity Market

Unlike the Irish government bond market, there are no primary dealers in Irish equities. Rather, the market in listed company shares is 'created' by the buy and sell orders that are generated by investors in Irish shares. The equity market may be characterised as an 'order-driven market'. In June 2000 the ISE moved to an electronic order-driven system called ISE Xetra. This system is the product of a strategic alliance between the ISE and the Deutsche Börse in Germany. The Xetra trading system is accessible by all member firms of the ISE through an IT package that provides their dealing rooms with direct access to the central trading system. Investors still give their buy and sell orders to stockbrokers, who then enter orders into the electronic system. Deals then occur when the system matches buy and sell orders. Use of the order book is governed by procedures, rules and market parameters. Each order must be:

- Firm.
- At the minimum size lot, or multiples of the lot size.

- For standard settlement.
- At a price that is an exact multiple of the tick size specified by the ISE.

The key advantage of this system is that it is cost-effective, as the cost of supporting primary dealers or market makers is avoided. A disadvantage is that there may be periods when it is difficult to trade in some shares, when there may be a very small number of active orders in the system.

The system does, however, offer the facility for market making to be conducted in one or more securities. Suitability criteria are laid down by the ISE and the market maker must at all times satisfy the ISE that it:

- Is appropriately authorised to deal on its own account.
- Has adequate systems and control procedures in place.
- Has suitably competent and experienced staff.

Settlement

Trades on markets run by the ISE use the following settlement platforms:

i) CREST for the settlement of equity and exchange-traded fund securities on the MSM and the ESM.
ii) Clearstream Bank Luxembourg, Euroclear Bank and Depository Trust Company (DTC) for the settlement of GEM securities.

SUMMARY

- Investment alternatives available to investors include fixed-interest securities (bonds), index-linked securities, equities, property, and cash or bank deposits.
- Equities and bonds are generally highly marketable and are easily traded on recognised stock exchanges.
- Deposits are non-negotiable, but are usually accessible at short notice and are therefore highly liquid.
- Property investments are marketable, but because of the large value per unit and high transactions costs property is a highly illiquid investment.
- Equity and property investments provide investors with returns that are closely linked to the performance of the overall economy and are therefore referred to as real assets. Cash and fixed-interest securities provide no such link to economic growth and may be referred to as nominal assets.
- The key risk facing investors in long-term, fixed-interest securities is that of unanticipated inflation. In contrast, index-linked securities promise

returns that rise in line with inflation and therefore offer investors a risk-free real return.

- Investors in bonds also face issuer risk, i.e. the risk that the issuer (corporate or government) defaults on its obligations.
- A market where a company or government issues new securities for the first time is referred to as a primary market and such issues are referred to as initial public offerings (IPOs).
- Once issued on a stock market, securities can be bought and sold by investors on a daily basis on what is known as the secondary market.
- Once listed on a stock exchange, companies can issue further tranches of securities through either a rights issue or through a placing of new shares with investors.
- The Irish Stock Exchange (ISE) is the designated competent authority for the listing of securities in Ireland.
- The ISE operates different dealing systems for Irish government bonds, and for equity and other quoted securities.
- The Irish government bond market revolves around the primary dealers who are recognised by the National Treasury Management Agency (NTMA) and who apply for registration by the ISE as a primary dealer for Irish government bonds.
- The market in listed company shares is 'created' by the buy and sell orders that are generated by investors in Irish shares. The equity market may be characterised as an 'order-driven market'. In June 2000 the ISE moved to an electronic order-driven system called ISE Xetra.

QUESTIONS

1. **Holding all other factors constant, which of the following is/are TRUE?**

    A. A bond sold at discount will experience a rise in price over time to reach par value.
    B. A bond sold at premium will experience a rise in price over time to reach par value.
    C. A bond sold at premium will experience a decline in price over time to reach par value.
    1. B & C only
    2. All of the above
    3. A & C only
    4. A only

2. **Why do investors invest in fixed-income securities?**

   A. A steady stream of income offered over the life of the bond's obligations.

   B. A return of principal when the bond matures.

   C. It is possible to earn capital gains when interest-rate movements are correctly predicted.

     1. None of the above

     2. A & B only

     3. All of the above

     4. B & C only

3. **Regarding bonds, which of the following statement(s) is/are FALSE?**

   A. The vast majority of fixed-income securities have a specified repayment schedule and must mature at some future date.

   B. Since stocks regularly pay dividends, stocks are fixed-income securities.

   C. At the time the bond is issued, the coupon payments for a typical bond are specified and remain fixed for the life of the bond.

   D. A buyer will get the principal back when a bond matures, assuming there is no default by the issuer.

4. **Regarding the holder of an ordinary share, which of the following is/are FALSE?**

   A. Is guaranteed a specified dividend return.

   B. Is senior to bondholders in terms of payment.

   C. As the owner, can best be described as the residual claimant.

   D. Has unlimited liability and is responsible for any loss created by the firm.

     1. A, B & C only

     2. A, B & D only

     3. None of the above

     4. D only

Questions 5 and 6 are based on the summary information below for ABC plc.

	€ Million
Sales	200
Operating Profit	30
Profit after Tax	20
Dividend	10
Retained Profits	10

ABC has 200 million shares in issue and the current market price is 100c.

5. **What are ABC's Earnings Per Share (EPS), and its dividend yield?**

   A. 1c; 2.5%
   B. 100c; 5.0%
   C. 10c; 5.0%
   D. 10c; 10%

6. **What is ABC's Price Earnings Ratio (PER)?**

   A. 20
   B. 6.7
   C. 10
   D. 13.3

7. **Which of the following statements is FALSE?**

   A. Investment returns from property investment depend on the success of the building in attracting tenants who over time will be willing to pay rising rents.
   B. Property unit-linked funds promoted by the life assurance industry enable small investors to invest in the commercial property market.
   C. Unlike equities, property returns are guaranteed and therefore property is a lower-risk investment than government bonds.
   D. Commercial property investments typically include offices, retail shops and industrial premises such as factories and warehouses.

8. **Which of the following statements regarding direct property investment is FALSE?**

   A. Location risk may be diversified away by building a portfolio of properties.
   B. Property prices, like quoted equity and bond prices, are marked to market on a continuous basis.
   C. By comparison with quoted property companies, Real Estate Investment Trusts provide superior tax transparency and narrower discounts to net asset values.
   D. Direct property investments are relatively illiquid.

9. **For index-linked government bonds, which of the following statements is TRUE?**

   A. The investor will earn the real yield originally purchased when the bond is sold in the market prior to redemption or on redemption.
   B. An attraction of index-linked bonds is that the investor will receive a return that is fixed in nominal terms.

C. The price of an index-linked bond will fluctuate over its life. Inflation is the only driver of these fluctuations.

D. Index-linked bonds protect the investor against the impact of inflation by linking both interest payments and the eventual payment on redemption to an index of retail or consumer prices.

Case Study Exercise: Aer Lingus IPO

Below are excerpts from various public announcements leading up to the Aer Lingus IPO.

28.08.2006: Announcement of Intention to Float

The Minister for Transport of Ireland and Aer Lingus Group plc today announce the intention to seek admission of the Company's ordinary shares to the Official Lists of the Irish Stock Exchange and the United Kingdom Financial Services Authority . . .

AIB Corporate Finance and UBS Investment Bank have been appointed as joint sponsors to the Offer. AIB Capital Markets and UBS Investment Bank have been appointed as advisers to the Irish Government, joint global co-ordinators and joint bookrunners to the offer. Goldman Sachs International and Merrion Stockbrokers have been appointed as joint lead managers to the offer and as advisers to the Company.

27.09.2006: Announcement of Offer Price of €2.20 per Ordinary Share

The Minister for Transport and Aer Lingus Group plc today announce an offer price of €2.20 . . .

- Based upon the Offer Price, the market capitalisation of the Company on Admission will be €1.13bn.
- The Offer Shares will comprise 292.76 million Ordinary Shares.
- The number of ordinary shares held by the Selling Shareholder represent 34.8% of the entire issued share capital.
- At Admission, the Company will, through the issue of New Ordinary Shares, raise . . . gross proceeds of €501.80m . . . the commissions, fees payable by the Company are expected to amount to €30m

02.10.2006: Admission to Official Lists of the ISE and the UK Financial Services Authority and Commencement of Unconditional Dealings on the Main Markets of the ISE and of the London Stock Exchange

Aer Lingus is pleased to announce that its ordinary shares have been admitted to the Official List . . . And to trading on the Irish Stock Exchange's main market . . . (ticker symbol EIL 1) and on the London Stock Exchange main market (ticker symbol AERL).

➡

1. Identify the main players and outline their respective roles in the Aer Lingus IPO (i.e. the originating investment bank, the seller of the shares, etc.).
2. Calculate the total proceeds raised in the IPO and the value of the selling shareholders' holding at the issue price.
3. Estimate the cost of the issue as a percentage of the gross proceeds. Does this seem a reasonable cost of flotation?
4. Construct a flow chart plotting the movement of shares and cash between the various players.

Chapter three

Investing in Bonds

This chapter extends the analysis of bonds begun in Chapter 2. The chapter has two parts. In the first part, issues such as the valuation of bonds and the calculation of the flat yield and the gross redemption yield (GRY) or yield to maturity (YTM) are examined in detail. The term structure of interest rates is discussed, as well as the important concept of duration. The second part looks at bonds as an asset class. Expected returns from bond portfolios are analysed relative to other asset classes. Strategies and techniques that investors use in managing bond portfolios are outlined.

Learning Objectives

After completing this chapter you should:
- Be familiar with the various bond yield measures, most importantly the gross redemption yield
- Have an understanding of how to value a bond, applying the time value of money concept
- Understand the nature of the inverse relationship between changes in interest rates and bond prices
- Be familiar with the term structure of interest rates
- Be able to use a bond's duration to estimate the impact of a change in yield on the price of a bond
- Appreciate the role played by bonds in asset allocation
- Be familiar with the main types of investment strategy adopted by bond investors.

Bonds (or fixed-income securities) usually provide a return in the form of regular interest payments and the repayment of their capital value on their maturity or redemption dates. Bonds are generally a more reliable source of ongoing income than many other asset classes, as they provide a predefined income stream and the repayment of principal at maturity. This sets them apart from equity securities, where the future dividend income stream is uncertain and where there is no maturity date. Likewise the certain future investment-income stream associated with bonds contrasts with the uncertain future rental-income stream associated with property. Not surprisingly, equities and property tend to be more volatile investment categories than bonds. Essentially bonds are loans with pre-specified terms and conditions; they have been used by borrowers and lenders for centuries and provide returns in the form of income and repayment at maturity. The early bonds were issued by governments, often for the purposes of funding wars or colonial escapades. The UK was a leader in this regard and by the nineteenth century there was an active market in British government securities. Title to these early bonds was by way of a certificate which was embossed with gilt edging. As a result British government securities came to be referred to as 'gilt-edged' securities and to this day are still referred to as such.

WHY BOND MARKETS HAVE DEVELOPED

The development of bond markets reflects the benefits that such investment securities offer to both the issuers (borrowers) and investors (lenders). In Ireland the vast majority of bonds are those issued by the Irish Government and this is a pattern that is common in most economies. Corporations also issue bonds and corporate bonds are identical to government bonds except for one important difference. Bonds issued by corporations are subject to default risk, the extent of which is determined by the financial strength of the respective company and an assessment of its future prospects. Investors (lenders) will require compensation for this credit risk in the form of a higher interest rate. Likewise, bonds issued by emerging market countries and weaker developed countries also carry higher yields. The default risk of bonds issued by most governments in the developed world is extremely low and these securities are viewed by investors as being risk-free. Our discussion on bonds that follows relates to government bonds and examples are confined to the Irish government bond market. However, the characteristics of bonds are generic and apply equally to bonds issued by a wide variety of issuers.

ATTRACTIONS TO ISSUERS AND INVESTORS

Cost and flexibility are the key attractions to the issuers of bonds. By funding their borrowing requirements in this way governments have created the conditions for the development of large and liquid bond markets, thus creating a very cost-effective way for governments to fund their borrowing requirements on an ongoing basis. The ability to issue bonds with varying maturity dates ensures that interest payments and eventual repayment of bonds can be timed to coincide with any specific set of cash-flow needs. For investors, bonds offer a steady and secure future income stream with extremely low default risk in the case of most government bonds. For corporate bonds the work of credit rating agencies such as Moody's and Standard & Poor's ensures that an efficient market exists that enables company credit risk to be priced. Furthermore, large institutional investors devote substantial resources to analysing and assessing the credit risk of individual companies. Because the characteristics of bonds are very different from other assets such as equities and property they are the key to enabling investors to diversify risk.

CHARACTERISTICS OF BONDS

Bonds are essentially loans that are negotiable, i.e. they can be bought and sold after they are issued, and therefore a bond has a set of terms and conditions that protects the purchaser or investor by obliging the borrower to repay specified amounts at certain intervals. Although the prospectus of any new bond issue is a long legal document, there are three key components that establish the essentials of the contractual relationship between the borrower and the lender. These are:

* par value
* coupon
* term to maturity.

Par Value: The par value is sometimes referred to as the face value, nominal value or redemption value of a bond. Irish government bonds typically have a par value of €100. One unit of a bond therefore has a nominal value of €100. The price at which a bond is issued may be higher or lower than this par value, and the market prices of bonds already in issue will usually diverge from the par value. As well as being a nominal unit of value, the par value has real economic significance, as this is the amount of money that the issuer will repay to the holder on the maturity date of the bond.

Coupon: The coupon is the interest rate set as part of a bond's terms and conditions. This interest rate is calculated on the *par value* of a bond and not the issue price of the bond. Therefore, the amount of interest paid by a bond issuer is calculated by multiplying the coupon interest rate by the par value of the bond. Irish government bonds usually pay this interest once a year.

A holder of €10,000 nominal of the 4.5% Treasury 2020 holds 10,000/100 = 100 units of this bond. Each unit will pay annual interest of €100 * .045 = €4.5. With 100 units this investor will receive annual interest on his holding of 100 * €4.5 = €450.

Time to Maturity: This is the length of time between the date the money is invested and the date it is subsequently repaid by the borrower. The maturity date or redemption date is the day the issuer repays the bond's par value.

For an investor the par value, coupon interest rate and the redemption date provide sufficient information to establish the investment parameters of a bond. A schedule of cash flows that are determined by the terms of the bond can easily be established, and this schedule provides the basis on which bonds can be valued and priced.

PRICING AND VALUING BONDS

An investor who wishes to put funds on deposit will generally look at interest rates offered on deposits in the marketplace and will place his funds with the institution that offers the highest interest rate for the particular period chosen. The deposit product that offers the highest rate of interest clearly is the one that offers the best 'value' to the prospective investor. Assessing the investment worth of bonds has similarities with the above but, given the characteristics of bonds, the process is much more complicated. A good starting point is to define the various interest rates or yields that apply to a fixed-interest bond; there are three of these.

i)   Coupon Rate: This is the annual interest paid divided by the par value of the bond, expressed as a percentage.
ii)   Flat or Running Yield: This is the actual annual coupon payable divided by the current market value of the bond, which usually differs from the par value, again expressed as a percentage.
iii)   Gross Redemption Yield: This takes into account all the future coupon payments due on the bond, together with the redemption value (which is the bond's par value), and relates these future payments to the current price of the bond in the market. The Gross Redemption Yield (GRY) is expressed as a percentage per annum and is the most useful measure of the worth or value of the bond. It is sometimes referred to as the Yield to Maturity (YTM).

Exhibit 3.1 contains the list of Irish government bonds that appears daily in the *Irish Times*. The information published for each bond includes:

• coupon
• redemption date
• market price
• yield (which is the GRY).

Exhibit 3.1 List of Irish Government Bonds

GOVERNMENT STOCKS		
	Euro price	**Yield**
Irish 4 11/11/11	100.18	3.705
Irish 3.9 03/05/12	99.44	4.464
Irish 8¾ 09/30/12	104.06	6.147
Irish 5 04/18/13	96.41	6.847
Irish 40 1/15/14	90.62	7.741
Irish 8¼ 08/18/15	101.11	7.925
Irish 4.6 04/18/16	84.35	8.473
Irish 4½ 10/18/18	77.98	8.530
Irish 4.4 06/18/19	75.46	8.654
Irish 5.9 10/18/19	83.26	8.728
Irish 4½ 04/18/20	73.51	8.840
Irish 5.4 03/13/25	72.67	8.880

Courtesy NCB Stockbrokers

The Flat Yield or Running Yield can be easily calculated for each bond; let's take the 4.6% Treasury 18/04/16 as an example. This bond matures on 18 April 2016, which is a crucial piece of information for the calculation of the GRY. However, the redemption date has no relevance to the calculation of the flat yield. For the above bond the flat yield is calculated using the formula:

$$\frac{\text{Coupon}}{\text{Price}} \times 100 = \frac{4.6}{84.35} \times 100 = 5.5\%$$

Because the bond is trading below par, the flat yield is higher than the coupon – 5.5% versus 4.6%. An investor who invests €1,000 in this bond will receive €55 interest for each year that he holds the bond (he holds €1,000/0.8435 = €1,185 nominal of the bond). This can be compared with deposit interest of €20 that would be received on a €1,000 deposit if the deposit interest rate were 2% per annum for the same period. While the flat yield is useful, it presents only part of the return picture of a fixed-interest bond. Figure 3.1 illustrates that the value of the bond will move from €84.35 to €100 if it is held to maturity.

Figure 3.1 4.6% Treasury 2016, Price Movement if Held to Maturity

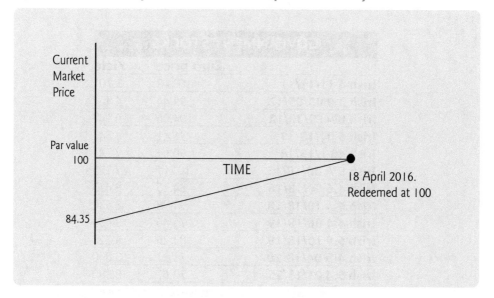

On the maturity date the bond will be redeemed at its par value of €100, so that a capital gain of €15.45 will be sustained if the bond is held until it matures. Clearly, in order to accurately assess the investment value of the bond, this future capital gain must be taken into account.

Gross Redemption Yield (GRY)

The GRY is calculated in a way that takes into account all the future cash flows that are associated with a particular bond. There are two very important assumptions made in the calculation of GRY. These are:

i)   The bond is held until its maturity date.
ii)   All coupons are reinvested immediately when received and achieve a
       GRY that is identical to today's GRY.

To understand the GRY concept, we need to digress into a discussion of the time value of money. It is intuitively clear that future or deferred income is not as valuable as immediate income. This manifests itself in the financial markets as a rate of interest on low-risk assets such as cash, and an expected rate of return on risky assets such as equities. In other words, savers or investors need a reward if they are going to save for tomorrow rather than spend today. Example 3.1 illustrates how the value of a deposit grows over time to a much larger future value.

Example 3.1 The Future Value (FV) of a Deposit

€1,000 is deposited at a fixed annual rate of interest of 5% with interest credited once a year. Deposit to last for a term of 10 years. Value of deposit after one year is calculated as:

€1,000 * (1 + r), where r = rate of interest expressed as a decimal
€1,000 * (1 + 0.05) = €1,050
Value of deposit after 10 years is calculated as:
€1,000 * $(1 + r)^n$, where n = term of deposit in years
€1,000 * $(1 + 0.05)^{10}$ = €1,629.

The process whereby money grows at a compound rate of interest to reach a future value as we move forward in time can be reversed if we examine what happens as we move back in time. Example 3.2 illustrates how a sum of money to be received in the future can be translated into the equivalent

Example 3.2 The Present Value (PV) of a Sum to be Received in the Future

A payment of €1,000 is to be received in exactly one year. The rate of interest or discount rate is 5%. The payment in today's money (the present value) may be calculated using the formula: €1,000/(1 + r), where r = the rate of interest or the expected rate of return, commonly referred to as the discount rate. Therefore, the PV of this expected receipt is €1,000/1.05 = €952.

If this payment were to be received in 10 years' time the PV may be calculated using the formula: €1,000/$(1 + r)^n$, where n = the number of years to wait before payment is received. Now the PV of this expected receipt becomes €1,000/$(1.05)^{10}$ = €614.

value in today's money.
This example illustrates that the PV of a future payment is calculated by dividing the expected payment by one plus the rate of interest to the power

of the number of years to wait for the payment. Clearly, the higher the rate of interest (discount rate) the lower will be the present value, and the longer the time period the lower will be the present value.

Example 3.3 sets out the future cash flows associated with the 4% Treasury 2014, taken from the list of Irish government bonds, assuming today is 15 January 2011.

Imagine the government is selling this bond for the first time and is seeking bids from investors. You are considering investing in this bond, but you have to decide on a price. What you need to do is to work out what the future pay-outs of the bond are worth in today's money. You therefore need to work out the present value of the interest payments and the final redemption amount. We can apply the technique illustrated in Example 3.2 to calculate the present value of each cash flow associated with this bond. To do this we need a discount rate. In this example, the discount rate should be the rate of return that we require if we are to be enticed to invest in this bond. Let's assume that we would be happy with a return of 3% per annum. This then becomes the discount rate that can be plugged in to our present-value calculations, as illustrated in Example 3.3.

Example 3.3 Calculating the Present Value of a Government Bond, 4% Treasury 2014

To calculate the present value we need to decide on a rate of discount; in this case $r = 3\%$

Cash flows	Year	Cash Flow	Present Value Calculation	PV of end Payment
	2012	4	$\dfrac{4}{1.03} =$	3.88
	2013	4	$\dfrac{4}{(1.03)^2} =$	3.77
	2014	104	$\dfrac{104}{(1.03)^3} =$	95.18
				102.83

We have now calculated the present value of the cash flows that will be generated by this bond at €102.83. We can interpret this as meaning that if we pay this price for the bond, it will deliver to us a return of 3% per annum.

If the government prices the bonds at 102.83, then an investment in this bond will yield an annual return of 3%. If the bond is priced lower than that, then it will deliver a return greater than 3% p.a. A price higher than 102.83 implies a return of less than 3% p.a. (in which case we would not invest in the bond).

Where the price of the bond is known, we can apply the same formula to establish the rate of return that this price implies. Example 3.4 illustrates this and it can be seen that when the price of the bond is known there is only one unknown to solve in the equation, namely the discount rate, r.

Example 3.4 Calculating the Gross Redemption Yield (GRY)

4% Treasury 2014

$$\text{Price} = \frac{\text{Coupon 1}}{1 + r} + \frac{\text{Coupon 2}}{(1 + r)^2} + \frac{(\text{Coupon 3} + \text{Par value})}{(1 + r)^3}$$

r = the discount rate, which is also the GRY of the bond.

If this is January 2011, and given the current price of the bond as 102.83, the GRY is calculated by inserting the known information into this equation:

$$102.83 = 4/(1 + r) + 4/(1 + r)^2 + 104/(1 + r)^3$$

This discount rate is in fact the gross redemption yield of the bond. It is quite a difficult equation to solve, but we can rely on financial calculators to do the job for us, or we will often be simply given information on both the price and GRY of the bond. From our previous workings we can see that in this example the GRY is 3%, which is the discount rate that brings the sum of the present values of the cash flows associated with the bond to the current price of €102.83.

Inverse Relationship between the Price and GRY of a Bond

Closer inspection of Examples 3.3 and 3.4 illustrates the relationship between changes in the discount rate (r) and the price of the bond. A rise in the interest rate or discount rate (r) will reduce the present value of each future cash flow. Since the price or value of the bond is equal to the sum of these present values, it is clear that any rise in interest rates will lead to a FALL in the price of a bond. Example 3.5 illustrates what happens to the price of a notional bond with a par value of €100 and an annual coupon of 3.25%, and which matures in three years. It assumes that the first coupon payment occurs in exactly one year.

Example 3.5 The Impact of a Higher GRY on the Value of a Bond

r = 3%   and   r = 4%

Cash flows	Year	Cash Flow €	Present Value	
			r = 3%	r = 4%
	2012	3.25	$\frac{3.25}{1.03} = 3.16$	$\frac{3.25}{1.04} = 3.13$
	2013	3.25	$\frac{3.25}{(1.03)^2} = 3.06$	$\frac{3.25}{(1.04)^2} = 3.01$
	2014	103.25	$\frac{103.25}{(1.03)^3} = 94.49$	$\frac{103.25}{(1.04)^3} = 91.79$

Sum of present Value of Cash Flows =
Price of Bond =   100.71   97.93

The present value of each expected cash flow falls and hence the price of the bond (which equals the sum of the PVs) falls to €97.93, compared with the price of €100.71 when r was 3%. Once a bond is issued, its price will constantly fluctuate in response to changes in long-term interest rates. A rise in interest rates reduces the price of a bond and a fall in interest rates increases the price of a bond. This is a precise mathematical relationship.

MANAGING A BOND PORTFOLIO

The inverse relationship between market yields and bond prices is the basis for understanding, valuing and managing bonds. A bond fund manager who correctly anticipates changes in market yields can exploit this relationship. In the decade to 2010 bond yields declined quite sharply, leading to an uplift in the value of fixed-interest bonds. The magnitude of change in the capital value of a particular bond in response to a change in market yields will depend on variables that are unique to each bond, i.e. the coupon and the time to maturity.

The Impact of Maturity

An important concept is that for a given change in market yields, changes in bond prices are directly related to time to maturity. From Example 3.5 we can see that the rise in GRY from 3% to 4% led to a fall in the price of this particular bond from 100.71 to 97.93, a decline of –2.8%. Given another bond with exactly the same coupon but with 4 years to maturity, we can calculate its value in the same way. With a discount rate of 3% the value of this bond is 100.92, which falls to 97.29 when the discount rate rises to 4%. This is a fall of –3.6% and in general it is the case that longer-dated bonds

Figure 3.2 Bond Prices, Time to Maturity and Interest Rate Changes

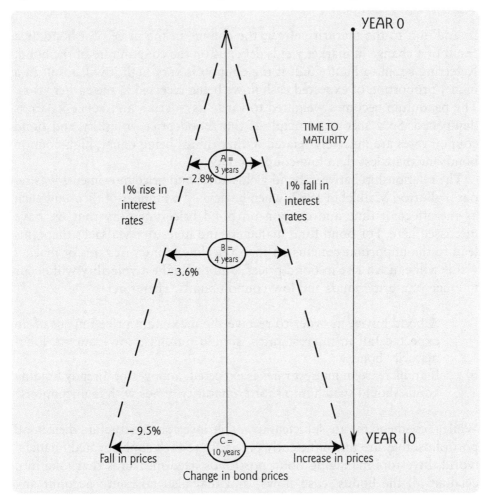

are more sensitive to interest-rate changes than are shorter-dated bonds. Figure 3.2 illustrates this relationship as a series of pendulums. Bond A is quite short and a rise in interest rates causes this pendulum to swing to the left, indicating a fall in price. For longer-dated bonds the pendulum becomes longer, and hence swings over a wider arc for the same change in market yields. Bond B is a 4-year bond which falls in price by –3.6% for the same 1% rise in yield. Bond C is a 10-year bond which falls in price by –9.5%. The greater sensitivity of longer-dated bonds is due to the longer wait for the receipt of the later coupons and particularly the longer wait for the final redemption amount, so consequently the discounting mechanism is working over a much longer period of time. The principle illustrated here is a stark one: other things being equal, bond price volatility is a function of maturity and therefore long-term bonds fluctuate more than do short-term bonds.

The Effects of Coupon

In addition to the maturity effect, the change in the price of a bond as a result of a change in market yields depends on the coupon rate of the bond. Referring again to Figure 3.2, if the coupon is very high it will result in a higher proportion of expected cash flows being received in the earlier years. The pendulum becomes weighted towards its fulcrum and hence its arc is dampened. So a second principle is that bond price volatility and bond coupon rates are inversely related. Other things being equal, high-coupon bonds fluctuate less than low-coupon bonds.

The relationship between bond yields and bond price movements was set out by Burton Malkiel in 1962, when he devised a number of theorems such as the effect of time and coupon on bond price volatility that we have discussed here. For bond fund managers and investors Malkiel's theorems lead to the important conclusion that a decline in interest rates or market yields will cause a rise in bond prices, and the highest volatility will occur in longer-maturity bonds and low-coupon bonds. Therefore:

i)   A bond buyer, in order to receive the maximum price impact of an expected fall in interest rates, should purchase low-coupon, long-maturity bonds.

ii)   If an increase in interest rates is expected, an investor already holding bonds should switch into shorter-maturity bonds with high coupons.

While these theorems are sufficient to enable investors to structure their bond portfolios, they are not sufficiently precise in today's sophisticated financial world. Investors managing bond portfolios need measures that take into account all the bonds' cash flows, and that also take into account any changes that occur in volatility as the overall level of market yields changes. Such measures are available and are called 'duration' and 'convexity'; they are explained later in this chapter.

The Term Structure of Interest Rates

So far our discussion has centred on the characteristics of a typical fixed-interest bond issued by the government of a developed economy. The fact that most governments have several bonds in issue, with different maturity dates, gives investors the ability to create bond portfolios that can closely match their respective investment objectives. Taking bonds issued by the Irish Government as an example, we can see that we have a set of bonds that are homogeneous in a number of important respects:

- They all have the same issuer, and therefore the risk of default is exactly the same for each bond.
- All these bonds are subject to the same tax, legal and regulatory regimes.

This homogeneity allows us to analyse the investment characteristics of a bond market as a whole, in addition to the characteristics of each individual bond. This provides a wealth of extra information regarding the current structure of interest rates. The relationship between time to maturity and yields for a particular category of bonds at a particular point in time is referred to as the term structure of interest rates. The term structure of interest rates is usually plotted as a yield curve and can be quite easily done by plotting pairs of yield and time to maturity on a scattergram. In Figure 3.3 yield curves for the German and US government bond markets are plotted.

In January 2008 we can see that the German yield curve was relatively flat, with the one-year yield at 3.8% and the ten-year yield at 4.1%; the spread between the one- and ten-year bonds was just +0.3%. At the time the European Central Bank (ECB) was adopting a relatively tight monetary stance, i.e. short-term interest rates were being maintained at a relatively high level to control inflationary expectations. By October 2010 the German yield curve had a very different shape. Although economies were recovering from the 2008/9 crisis, most central banks, including the ECB, were adopting very easy monetary policies in order to support the fledgling economic recovery. Hence very low short-term interest rates were leading to a steeply upward sloping yield curve. The spread between the one- and ten-year bonds stood at +1.6%. The US yield curve at that time exhibited an even steeper upward slope with the spread between the one- and ten-year bonds at +2.2%. This reflected an even easier monetary stance being adopted by the Federal Reserve, with short-term interest rates being kept at close to zero.

The shape of the yield curve is something that is closely watched by economists and investors alike. The shape of the curve reflects the spreads between bonds of different maturities. These spreads are a function of fundamental factors such as the time value of money, the current stage of the economic and business cycle and, crucially, expectations regarding future interest rates.

Figure 3.3 Yield Curves — Germany and US

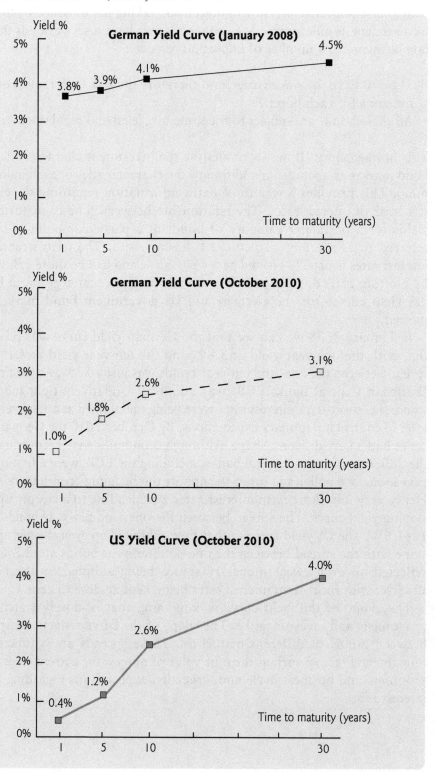

Term Structure Theories

There are several theories advanced to explain the shape of the yield curve and why it shifts over time. They can be categorised into the following:

- the pure expectations theory
- expectations with a risk premium theory
- the market segmentation theory (a variation is the preferred habitat theory).

According to the pure expectations theory, long-term interest rates can be seen as averages (calculated as geometric means) of the current short-term interest rate and future short-term interest rates. Assume that today is end-January 2011, that the current 1-year rate is 3%, and that the 1-year rate that will prevail at end-December 2012 for the following 12 months is 4%. An investor who wishes to invest funds for two years can place funds on deposit at the current 1-year interest rate, and then reinvest at end-December 2012 for the following year. Alternatively, the investor can place funds on deposit at the current 2-year rate of interest. According to the pure expectations theory investors are indifferent between these two alternatives. The implication of this is that the current 2-year interest rate must equal the geometric mean of these 1-year rates. The geometric mean of the current 1-year rate and the forward 1-year rate is:

$$\sqrt{(1.03 \times 1.04)} - 1 = .035 \text{ or } 3.5\%$$

If the pure expectations theory is an accurate explanation of the level of long-term interest rates, then the yield curve can be used to infer market expectations of future interest rates. In the example above, if we know the 1-year rate of 3% and the 2-year rate of 3.5%, we can deduce the 1-year forward rate as:

$$\sqrt{1.03 \times (1 + f)} = 1.035, \text{ where } f = \text{1-year forward rate}$$
$$[1.03 \times (1 + f)] = (1.035)^2 = 1.07$$
$$1 + f = (1.07)/(1.03) = 1.04$$

Therefore   f = .04 or 4%.

While this equation has been limited to just two years, it does apply more generally, so that forward rates of interest can be calculated for virtually any chosen period of time. Several governments now issue bonds with a maturity of 50 years, so that we have yield curves in some markets that stretch out to 50 years. There is one important caveat regarding the pure expectations theory, which is that it assumes that investors are risk-neutral. A risk-neutral investor is defined as one who is not concerned about the possibility that interest-rate expectations will not prove to be correct, so long as potential favourable deviations from expectations are as likely as unfavourable ones. However, it is generally assumed that investors are risk-averse. Risk-averse investors are prepared to forgo some investment return in order to achieve greater certainty in regard to the value of investments and the income from them.

The likely existence of risk aversion leads into the expectations with a risk premium theory. This could mean that the yield curve should normally slope upwards, because longer-dated maturities have higher volatility than shorter-dated ones. Risk-averse investors will demand a risk premium for the longer-dated bonds, thereby pushing up their yields relative to shorter-dated bonds. This theory provides a logical explanation as to why a yield curve normally slopes upwards. The tendency towards an upward slope could be further reinforced by borrowers' preference to borrow for long periods in order to reduce uncertainty. Such borrowers would presumably be prepared to pay a premium for longer-dated issues. However, the other side of this coin is that some investors may prefer long-dated bonds because they provide greater certainty of income flows compared with other assets. For example, bank deposits over the long term provide a very uncertain stream of future income. Therefore, such investors may be prepared to pay a premium (accept a lower yield) for longer-dated bonds, which would tend to flatten the shape of the yield curve.

The third theory of the term structure of interest rates is the market segmentation approach and a variation called the preferred habitat hypothesis. The essential idea here is that demand and supply conditions may vary across the maturity spectrum, and it is excess demand or supply that determines yields for different maturities. Therefore, short-term yields are determined by the interaction of supply and demand for short-term funds. Long-term yields are determined by the interaction of a different set of borrowers and lenders. Under this hypothesis the yield curve could have almost any shape, depending on the number of different maturity segments.

Concluding Comments on Yield Curve Theories

This discussion highlights the fact that there is no single, elegant explanation for the behaviour of the term structure of interest rates. Indeed, the 'theories' discussed here are really a series of explanations for the observation that yield curves change shape on an ongoing basis. Each 'theory' has its merits, but none is capable of providing a comprehensive explanation of the yield curve. These theories can provide a checklist for the important task of analysis of the term structure of interest rates.

Figure 3.4 Term Structure Theories and Slope of the Yield Curve

Implications of theories of the term structure of interest rates	Impact on the slope of the yield curve
Expectations regarding future short-term interest rates • expectations for a rise • expectations for a fall	• Upward slope • Downward slope (inverted)
Capital risk	Upward slope
Income risk	Downward slope (inverted)
Excess demand for long-dated bonds (15 years +)	Inverted from 15 years out
Excess supply of medium-term bonds (5–15 years)	Yield curve with a humped shape

The Measurement of Bond Price Volatility

Earlier in this chapter we identified maturity and coupon as being the determinants of the sensitivity of a bond's price to changes in the overall level of interest rates. A single statistic that captures the impact of both coupon and maturity would be very useful when it comes to managing bond portfolios. Fortunately there is such a concept, called 'duration', which was conceived over 50 years ago by Frederick Macauley.

Duration Defined: Duration can be thought of as the average number of years it takes for an investor to get his money back. More formally, it measures the weighted average maturity of a bond's cash flows on a present-value basis. Duration is expressed in years and Example 3.6 illustrates how it is calculated.

Example 3.6 Calculating Duration

3¹/₄ % Treasury 2014 (redeems in exactly three years)   r = 3%, Price = 100.71

Period (t)	Cash Flow	Present Value Cash Flow (PVCF)	t × PVCF
1	3.25	3.16	3.16
2	3.25	3.06	6.12
3	103.25	94.49	283.47
Total		100.71	292.75

Macauley Duration = 292.75/100.71 = 2.9 Years

3¹/₄ % Treasury 2009 Cash Flows

$$\text{Macauley Duration} = D = \sum_{t=1}^{n} \frac{PV(CF_t)}{\text{Market Price}} \times t$$

[*Equation 3.1*]

This example illustrates that the present value of each cash flow is weighted by the time (in years) to wait for the receipt, and these weights are totalled and divided by the price of the bond to give the Macauley Duration of the bond in years.

Understanding Duration

An examination of the Macauley Duration equation shows that the calculation of duration depends on three factors:

i)   The maturity of the bond: duration lengthens with time to maturity, holding the GRY and coupon payments constant.
ii)   The coupon payments: higher coupons lead to a faster recovery of money invested, so that higher coupons result in shorter duration compared with lower-coupon bonds. Therefore, coupon is inversely related to duration.

iii)   The gross redemption yield, GRY, is inversely related to duration
        (holding coupon and maturity constant).

Uses of Duration

The two most important uses of duration are: first, it gives us the *effective life* of a bond; and second, it is a measure of bond price sensitivity to interest-rate movements. Regarding the former, duration allows us to compare bonds with different maturities and coupons on a consistent basis. Furthermore, the duration of a bond portfolio can also be calculated, so that different portfolios can be compared with one another and bond portfolios can be compared with the duration of the respective liabilities that they may be seeking to match.

Regarding the latter, bond price changes are directly related to duration. More precisely, the percentage change in a bond's price, given a change in interest rates, is proportional to its duration, so that duration can be used to measure interest-rate exposure. A modification needs to be made to duration in order to apply it for this purpose, whereby Macauley Duration is divided by one plus the GRY (1 + GRY) to give what is termed Modified Duration:

$$\text{Modified Duration} = D^* = D/(1 + GRY)$$

Referring to Example 3.6, we can calculate the modified duration of this bond as:
$$MD = 2.9/(1 + .03) = 2.82$$

How do we interpret this number for modified duration? Unlike duration it is not a period of years; rather, it is a number that when multiplied by a change in the yield of a bond gives us the percentage change in the price of the bond. Referring again to Example 3.6, we can calculate the change in the price of this bond for any given change in yields (or interest rates) by applying the equation:

$$\Delta P/P = -D^* \, \Delta r$$

where: ΔP = change in price
          P = price of bond
          $-D^*$ = modified duration with a negative sign
          Δr = instantaneous change in yield in decimal form.

[Equation 3.2]

If there was an instantaneous rise in yields of one percentage point, then the price of the 3.25% Treasury 2009 would change as follows:

$$\text{Change in price} = -2.82 \times .01 = -.0282 \text{ or } -2.82\%$$

Therefore, a one-percentage-point rise in yields would lead to a fall in the price of this bond of $(100.7 \times .0282) = €2.84$ per €100 nominal. On this basis it would seem that we can interpret the modified duration number as being the percentage change in the price of a bond for a one percentage point change in yield. Unfortunately, Equation 3.2 is only an approximation. For very small changes in yield (up to about 20 basis points) it gives a result that is very close to being correct. For changes in yield of one or two percentage points there will be quite a large discrepancy compared with the true actual change in the price of a bond. However, we can interpret a bond's modified duration as giving us the percentage change in the price of a bond for a one percentage point change in yield, as long as we remember that this is an approximation.

While the modified duration number may be sufficient in many situations, the effective management of bond portfolios requires a more precise calculation.

The reason why modified duration is an approximation is that it produces symmetric percentage price change estimates. In the example above, applying the equation to a percentage point fall in yield would produce the same absolute bond price change (+2.82%). In other words, it operates as if the price–yield relationship were linear, whereas this relationship is not in fact linear, but is curvilinear.

Convexity

We refer to this curved nature of the price–yield relationship as the bond's convexity. More formally, convexity is the term used to refer to the degree to which duration changes as the GRY changes. Figure 3.5 illustrates why an adjustment to the modified duration calculation needs to be made for the convexity of a bond.

The MD calculation results in a fall in the price of the three-year bond to 97.86 from 100.7 for a rise in GRY to 4% from 3%. The MD relationship is represented by the line AB, whereas the true relationship at the 3% GRY is more properly represented by the curve XY. This curve indicates that the price fall should be read from point P (indicating a fall in price to 98.77). In general, modified duration overestimates price falls (rising yields) and underestimates price rises (falling yields). For very small changes in yield the discrepancy is immaterial, but for larger changes in yield it becomes significant.

Figure 3.5 Using Modified Duration 3.25% Treasury 2009

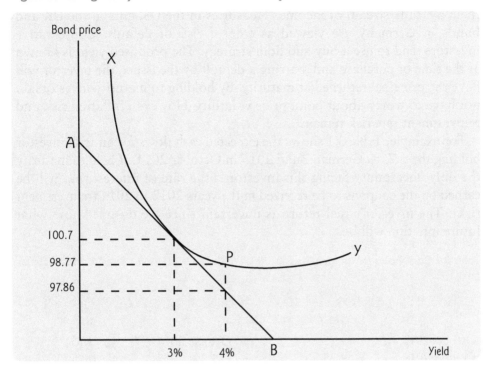

Convexity varies for different bonds and, just like duration, it is a function of coupon, maturity and yield. Convexity:

* is positively related to maturity, therefore it is larger for long-dated bonds;
* is negatively related to coupon; it is larger for low-coupon bonds;
* is negatively related to yield; it is larger when yields are low.

Convexity calculations can be made, similar to those for modified duration, to give a percentage change in the price of a bond due to a change in yield. This can be added to the approximate price change calculated using duration. The result will still be an approximation, but it will be a big improvement on the calculation based solely on duration.

BONDS AS AN ASSET CLASS

So far in this chapter we have focused on the characteristics of individual fixed-interest bonds. In the following sections we examine issues arising from the perspective of asset allocation and portfolio management. First, we need to address the question as to why investors buy bonds. The answer, of course, depends upon the different perspectives of different types of investor.

Conservative investors view bonds as fixed-income securities that will pay them a steady stream of income. Treasuries in the US, gilts in the UK and bunds in Germany are viewed as free of risk of default. Conservative investors tend to use a buy and hold strategy. The promised yield is known at the time of purchase and, barring a default by the issuer, the investor will have the principal returned at maturity. By holding to maturity investors do not have to worry about bond price volatility. However, inflation risk and reinvestment rate risk remain.

For example, Table 3.1 shows the expected cash flows for an Irish investor holding the 1.75% German Bund 2015 in October 2011. If held to maturity the only uncertainty facing this investor is the rate of interest that will be earned on the coupons to be received in the years 2012 to 2014 (reinvestment risk). The investor's real return is uncertain since we do not know what future inflation will be.

Table 3.1 Cash Flows for an Irish Investor Holding the 1.75% German Bund 2015 in October 2011

Date	Cash € per €100 nominal	Date	Cash € per €100 nominal
October 2012	1.75	October 2014	1.75
October 2013	1.75	October 2015	1.75

Of course, over its life the market price of a bond fluctuates inversely with the interest rate cycle. Some investors are interested in bonds for this very reason – by anticipating changes in interest rates, aggressive investors aim to make capital gains through the active trading of bonds.

The period from 1970 to 2000 saw unusually large volatility in the price of fixed-interest bonds. Data for the UK gilt market during this period illustrate this price volatility, and the consequent scope for making capital gains (or suffering capital losses) over particular time periods. Table 3.2 presents the price behaviour of UK long gilt price indices for a selection of the more volatile years.

Table 3.2 Gilt Price Volatility

	Gilt Price Index December Annual % Change	Yield %
1976	−1.1%	15.0
1977	+30.6%	10.9
1978	−13.3%	13.2
1981	−12.1%	15.8
1982	+36.2%	11.1
1998	+18.6%	4.4
1999	−8.4%	5.3

Source: *Barclays Capital Gilt Equity Study.*

Between 2000 and 2010 the volatility of returns from bond markets declined, reflecting a more stable interest rate and inflation rate environment. Nevertheless, returns from UK gilts ranged from a high of +8.3% in 2008 to a low of –5.0% in 2009.

Expected Returns from Bonds

In trying to assess expected potential returns from assets investors will often rely on long-run historical data. For bonds in particular, care needs to be taken in relying on such data as for any specific investment time horizon, the return from holding bonds will be a function of the GRY on the purchase date and the GRY on the end date. For example, at end-1981 the gilt yield stood at 15.8%. If yields in 1982 stood still the return from holding the gilt would have been an income return of 15.8%. However, yields fell sharply in 1982 to finish the year at 11.1%. This dramatic fall in yields led to a price appreciation in the gilt index of 36.2%. Therefore the total return from holding gilts in that year would have been an income return of 15.8% plus a capital gain of 36.2% to give a total return of 52%. So, when trying to assess expected returns from a bond investment over a particular holding period, be it one, five or ten years, the actual market yield at the end of the period will have a large impact on the expected holding period return.

We simply do not know what yields will be in the future, although we do know that they fluctuate quite considerably depending on economic circumstances. Where we expect to hold a particular bond to maturity, the GRY provides us with a good estimate of the likely prospective return. Where our holding period is less than the bond's term, then our expected return will be a probability distribution just like other risky assets, with the risk dependent on the probability distribution of yields at the end of our particular holding period.

Important Considerations in Managing a Bond Portfolio

The first consideration is understanding the relationship between the bond market and the economy as a whole. If the economy is growing slowly, then interest rates may decline and bond prices rise. An even more important relationship is between bond yields and inflation. If investors anticipate a rise in inflation they will demand a higher yield from a bond to compensate for the expected decline in the purchasing power of their cash flows from the bond investment. Therefore, an increase in expected inflation will tend to depress bond prices and increase yields.

Bond Strategies and Techniques

Different bond investors have adopted different strategies, depending on their risk preferences, their knowledge of the bond market and their investment objectives. The choices and issues that bond investors face may be summarised as:

- Adopt a passive or active strategy or some combination of both.
- Include corporate bonds in the strategy.
- Include emerging market bonds in the strategy.

Irrespective of the particular strategic approach adopted, bond investors need to make an accurate assessment of the price volatility of their portfolios in response to interest rate changes. Various techniques have evolved to protect portfolios against interest rate movements, which we will examine below.

Passive Management Strategies

Many investors agree that securities are fairly priced in the sense that the expected return is commensurate with the risk taken. Passive management strategies are based on inputs that are known at the time, rather than on expectations. Indexing is possibly now the more common passive strategy: investors invest in a strategy where their portfolio, or the fund that they are investing in, consists of bonds that replicate a chosen bond index.

Active Management Strategies

These strategies seek to profit from active management of bonds by activities such as: forecasting changes in interest rates; identifying abnormal yield spreads between bond sectors and taking advantage of them; and identifying relative mispricing between various fixed-income securities.

Just like active equity managers, active bond managers seek to find an 'edge' that will result in them being able to outperform passive investment strategies. Bond fund managers will typically rely on fundamental analysis of the business and interest rate cycle, detailed analysis of the term structure of interest rates and research into those specific factors driving individual bond markets. Implementing strategies involves detailed knowledge of the characteristics of particular bonds and of bond markets such as duration and convexity.

Private investors often adopt a buy and hold strategy when it comes to bond investment. For example, a private investor who has just retired may decide to invest in a ten-year bond with a view to supplementing his or her pension with the bond coupons over its ten-year life.

Immunisation

Immunisation is a particular strategy where the bond manager aims to protect the bond portfolio against interest rate risk. This relies on the fact that interest rate risk has two parts: price risk and reinvestment risk. Crucially, these risks have opposite signs for any given change in interest rates. For example, if bond yields rise by 1%, the value of a portfolio will fall. The magnitude of this fall will depend on the duration of the portfolio. However, if this rise in yield persists, then there will be a higher return on the reinvestment of the coupons as they arise.

Corporate Bonds

For some investors, investing in bonds is synonymous with investing in fixed-interest bonds issued by developed countries. However, bond investment is much wider than this and a large portion of global bond issuance is accounted for by bonds issued by corporations rather than governments. Just like governments, corporations issue debt securities to fund their long-term financial requirements.

Corporate bonds (i.e. debt financing) are a major source of capital for many businesses, along with equity and bank loans/lines of credit. Generally speaking, a company needs to have some consistent earnings potential to be able to offer debt securities to the public at a favourable coupon rate. The higher a company's perceived credit quality, the easier it becomes to issue debt at low rates and to issue higher amounts of debt.

The corporate bond market in the US is very large and varied. Corporate bonds are issued in blocks of $1,000 in par value, and almost all have a standard coupon payment structure. Corporate bonds may also have call provisions to allow for early prepayment if prevailing rates change. Corporate bonds are considered higher risk than government bonds. As a result, interest rates are almost always higher, even for top-flight credit quality companies.

Corporate bonds offer a higher yield than some other investments, but the higher yield is not risk-free. Investors of such bonds must assume not only interest rate risk but also credit risk, the chance that the corporate issuer will default on its debt obligations. Therefore, it is important that investors in corporate bonds know how to assess credit risk and its potential pay-offs: while rising interest rate movements can reduce the value of their bond investment, a default can almost eliminate it. Holders of defaulted bonds can recover some of their principal, but it is often pennies on the dollar.

Many investors in corporate bonds rely on the credit ratings agencies to assess the risk of issuers of corporate bonds. These ratings agencies also assign credit ratings to bonds issued by governments. See page 17 for the system of credit ratings of the main credit rating agencies.

Assessing Credit Risk

Credit ratings published by Moody's, Standard & Poor's and Fitch IBCA are meant to capture and categorise credit risk, but institutional investors in corporate bonds often supplement these agency ratings with their own credit analysis. The credit analyst does a job that is similar to that of the equity analyst. Both analyse and assess the fundamental strength of the company, relying heavily on accounting information such as the company's profit and loss account and balance sheet statements. However, the perspective of each is different: the equity analyst's primary interest is on the bottom line profits after tax generated by the company, whereas the credit analyst is more interested in the company's free cash flow.

Figure 3.6 shows a simplified profit and loss account. The credit analyst will focus on operating profit and depreciation (free cash flow), whereas the equity analyst will focus on PAT (profits after tax). Typically, credit analysts will focus on the interest cover ratio (free cash flow/interest payable). In contrast, the equity analyst will take account of interest cover as one of many financial ratios; however, the key issue for the equity analyst is how profitable the company is and how fast it can grow its profits over time.

Figure 3.6 ABC plc Profit and Loss Account 2010

Excerpts from the Profit & Loss Account 2010	€m	Per Share
Sales	2000	200c
Operating Costs	(1650)	
Operating Profit	350	
Depreciation	(75)	7.5c
Interest Charge	(125)	
Pre-tax Profit	150	
Taxation	(30)	
After-tax Profits	120	12.0c
Dividend	(40)	4.0c
Retained Profits	80	

Investment in corporate bonds may involve close examination of the bond prospectus, which outlines in detail the bond's characteristics and the rights, priorities and obligations of the issuer and bondholder.

Other Risks

Investors should be aware of some other risk factors affecting corporate bonds. Two of the most important ones are call risk and event risk. If a corporate bond is callable, then the issuing company has the right to purchase (or pay off) the bond after a minimum time period. Event risk is the risk that a corporate transaction, natural disaster or regulatory change will cause an abrupt downgrade in a corporate bond. Event risk tends to vary by industry sector. For example, if the telecom industry happens to be consolidating, then event risk may run high for all bonds in this sector. The risk is that the bondholder's company may purchase another telecom company and possibly increase its debt burden (financial leverage) in the process.

Credit Spread: The Pay-off for Assuming Credit Risk

The pay-off for assuming all these extra risks is a higher yield. The difference between the yields on a corporate bond and on a government bond is called the credit spread (or sometimes just the yield spread).

Table 3.3 Global Investment Grade Bonds

Bond – Currency; Issuer; Redemption Date	Yield to Maturity (%)	Spread versus Government (%)
$ Goldman Sachs 4.75% 07/13	2.55	1.75
$ GE Capital 5.0% 01/16	3.35	1.83
$ Goldman Sachs 6.13% 02/33	5.79	1.50
€ HSBC Fin 3.38% 06/12	2.30	1.59
€ Unicredit 4.38% 01/20	4.35	1.65

Source: *Financial Times*, 26 November 2010.

Predicting changes in a credit spread is difficult because it depends on both the specific corporate issuer and overall bond market conditions. For example, a credit upgrade on a specific corporate bond, say from S&P BBB to A, will narrow the credit spread for that particular bond because the risk of default lessens.

After purchasing a corporate bond, the bondholder will benefit from declining interest rates and from a narrowing of the credit spread. This in turn drives up the price of the bondholder's corporate bond. On the other hand, rising interest rates and a widening of the credit spread work against the bondholder by causing a higher GRY and a lower bond price.

Managing Corporate Bond Portfolios

Just like every other asset category, investors can adopt a passive or an active approach when investing in corporate bonds. For active managers, corporate bond markets present a wide array of opportunities and challenges.

Inefficiencies in credit markets are generally viewed as being greater than in government bond markets or indeed in the major equity markets. Information on specific bond issues may not be widely available and investor inexperience may result in markets with many pricing anomalies. Therefore, fund managers who commit resources to intensive research and trading resources can exploit such inefficiencies to create added value.

The credit investment process involves a mixture of analysis of the financial strength and business prospects of the issuing company, and the prospects for overall interest rates and bond yields. Therefore, managing a corporate bond portfolio requires skills associated with detailed analysis of individual companies as well as skills associated with analysing the overall economic cycle. Table 3.4 summarises the 'stock selection' skill set required.

Table 3.4 Corporate Bonds Stock Selection

Company (Issuer)	Qualitative analysis	Management Regulatory environment Industry and company risks
	Quantitative analysis	Balance sheet Profit and loss account Cash flows Key ratios
	Bond-specific analysis	Prospectus Capital structure Liquidity

In Chapter 13 we analyse the economic cycle and its impact on the major asset categories. Figure 13.2 (see page 285) shows the typical behaviour of the different asset classes over the course of the cycle. We can see that bond markets typically perform well (bond prices rise, yields fall) as an economy heads into recession. In contrast, as the economy heads towards a peak in activity, bond prices fall (yields rise). As part of the widely defined 'bond asset class', corporate bonds are subject to the same influences. However, the behaviour of corporate bonds is more complicated than this over the course of the cycle. This is because changes in spreads will have a material impact on corporate bond prices through the course of the economic cycle. As an economy heads into recession, there will be a general downward pressure on yields. However, corporate failure and bankruptcy will tend to increase, leading to an increase in the rate of corporate defaults. As a consequence, investors will look for higher yields from corporate bonds to compensate for the higher risk of default. In contrast, during the growth phase of the economic cycle, corporate health improves and investors will be prepared to accept lower risk premiums from corporate bonds as default rates decline.

Index-Linked Bonds

Our discussion so far has related to bonds (government and corporate) that pay a fixed nominal coupon and repay par value on the maturity date. Index-linked bonds are identical to fixed-interest bonds in terms of structure: they pay a regular coupon and have a fixed maturity date. However, index-linked bonds are fundamentally different investment vehicles because:

* The coupon is not fixed but increases in line with the rise in general inflation.
* At maturity the investor receives the par value of the bond, which will have been uplifted by the cumulative increase in the general price level over the life of the bond.

Therefore, index-linked gilts have very different investment characteristics to those of conventional bonds and should be considered as a separate asset class: see Table 3.5.

Table 3.5 Index-Linked Bonds versus Conventional Bonds

	Fixed-Interest Bonds	Index-Linked Bonds
Inflation Risk	Extremely high	Fully protected
Income	Nominal income flows known	Uncertainty regarding nominal flows
Price Volatility	Fluctuation driven by change in nominal yield	Fluctuation driven by change in real yield
Duration		Longer duration asset as cash flows weighted towards later dates

Index-linked bonds account for around one-quarter of UK government debt. The UK was one of the first developed economies to issue index-linked bonds in 1981, and has issued nineteen index-linked bonds since that date. Like conventional gilts, index-linked gilts pay coupons that are initially set in line with market interest rates. However, their semi-annual coupons and principal payment are adjusted by the Retail Prices Index (RPI). In September 2005 the UK Government issued the longest ever index-linked government bond: 1.25% Index-Linked Treasury Gilt 2055, maturing on 22 November 2055.

The most liquid index-linked market is Treasury Inflation-Protected Securities (TIPS), issued by the US Treasury. Other countries with significant index-linked markets are France, Canada, Germany and Australia.

SUMMARY

- Both lenders and borrowers benefit from the existence of well-developed bond markets.
- Bonds are essentially loans that are negotiable and the three key components that define the contractual relationship between the issuer and investor are par value, coupon and term to maturity.
- The yield measures that investors look to are the flat or running yield and, more important, the gross redemption yield (GRY).
- Bonds are valued using present-value techniques, whereby the bonds' cash flows are discounted at an appropriate rate of interest.
- The inverse relationship between market yields and bond prices is the basis for managing bond portfolios.
- Where we have a homogeneous set of bonds, such as Irish government bonds, we can analyse the characteristics of a bond market as a whole; the relationship between time to maturity and yields is referred to as the term structure of interest rates and is normally depicted as a yield curve.
- Duration can be thought of as the average number of years that it takes for an investor to get his money back.
- Modified Duration can be used to calculate the sensitivity of bond prices to changes in interest rates for small changes in rates.
- For large changes in yield, the convexity of a bond needs to be used to adjust the duration calculation.
- Evaluating credit risk is vitally important for investors in corporate bonds.
- The expected return and risk characteristics of index-linked bonds are fundamentally different from those of conventional fixed-interest securities.

QUESTIONS

1. A two-year government bond (3% Exchequer 2005) has a fixed coupon of €3 per €100 nominal of the bond. Your broker has quoted you a purchase price of €98 per €100 nominal but you don't trust him. The two-year rate of interest offered by your bank is 4% p.a. Is your broker offering you a better deal than that offered by the bank?

A. Yes

B. No

2. 10% is equivalent to _____ basis points.

A. 10

B. 100

C. 1,000

D. 10,000

3. Irish 10-year Government Bonds typically yield more than 6-month Irish Exchequer Bills primarily because of the:

A. Default risk differential

B. Expected inflation premium differential

C. Liquidity differential

D. Maturity differential

4. Holding all other factors constant:

A. A bond sold at a discount will experience a rise in price over time to reach par value.

B. A bond sold at a premium will experience a rise in price over time to reach par value.

C. A bond sold at a premium will experience a decline in price over time to reach par value.

D. Both A and C are true statements.

5. Why do investors invest in fixed-income securities?

A. A steady stream of income offered over the life of the bond's obligations.

B. A return of principal when the bond matures.

C. It is possible to earn capital gains when interest-rate movements are correctly predicted.

D. All of the above.

6. Which of the following statement(s) is/are TRUE?

A. Investors should shorten the maturity of the portfolio when interest rates are expected to fall.

    B. Investors should lengthen the maturity of their portfolio when interest rates are expected to rise.

    C. Investors will have a preference for low-coupon bonds over high-coupon bonds when interest rates are expected to rise.

       1. C only

       2. None of the above

       3. All of the above

       4. A & B only

7. **If interest rates are expected to fall, which of the following bond strategies yields the largest capital gains?**

    A. Buy short-term and high-coupon bonds.

    B. Sell long-term and low-coupon bonds.

    C. Buy long-term and low-coupon bonds.

    D. Sell short-term and high-coupon bonds.

8. **'Duration' is:**

    A. Always equal to the maturity of the bond

    B. Equal to double the maturity of the bond

    C. The weighted average of time to full recovery of the principal and interest payments on a bond at a present-value basis

    D. The weighted average of time to full recovery of the principal on a bond at a present-value basis

9. **The duration of a zero coupon bond is:**

    A. Less than its maturity

    B. Equal to its maturity

    C. Greater than its maturity

    D. Impossible to determine

10. **Regarding duration, please select the TRUE statement(s).**

    A. Other things being equal, the shorter the maturity, the longer the duration.

    B. Duration can measure the bond price sensitivity.

    C. Other things being equal, duration is positively related to coupon payment.

    D. Other things being equal, duration is positively related to GRY.

11. Which of the following is closest to the duration of the under-mentioned bond?

    4% Treasury 2014, which will be redeemed in exactly three years. The GRY is currently 2.5%.
    A. 3 years
    B. 4%
    C. 2.89 years
    D. 100.00

12. The 3.25% Treasury 2014 fixed-interest bond is currently trading on a GRY of 3%. The Macauley Duration of the bond is 2.9 years. If there is a one percentage point increase in the GRY, which of the following is closest to the percentage change in the price of this bond?

    A. +2.90%
    B. −2.90%
    C. +2.82%
    D. −2.82%

Chapter four

Investing in Equities

In Chapter 2 we discussed the basic characteristics of equity securities and how they are issued and traded on stock exchanges. Here we examine ways in which we can analyse and assess the investment merits of a company's shares. The questions that investors are interested in seeking answers to include:

- What is the fair price for a share and how can we calculate it?
- What are the key financial ratios relevant to an analysis of the investment prospects of a company?
- What yardsticks should be employed to compare one share with another?
- Are there ways to establish the investment value of an equity market?
- How can equity markets in different countries be compared with one another?

In this chapter we first apply the discounted cash-flow technique to estimate the fair price of a share. We then go on to describe the most commonly used relative valuation techniques. Chapter 5 provides a fuller list of definitions and descriptions of the most widely used financial and accounting ratios.

Learning Objectives

After reading this chapter you should:
- Understand the dividend discount model (DDM) and be able to use the model to estimate the fair value of a share
- Use the DDM as an analytical tool to infer market expectations regarding long-term dividend growth and expected market returns
- Be familiar with the price earnings ratio (PER) and its application to share valuation
- Be aware of relative valuation techniques as an approach to share valuation.

DISCOUNTED CASH FLOW TECHNIQUE

The analysis of bonds in Chapter 3 showed how the fair price of a bond could be calculated using the discounted cash flow technique. The basic underlying principle is that the price of any security can be determined by its estimated value. This estimated value may be calculated using the discounted cash flow technique. In the case of bonds this technique can be applied relatively easily, because the expected cash flows from bonds are known precisely. Equation 4.1 expresses the concept more generally:

$$\text{Today's Value of a Security} = \sum_{t=1}^{n} \frac{\text{Expected Cashflows}}{(1+r)^t}$$

[Equation 4.1]

where:
Cash flows = future cash flows resulting from ownership of the asset;
r = the appropriate interest rate or expected rate of return used as the discount rate;
n = number of periods (usually years) over which the cash flows are expected.

It is worth examining again Example 3.3 (reproduced below), where the discounted cash flow technique was applied to estimating the price of the 4% Treasury 2014.

Example 3.3 Calculating the Present Value of a Government Bond, 4% Treasury 2014

| Interest | | | €4 | €4 | €4 | |
| Redemption Amount | | | | | €100 | |

```
        +--------------+----------+----------+-----------------+-------->
        15 January     2012       2013       15 January        Time
        2011                                 2014
```

To calculate the present value we need to decide on a rate of discount, in this case r = 3%

Cash flows	Year	Cash Flow	Present Value Calculation		PV of end Payment
	2012	4	$\frac{4}{1.03}$	=	3.88
	2013	4	$\frac{4}{(1.03)^2}$	=	3.77
	2014	104	$\frac{104}{(1.03)^3}$	=	95.18
					102.83

In this example, cash flows are received over the next 3 years and the estimated price of the bond has been calculated using a discount rate of 3%. This approach applies to bonds of any maturity, so for a 50-year bond there will just be more calculations. However, financial calculators or interest tables make such calculations fast and accurate.

For other securities, such as equities, the valuation approach expressed in Equation 4.1 can also be applied. However, compared with bonds there is a major obstacle to using this technique – the cash flows that are expected to be generated from ownership of shares are unknown. They are expected cash flows with a high degree of uncertainty, rather then the definite income flows generated by bonds. Therefore, the future expected stream of investment income from an equity has to be estimated from an analysis of the underlying business and an assessment of prospects for the overall economy. This is a very difficult task and, not surprisingly, several approaches have been developed to estimate the value of company shares. There is no one approach that answers all the questions, and most investors and investment analysts apply several techniques in their quest to value company shares. In this chapter we discuss the three most commonly used approaches to share valuation:

i)   The traditional discounted cash flow technique based on the dividend discount model (DDM).
ii)   The price earnings ratio (PER) or earnings multiplier approach.
iii)   Relative valuation techniques.

THE DIVIDEND DISCOUNT MODEL (DDM)

Discounted cash flow techniques require two key pieces of information to work effectively:

• the future stream of income that is expected to be generated by a security and its timing;
• a discount rate (r) that is used to calculate the present value (PV) of each cash flow.

We leave until later in this chapter the question of what discount rate to apply. First, let's tackle the thorny issue of estimating the future stream of income that we expect the equity security to generate. Fortunately the DDM provides us with a solution that is conceptually well grounded and is relatively easy to implement once we make some simplifying assumptions. The critical premise underlying this model is that the only cash flows that are relevant to investors in company shares are dividends. At first glance this may seem like an unrealistic assertion, as most investors probably look at equity investment in terms of achieving capital growth. In other words, most investors think of the prospective return from equity investment in terms of the holding period return (HPR). For any security this is defined as:

$$\frac{\text{(Sale Price} - \text{Purchase Price)} + \text{Investment Income}}{\text{Purchase Price}}$$

and is usually expressed as a percentage.

Of course the big problem is trying to estimate the future sale price of a security. The DDM looks at the question of share valuation from an altogether different angle. It views a share in terms of a very long holding period – in fact it addresses the issue based on the viewpoint that a company share generates a stream of cash flows that will stretch out to infinity! Conceptually this is in fact correct; unlike bonds, equities have no terminal or redemption date. As long as the underlying business thrives, shares in a company exist for ever. If we also assume that an investor holds shares for a very long time, then the only investment return that such an investor can expect to receive is the future stream of dividend payments from the company. This assumption is not as unrealistic as it may seem at first blush. A substantial proportion of the money invested in the stock market comes from investors that have a very long investment time horizon. Pension funds, insurance companies and many private investors would fall into this category. The DDM does go a step further than the very long term and assumes that the dividend stream from an equity stretches to infinity. We will see that this assumption enables us to use a mathematical equation that simplifies enormously the task of estimating the fair value of a share. In a practical sense, extending the time horizon to infinity is not too troublesome. This is because the present value of income due to be received in (say) 50 years' time is tiny. So while the model does include these theoretical, faraway payments, the fact is that most of the estimated value of a share is accounted for by dividends expected to be received over the first 20 to 25 years.

Therefore dividends, as the only cash payment a shareholder receives from a company, are the foundation of valuation using the discounted cash flow technique. The DDM equation (4.2) is conceptually exactly the same as the approach used to value bonds and may be written as:

$$\text{Fair Value of a Share} = \sum_{t=1}^{n} \frac{D_t}{(1+r)^t}$$

[*Equation 4.2*]

where:

$D_1, D_2 \ldots D_n$ = dividends expected to be received in each future period;
r = the discount rate: the rate used is often referred to as the required rate of return. There are two differences compared with bonds:

- The dividend stream is uncertain, and where a company gets into financial difficulty no dividend at all may be paid.
- Because company shares have no terminal date, Equation 4.2 indicates that investors are dealing with infinity.

The latter issue is in fact less troublesome than it may seem, as we alluded to above. This is because the present value of a dividend expected to be received a long time into the future is very low. For example, imagine we are analysing CRH and we estimate that the dividend to be received in 50 years' time is €10 per share. Assume a discount rate of 10% and the present value of this dividend is only 9c! (CRH's dividend in 2009 was 62.5c per share):

Example 4.1 Present value of Dividend to be Received in 50 Years

$$PV = D_{50}/(1 + r)^{50} = 10/(1.1)^{50} = 10/(111.1) = .09$$

Therefore, we know that in any analysis the dividend income to be received over the first 15–25 years will account for the lion's share of the estimated intrinsic value of an equity. Detailed analysis of a company and its prospects can yield reasonably accurate forecasts of dividends over the first 3–5 years, particularly for long-established companies with a record of steady and stable growth in dividend payments. However, any forecasts of dividend payments beyond this timeframe will be subject to huge margins for error.

The DDM enables investors to get around this seemingly intractable problem by making assumptions about the expected long-term growth rate in dividend payments. The starting point is the most recent dividend paid by a company, which is known. Then an investor or analyst attempts to estimate the future growth rate in that dividend. The simplifying assumption is made that a company will grow its dividend at a *constant* rate of growth. This assumption is not as far removed from practice as it seems. Many companies seek to grow their dividend payments at a stable long-term rate that is in line with the long-term rate of growth of the underlying business. Also, because we are dealing with infinity, even companies that are currently growing rapidly will eventually converge on some long-term sustainable rate of growth. The DDM model is usually framed in terms of three different growth scenarios, namely:

- no growth;
- constant growth;
- variable growth.

No-Growth Model

If we have a company where we expect no growth in the dividend stream, we can represent the dividend stream as:

Figure 4.1 No-Growth Dividend Stream

$$\text{Value of a share} \quad = \quad \frac{D_0}{1+r} \quad + \quad \frac{D_0}{(1+r)^2} \quad \cdots \quad \frac{D_0}{(1+r)^n} \quad \infty$$

To estimate the intrinsic value of the share we can calculate the present value of each expected dividend by dividing each payment by $(1+r)^t$ and then summing all of these payments. The no-growth dividend model is essentially a fixed perpetual income stream. Fortunately, there is a simple equation to estimate the present value of a perpetuity that can be applied to this infinite stream of constant cash flows as follows:

$$\text{Value of a share} \quad = \quad \frac{D_0}{r}$$

where:
D_0 = constant dividend payment;
r = the required rate of return, which is used as the discount rate.

Therefore, the estimated value of a share which has just paid a dividend of €1 that is expected to remain constant to infinity, can be calculated as €1/r. If we assume that 10% is the required rate of return, this results in a fair price for this company's shares of €1/0.1 = €10.

This model is of little practical benefit, since it is the ability of equities to grow their dividend over time that makes them an attractive investment. However, when we assume that dividend payments grow at a constant growth rate out to infinity we get an altogether more interesting equation.

Constant-Growth Model

When we assume that a company will grow its dividend at a constant growth rate into the future, we can then represent the expected flow of dividend payments as follows:

Figure 4.2 Constant-Growth Dividend Stream

$$\text{Value of a Share} \quad = \quad \frac{D_0(1+g)}{(1+r)} \quad + \quad \frac{D_0(1+g)^2}{(1+r)^2} \quad + \quad \frac{D_0(1+g)^3}{(1+r)^3} \quad \cdots \quad \infty$$

where:
D_0 = the most recent dividend paid;
g = projected constant rate of growth in the dividend.

From this equation we can see that the next dividend to be received is projected as last year's dividend multiplied by one plus the assumed growth rate. Each subsequent dividend can be estimated by multiplying the previous payment by $(1 + g)$. We can calculate the present value of each dividend by dividing each cash flow by $(1 + r)^t$ and then summing each present value. While the cash flows in the model go to infinity, we may take (say) 50 years as a cut-off given that we know the faraway cash flows will have very little value today. Fortunately we don't have to calculate the value of a share in this painstaking way, as the constant growth DDM simplifies to the following equation:

$$\text{Value of a share} = \frac{D_1}{r - g}$$ [Equation 4.3]

where:
D_1 = the dividend expected to be received at end-year one;
r = the discount rate;
g = growth rate of future dividends, which is assumed to be constant.
Note: r must always be greater than g.

This equation is also 'more correct' than doing lengthy hand calculations, as it includes all dividend payments expected to be received to infinity. As long as the assumption regarding the dividend growth rate is reasonably accurate, then Equation 4.3 provides a simple and conceptually elegant valuation tool.

Example 4.2 CRH Fair Value

CRH has just paid a dividend of 60c per share and investors expect dividends to grow at a constant long-term rate of growth of 9% per annum. For investments of CRH 's risk level investors require a return of 12% per annum. Using the constant growth DDM to estimate the value of a share in CRH we have:

$$\text{Share Value} = \frac{D_1}{r - g}$$

where:
D_1 = the dividend expected to be received one period from now, which may be calculated as last year's dividend (D_0) multiplied by the assumed growth rate $(1 + g)$ and the estimated value per CRH share is:

$$\frac{60c\,(1 + 0.09)}{0.12 - 0.09} = €21.80$$

Estimating the Discount Rate

So far we have not discussed how we estimate the discount rate (r). For government bonds r could be quite easily established from the current level of gross redemption yields on bonds of a maturity similar to the bond in question. For equities the issue is far more problematic, since the variability of expected returns associated with equity securities means that there is no equivalent of the GRY for equities. The approach adopted by most investors is to think in terms of that long-term rate of return that an equity needs to generate if it is to reward an investor for the risk taken. Equity investment involves risk that must be rewarded through a commensurately higher rate of return. In principle, companies can be ranked in terms of their risk level. For example, most investors would assign a lower degree of risk to CRH than they would to (say) a small oil exploration company. We can think of that rate of return which compensates investors for the investment risk taken as the required rate of return. A starting point in estimating r can be the long-term historical returns achieved by the overall equity market. For example, over the very long term equity markets have delivered average annual returns of approximately 10% per annum. If we assume that CRH has a risk level higher than the market as a whole we may assign a required rate of return of 12% to CRH. This then becomes the appropriate discount rate to use in the DDM.

Variable Growth Dividend Discount Model

In estimating the fair value of equity the assumption of constant growth out to infinity is quite restrictive. One way of improving the usefulness of the model is to make the growth assumption more realistic. Most companies go through different development phases. Typically companies may go through an initial period of fast growth that eventually slows to a rate of growth in line with the sector or the overall economy. The future growth pattern of dividends may be modelled to include different rates of growth for different sub-periods. For example, we could take market consensus forecasts of earnings and dividends for an initial period of up to five years, with a constant rate of dividend growth assumed thereafter.

Here, we will look at the simplest refinement of the constant growth DDM, namely a two-stage variable growth model. Instead of conceptualising the future dividend payments of a stock in terms of a stream of income growing at a constant rate to infinity, we now think of the cash flows occurring over two distinct periods:

Period 1: Today is t_0 and we expect dividends to grow at an annual rate of g for N years.

Period 2: From year N+1 to infinity dividends are expected to grow at a different (usually lower) constant rate g_c

The estimate of the fair value of a stock thus becomes a function of two dividend flows:

i)   The flow from period 1 to N, which we call V_1.
ii)   The flow from period N+1 to infinity, which we call V_2.

Part 2 can be thought of as the constant growth DDM except that it puts a capital value at year N on all dividends expected to be received from period N+1 to infinity.

Thus our estimate of fair value or fair price for a stock becomes:
$$P = V_1 + V_2$$

Algebraically, the first stage of growth may be expressed as:

$$V1 = \sum_{t=1}^{N} \frac{D_0(1+g)t}{(1+r)t}$$

where D_0 = last dividend paid
g = growth rate of dividend in the first sub-period
t = time (in years)
N = number of years in the first period.

Example 4.3: CRH

Assume that our investment research department has provided the following forecasts for CRH:
- Dividend to grow by 50% over the next two years and at a constant rate of 3% per annum thereafter.
- A dividend of 63c has just been received.
- Investors' required rate of return is 10%.

Therefore the expected dividend income stream for the first period is:

D_0 =   63c
D_1 =   63(1+g)   =   63(1.5)   =   94.5c
D_2 =   63(1+g)^2 =   63(1.5)^2 =   142.0c

Applying the formula $VI = \sum_{t=1}^{N} \frac{D_0(1+g)t}{(1+r)t}$ we have

$$V_1 = \sum 94.5/1.1 + 142.0/(1.1)^2 = 85.9 + 117.4 = 203.3c$$

For V_2 we can apply the standard constant growth DDM with just two refinements:

i)   The first dividend to go into the equation is not D_1, but the forecast dividend at year N+1.
ii) The estimated capital value needs to be divided by $(1+r)^N$.

Staying with the CRH example, the dividend at year N+1 may be calculated by taking the forecast dividend at the end of year 2, $\mathbf{D_2}$ = 142, multiplied by one plus the period 2 constant rate of growth $\mathbf{g_c}$. The constant rate of growth is 3%, so the forecast dividend at year N+1 is:

$$142 * 1+.03 = 146.3$$

Algebraically, this may be written as:

$$D_3 = D_0 (1+g)^N * (1+g_c)$$

Then, applying the constant growth DDM formula, we divide this dividend by what is sometimes called the **capitalisation rate (r-g_c)**. In our CRH example this is:

$$146.3/r-g = 146.3/ 0.1 -0.03 = 146.3/ .07 = 2090c$$

Algebraically, this may be written as:

$$P_N = \frac{D_0 (1+g)^N * (1+g_c)}{r - g}$$

This is sometimes referred to as the **terminal value (P_N)** as it represents the present value of all future dividends expected to be paid by CRH at the end of year 2. Remember that our equation for the fair value of CRH shares is $P = V_1 + V_2$. We have calculated V_1 above as 203.3c. V_2 may be calculated as the terminal value discounted back to today's present value:

$$P_N / (1+r)^N$$

which is $2090c/(1.1)^2 = 1727c$.
Thus our estimate of the fair price of CRH's shares using the two-stage variable growth DDM is:

$$P = V_1 + V_2 = 203.3 + 1727 = 1930.3c$$

$$P = \sum_{t=1}^{N} \frac{D0(1+g)t}{(1+r)t} + P_N / (1+r)^N$$

Advantages and Usage of the DDM

The constant-growth DDM is theoretically sound and requires only three inputs – the most recent dividend paid, the appropriate required rate of return and an estimate of the future growth rate in dividends. The DDM is used extensively by investment analysts and investors, although it is usually used in conjunction with other models. For many analysts the assumption that dividends will grow at a constant rate of growth to infinity is too restrictive. They often fine-tune this assumption by modelling different rates of growth for different sub-periods. For example, an initial period of high growth may be assumed if a company is at an early stage of its development, and after a period of (say) 5 years a constant growth rate closer to the market average may be assumed. This is referred to as the variable growth model. It allows analysts to refine their growth forecasts, but it exhibits the same advantages and disadvantages as the basic constant-growth model.

Disadvantages of the DDM

The drawbacks of the DDM hinge on the fact that the estimate of fair value that the model produces is extremely sensitive to the values input for r and g. To get some feel for this let's go back to Example 4.2, where we used inputs of 9% for g and 12% for r for CRH. In practice the values chosen for these variables will be subject to substantial judgment on the part of the investor. Let's assume that in this case we are told that any values for r and g within a range of +/−1% would be reasonable. Let's reduce g to 8% and increase r to 13%. These are apparently quite small adjustments in variables that are, after all, subjective estimates. Plugging these new figures into the DDM now results in a very different estimate of fair value for CRH:

$$\text{Share Value} = \frac{60c\,(1 + 0.08)}{0.13 - 0.08} = €12.96$$

It is instructive to establish what happens to the estimate of fair value when we increase g by 1% and leave r at 12%:

$$\text{Share Value} = \frac{60c\,(1 + 0.10)}{0.12 - 0.10} = €33.00$$

The apparently small changes to our input values have resulted in a very wide price range. This highlights the key weakness of the DDM, which is that it is not robust. In other words, small changes to the estimates of r and g can lead to disproportionately large changes in the estimates of fair value. In itself this does not give sufficient cause to discard the model as a valuation tool; rather it emphasises the need to expend substantial effort in estimating the inputs that go into the model.

The DDM as an Analytical Tool

Like any theoretical model the DDM has its flaws, particularly if the objective is to get a precise estimate of the fair value of a share. However, it is a very flexible model and the basic equation can be easily manipulated to help answer a variety of questions concerning individual equities and the market as a whole.

What is the Market Saying about r?

We can manipulate the basic DDM equation to enable us to infer the required rate of return that is built into current market levels, once we assume a value for the growth rate (g).

$$r = D_1/MV + g$$

[Equation 4.4]

Returning to CRH, if the share price today is €18 and we estimate dividend growth of 8% per annum, we can derive the required rate of return based on the market price of the shares using Equation 4.4:

$$r = \frac{60}{1800} + .08 = .03 + .08 = .11 \text{ or } 11\%$$

If the assumption regarding g is correct, then investors who buy shares in CRH at €18 can expect to receive a long-term rate of return of 11%. This equation can also be used to infer what the expected return is on the overall equity market. Given the information below for the overall Irish equity market, using Equation 4.3 we can estimate the expected long-term rate of return implied by the current level of the market.

ISEQ Overall Index – Current Data
Prospective Dividend Yield (D_1/MV) = 3% or .03
Constant Growth Rate of Dividend = 7% or .07

where MV now is the current level of the index and D_1 is the aggregate level of dividends expected to be paid next year.

$$r = .03 + .07 = .10 \text{ or } 10\%$$

Again, confidence in the estimated value for r depends on how valid the assumption regarding g turns out to be. For the overall equity market the assumed value for g is normally based on an assessment of the long-term rate of growth in nominal GDP and of long-run inflation expectations.

What is the Market Saying about g?

In order to answer this question we can rearrange the DDM equation to give:

$$g = r - D_1/MV$$

[Equation 4.5]

To solve for g we must make an assumption about r. Usually analysts estimate r on the basis of the very long-run historical average annual rate of return delivered from an overall equity index. Let's assume that on the basis of our historical investigation of returns we believe that it is reasonable to expect a long-term rate of return of 10% per annum from the Irish market. We also learn that the prospective dividend yield (D_1/MV) is 3%, and armed with these two items of information we can now use Equation 4.5 to generate a value for g:

$$g = .10 - .03 = .07 \text{ or } 7\%$$

This indicates that the current level of the Irish equity market implies that dividends will grow at a long-term rate of growth of 7% per annum.

DDM: How It Is Used

ESTIMATE FAIR VALUE OF AN EQUITY	• Assume required rate of return. • Assume constant growth rate in dividends.	• Compare 'fair price' with market price.	• Assumptions may be varied to check for 'reasonableness'.
ESTIMATE GROWTH RATE IN DIVIDENDS (g) IMPLIED BY CURRENT MARKET LEVELS	• If g is high relative to historical norms, it suggests investors may be disappointed as actual growth reverts to historical norms – signals that market may be too high.	• If g is low relative to historical norms, it suggests that market may be too low and could be due a rise.	
ESTIMATE EXPECTED RETURN (r) IMPLICIT IN CURRENT MARKET PRICES	• Constant growth rate in dividends must be assumed. • Current level of market is input.	• If r is high relative to historical norms, it indicates that the share or market offers above-average long-term returns.	• If r is low relative to historical norms, it indicates that current prices are high, thus offering poor future returns.

In summary, the DDM provides a solid conceptual framework whereby assumptions can be tested in a rigorous way and a variety of information can be gleaned based on market prices. The DDM is an extremely useful analytical tool but is most effective when used in conjunction with other valuation tools.

THE PRICE EARNINGS RATIO (PER) OR EARNINGS MULTIPLIER

The PER was defined in Chapter 2 and is reproduced below:

The Price Earnings Ratio (PER)

The most commonly used convention for measuring and comparing company valuations is the Price Earnings Ratio or PER.

A company may be expected to generate a stream of profits into the future. The shareholder is a part-owner of that stream of profits.

Earnings per share is a measure of the amount of profit after tax earned in a financial year, which is attributable to each share issued by the company.

The PER is a profit-based measure of the company's perceived worth that relates share price to earnings per share.

With ABC plc's share price at 200c and EPS of 12c in its most recent financial year:

Price Earnings Ratio: $\dfrac{200c}{12c}$

$= 16.7$ times

The PER is the best-known and most widely used valuation technique. Analysts, company executives and active private investors are comfortable with earnings per share (EPS) and PERs. Despite its more widespread use, the conceptual framework for the earnings multiplier model is not as solidly based in economic theory as is the DDM. The P/E Model is based on a simple identity:

$P = EPS \times PER$ where:

P = current market price;

E = most recent 12-month earnings;

EPS = earnings per share.

Therefore, the price of a share is viewed as the product of two variables:

i)   EPS
ii)   PER

Investment analysts will often use the model to establish a price target for a company's shares. First, EPS are forecast for (say) the next two years. This forecast will usually be based on a detailed analysis of the company's historical performance and an assessment of its prospects over the next 2–3 years. The second step is to apply a forecast PER to these EPS estimates, which results in a target price for the shares in one year's and two years' time.

Example 4.4 Forecasting CRH's PER

You are an investment analyst in a stockbroking firm and after lengthy analysis you forecast EPS for CRH as follows:

	Last Year (actual)	This Year (forecast)	Next Year (forecast)
EPS (c)	63	63	69

The current market price of CRH's shares is €13 and, armed with this information, you calculate CRH's PER as:

$$1300/63 = 20.6$$

This is sometimes referred to as CRH's historic PER. You now assume that CRH will trade on the same PER this time next year and in two years' time. Therefore, you put a price target on the shares of:

Price Target in year 1: $EPS1 \times PER1 = 63 \times 20.6 = €13.00$
Price Target in year 2: $EPS2 \times PER2 = 69 \times 20.6 = €14.20$

The degree of confidence that can be attributed to these price targets depends on the accuracy of the EPS forecasts and the validity of the assumption regarding the PER that is attributed to CRH. The degree of error of EPS forecasts increases with time and varies enormously from company to company. Greater confidence can be placed in forecasts for long-established companies that operate in relatively stable business sectors. Overall market PERs expand and contract depending on investors' expectations regarding overall economic and market developments. PERs for individual companies are influenced by these overall market trends and by the ebb and flow of investors' assessment of the prospects for each individual company. Therefore, forecasting the PER that will apply to CRH in one year is usually more difficult than forecasting CRH's EPS! Analysis of historical trends and an assessment of where we are in the economic cycle is one way to tackle this forecasting problem (see Chapter 13). Analysis of these macro trends would then need to be combined with a historical and peer-group analysis of the particular company.

What Factors Determine the PER?

Most investors intuitively realise that the PER should be higher for companies whose earnings are expected to grow rapidly. Figure 4.3 lists the ten largest Irish quoted companies at end-January 2011 and we can see how the PER ranges from a low of 11.3 for DCC to a high of 20.6 for CRH. Other things being equal, this indicates that investors expect CRH to grow its EPS at a faster rate than DCC and are therefore prepared to pay a price for CRH shares that represents a much higher multiple of its current earnings.

Figure 4.3 Top Ten Irish Quoted Companies

Company	Share Price (€c)	Market Capitalisation € million	Price Earnings Ratio 2010
CRH	1564	11,087	20.6
Ryanair Holdings	365	5,424	13.6
Kerry Group	2367	4,151	12.4
Dragon Oil (USc)	928	3,466	12.2
Elan Corp (USc)	675	2,886	N/A
ARYZTA	3175	2,629	13.0
Smurfit Kappa Group	873	1,910	14.5
DCC	2160	1,799	11.3
Bank of Ireland	30	1,611	N/A
Paddy Power	2880	1,390	16.5
Top Ten Companies		**36,354**	

Source: Davy Stockbrokers

In the CRH example above we used the current or historic PER as our estimate of the future PER to generate a price target for CRH. However, we are still faced with the question as to whether the current price and PER of CRH is appropriate. Compared with the DDM an apparent advantage of using the PER is that we don't have to estimate or assume values for growth (g) and the required rate of return (r). Ironically, in order to try to understand what factors determine a company's PER it is in fact instructive to derive the PER from the constant-growth DDM.

First, we can think of the value of a share today as a function of forecast earnings per share and the prospective PER. A share price is a function of its future performance and not its historical returns, so we must therefore look to the future to estimate share values. Since we are considering a stock with a constant growth rate we can calculate next year's expected earnings as:

$$E_1 = E_0 (1 + g)$$

Now instead of expressing the current market price as:

$$P = E * PER$$

where:
P = current market price,
E = most recent 12-month earnings per share,
we can express it slightly differently as:

$$P = \text{value of stock today} = E_1 \text{ * } P/E_1$$

We are now estimating the current value of the share in terms of forecast EPS and the 1-year prospective PER. We can compare this value with the current market price in order to determine whether the shares should be purchased or sold. In order to establish the 'fair value' of a share in this way we must establish a value for the prospective PER. In the CRH example above we simply used the historic PER as our estimate of future PERs. Clearly we need to do more than this, so let's start with the constant-growth DDM equation, which as we've seen is the foundation of valuation of equity securities:

$$\text{Value of a share (P)} = \frac{D_1}{r - g}$$

[Equation 4.6]

where:
D_1 = the dividend expected to be received at end-year one;
r = the discount rate;
g = growth rate of future dividends.

Remember that this equation provides us with an estimate of the value of a stock today. Dividing both sides of this equation by expected earnings (E_1) we get:

$$\frac{P}{E_1} = \frac{D_1/E_1}{r - g}$$

[Equation 4.7]

The left-hand side of Equation 4.7 is nothing other than the prospective PER, and the right-hand side allows us to focus in on those factors that determine the prospective PER, which are:

i)   The *expected* dividend payout ratio (D_1/E_1).
ii)   The *estimated* required rate of return.
iii)   The *expected* growth rate in dividends.

Looked at in this conceptual framework we can see that the PER is a function of the above three variables, and holding the relevant other two variables constant, the following relationships should hold:

i)   The higher D_1/E_1 (the expected payout ratio), the higher the PER.
ii)   The higher the expected growth rate, the higher the PER.
iii)   The higher the required rate of return, the lower the PER.

While the above relationships do hold, it must be emphasised that these three variables interact with one another in terms of their impact on the PER. When a firm raises its payout ratio it usually improves sentiment towards the stock and leads to an expansion in the PER. However, if the rise in the pay-out ratio results in the firm investing less, then this will lower its prospective growth rate. A lower g will lead to a contraction in the PER and a lower share price! By the same token, when a firm tries to increase its prospective growth rate by investing in risky projects it should lead to an expansion in its PER. However, in this scenario investors will demand an increase in the required rate of return, which will act to lead to a contraction in the PER! We can see that, just like the DDM, the key variables that influence a firm's prospective PER are g and r.

Therefore, while the earnings multiplier approach to share valuation may be intuitively easier to grasp than the DDM, the actual estimate of share value is critically dependent on the assumptions made regarding expected returns and forecast growth in earnings. Because of these difficulties many investors and investment analysts concentrate on relative valuations rather than absolute valuations.

Relative Valuation Techniques

Example 4.5 Forecasting CRH's Share Price

From the previous example you know that CHR at its current market price of €13 is trading on a historic PER of 20.6. You have gleaned the information below from various market sources:

Historic PERs for:

	CRH	European Building Materials – Sector Average
2 years ago	17.4	18.6
1 year ago	16.2	14.4
Current	20.6	13.2
Average	18.1	15.4

It is apparent that CRH is trading on a PER that is significantly higher than its recent historical average. If it were to revert to this average of 18.1, the share price would fall to:

CRH Share Price : EPS * PER = 63c * 8.1 = €11.40

If, instead of applying CRH's historical average PER, we use the historical average for the European building materials sector, our share price forecast now becomes:

CRH share price: 63c * 15.4 = €9.70

This much lower share price estimate highlights a very important point. Detailed analysis on the company in question and on the overall business cycle is required before we can have confidence in our share price estimate. Imagine that you are employed as an investment analyst and you are given the task of producing a share price target for CRH in one year, using the PER model. You need to make two estimates: a forecast for CRH's EPS for next year, and an estimate of the PER that will apply to its shares in one year's time. CRH operates in a cyclical business sector and your analysis may lead you to conclude that as economies come out of recession CRH will benefit with a big bounce-back in earnings. While the average forecast of next year's EPS may be 69c, you may take a more optimistic view with a forecast of 73c per share.

Next you will need to make a judgment about the appropriate PER to apply. You will note that during recessions cyclical companies such as CRH trade on a very high PER. This is not due to a fundamental reassessment of the company's long-term prospects. Rather, it reflects the fact that earnings of cyclical companies fall sharply during recessions, pulling down EPS. However, share prices fall by a much smaller percentage amount since investors 'see through' what they believe will be a temporary fall in earnings. Therefore, the higher PER in recessionary times is arithmetic. If your analysis concludes that we are currently near the bottom of the business cycle, then you are likely to conclude that the average PER based on the past three years is too high an estimate to apply to next year's data.

In practice you will look at a much longer time period of perhaps ten years or more, and you will also analyse CRH's peer companies. Your forecast PER for next year will therefore be a function of three key pieces of analysis and judgment:

i)   Fundamental analysis of CRH and an estimate of its historical PER based on a long period of time.
ii) Analysis of the building materials sector and its historical PER.
iii) Assessment of the overall market PER and analysis of how CRH's PER has historically moved relative to this market PER.

If, after all this analysis, you conclude that the appropriate PER to apply is a 10% discount to the building materials sector average calculated in the example above, which is 15.4 / 1.1 = 14, your share price target for next year then becomes:

CRH one-year share price target: 73c * 14.0 = €10.22

Because of the difficulty in forecasting PERs and the consequent unreliability of resultant share-price targets, the investment community often assesses the prospects for a share relative to the company's average PER in the past, and to the average PER of a peer group of companies. Applying this approach involves analysing additional variables to those in the previous example. Example 4.5 stays with CRH and we can see that the object of the exercise is to establish whether CRH at its current share price is a BUY, HOLD or SELL.

The advantage of this approach is that it is not necessary to make explicit assumptions regarding r and g. The assessment of the appropriate PER is couched in the context of historical analysis of the company and the sector and/or market in which it operates. As well as the relative PER, several other investment ratios are normally analysed; these include Price/Book, Dividend Yield and a variety of cash flow-related ratios (see Chapter 5).

Inverting the PER to give the Earnings Yield

Investors often express the relationship between a share price and earnings per share in terms of the Earnings Yield. For the CHR example cited here, we now calculate EPS as a percentage of the share price. Above, we calculated CRH's PER as:

$$1300/63 = 20.6, \text{ i.e. Market Price/EPS}$$

and we calculate the Earnings Yield as:

$$63/1300 = .049 \text{ or } 4.9\%, \text{ i.e. EPS/Market Price}$$

The Earnings Yield is useful in that investors can often more easily relate to a percentage rate of return, and it can be compared with rates of return on other assets. The earnings yield can be calculated for individual equities and for equity indices. In particular the earnings yield of an equity index is often compared with the yield on long-term government bonds, and we would normally expect the earnings yield to be significantly higher.

The Earnings Yield can be particularly useful in the context of relative valuation techniques. It is all very well to come to a conclusion that a share is cheap relative to the overall equity market; but what if the market itself is overvalued? One way to assess this is to plot the historical relationship between the Earnings Yield and long-term bond yields. Many analysts believe that there will be a tendency for this relationship to revert to the mean.

SOME CONCLUDING THOUGHTS ON VALUATION

This chapter has covered three approaches to equity valuation:
i)   The dividend discount model.
ii)   The price earnings ratio or earnings multiplier approach.
iii)   The relative valuation approach.

These are not mutually exclusive and neither are they exhaustive. Each approach has its positives and negatives and those involved in investment analysis will generally use some combination of these techniques. In theory the DDM is the best model, as conceptually the best estimate of the current value of a company's shares is the estimated cash flows to be generated by that company. However, as we saw, any estimate of the company's present value is very dependent on a subjective assessment of future dividend growth and the risk-adjusted rate of return appropriate to the company in question. Because of these difficulties the PER model, when used as a relative valuation technique, has more widespread appeal and is easier to calculate. It has more intuitive appeal and can generate investment conclusions with a clearly articulated logic. The main danger of relying too heavily on relative valuation techniques occurs when the overall market is at a valuation extreme. This occurred at the height of the technology, media and telecom (TMT) bubble in the early 2000s, when many internet stocks were being sold at extremely high valuations. Investment banks and stockbrokers justified these valuations on the basis that they were 'cheap' compared with other similar stocks. This of course missed the really important reality at the time, which was that these comparator stocks were already ridiculously overvalued. Many investors had their fingers burned during this period, and with the benefit of hindsight the application of the DDM fundamental approach to valuation would have generated warning signals to anyone prepared to take notice.

Another important health warning when using the PER model is the importance of assessing the quality of earnings. In the era of cheap and plentiful credit up to the financial crash in 2008, most financial companies were trading on what seemed to be attractive PERs or earnings yields. However, subsequent events have shown that a large proportion of these earnings were illusory. Therefore, the reported accounting earnings drastically overstated the true long-term earnings power of these companies.

It should now be clear that just as a tradesman goes to work with a selection of tools, so too must the equity investor and analyst. There are a variety of tools available, and usually each one can play a part in solving the riddle of valuing equity securities. However, they are only tools and the quality of the outputs will depend on the quality of the inputs and the skills brought to bear on the analysis by the investment analyst, fund manager or private investor.

QUESTIONS

1. Which of the following statements is FALSE?

   A. The value of a share is the discounted present value of the stream of future earnings attributable to it.
   B. The price of a share results from the interplay of market supply and demand.
   C. Price and value can diverge dramatically for quite prolonged periods.
   D. At an equity-market peak, share prices will tend to be lower than value estimates based on discounted present values.

2. Which of the following statements is FALSE?

   A. Companies with high PERs are usually expected to grow faster than low-PER companies.
   B. Growth investing focuses on stocks that have potential for persistent and high earnings growth.
   C. The dividend yield and the price earnings ratio are two commonly used measures of value.
   D. Value investing focuses on stocks that are highly rated (they have high PERs) relative to the market.

3. Please select the FALSE statement:

   A. The discounted cash flow technique is used to evaluate stocks' prices.
   B. Present-value analysis is used to evaluate stocks' prices.
   C. The P/E approach is used to evaluate stocks' prices.
   D. The profit maximisation approach is used to evaluate stocks' prices.

4. Which of the following factors is NOT required for the calculation of securities' value in the present-value approach?

   A. The required rate of return
   B. The timing of future cash flows paid to shareholders
   C. The amount of future cash flows
   D. The par value of the shares in issue.

5. Which of the following dividend discount model formulae is/are correct (where D_0 = last dividend paid, and D_1 = next dividend to be received)?

   A. $D_0 (1+g)/(r-g)$
   B. $D_0 /(r-g)$
   C. $D_1 /(r-g)$
   D. D_1 /g

      1. A & C only
      2. All of the above
      3. A & B only
      4. A only

6. Kerry Group has just paid a dividend of €1.5 per share. Owing to the increasing popularity of cider drinking, Kerry expects to see a future growth rate of 10% per year. Given an average market required rate of return of 15%, what is the estimated current price of Kerry Group?

   A. €33
   B. €30
   C. €4
   D. €53

7. If Kerry Group trims its future outlook from a 10% growth rate to a 5% growth rate, what is the impact on its valuation? (Assume other things hold constant.)

   A. Stock price drops by 50%, that is, the new price is €16.50.
   B. Stock price remains the same.
   C. Stock price drops by about 52.27%; that is, new price is €15.75.
   D. Stock price increases by 50%; that is, new price is €49.50.

8. Regarding ordinary shareholders, which of the following statement(s) is/are TRUE?

   A. Their shares entitle them to a guaranteed dividend return.
   B. They are senior to bondholders in the event of the company going bankrupt.

➡

C. As the owners, shareholders may be described as the residual claimants on the assets of the company.

D. Limited liability means that shareholders are not responsible for the debts that a company takes on and therefore they cannot lose more than they paid for their shares.

1. All of the above
2. C & D only
3. A, C & D only
4. B & D only

9. The current dividend on a stock is 10c per share, growing at 10% p.a. What is the price of the stock if the discount rate is 12%?

A. 550c
B. 500c
C. 110c
D. 85c

10. Which of the following statement(s) is/are TRUE?

A. When intrinsic or fair value is larger than current market price, it suggests that the asset is undervalued.
B. When intrinsic or fair value is smaller than current market price, it suggests that the asset is undervalued.
C. When intrinsic or fair value is larger than current market price, it suggests that the asset is overvalued.
D. When the current market price is higher than intrinsic or fair value, it suggests that the asset is undervalued.

11. A firm has just paid a dividend of 33c. Investors expect the dividend to grow at a constant rate of 8% p.a. As the company is in a medium-risk sector, investors' expected return from such a share is 11% p.a. What is your estimate of the fair market value using the dividend discount model?

A. 446c
B. 1188c
C. 1100c
D. 324c

Exercise: Dividend Discount Model

You have estimated that Analog Devices has a sustainable return on equity (ROE) of 9% per annum. The company is in a fast-growing but low-margin segment of the computer industry and its management have stated that they intend to reinvest 60% of earnings indefinitely. An annual dividend of €1 has just been paid. Analysts view Analog as a moderately risky company so you have decided that an appropriate required rate of return is 12%. The shares are currently trading on the market at a price of €12.

1. Estimate the intrinsic value or fair price of an Analog share. Based on your estimate, would you invest in Analog at its current share price?
2. If you invest in Analog at the current price of €12, what is your expected long-term rate of return?
3. Calculate Analog's PER using your forecast of next year's earnings.
4. Suppose the company decided to increase the pay-out ratio to 80%. What impact would this have on your estimated PER for the company? (assuming no change in the constant growth rate of dividend, g)
5. Critically compare your estimates of Analog's PER. Do you need to do further analysis before concluding on your final estimate of a justifiable PER for Analog?
6. If you were analysing Analog Devices, what aspects of its business and financial performance would you concentrate on to help in determining the most appropriate PER to apply to value the company's shares?

Chapter five

Investment Arithmetic

This is a catch-all chapter that sets out to bring together the key quantitative yardsticks and financial ratios that are commonly used by investment practitioners. A brief description is provided for each concept together with illustrative examples where appropriate. Many, but not all, of the definitions outlined here appear in other chapters.

ACCOUNTING RATIOS

There are many ratios derived from published company accounts. The more important ones are described here by reference to information relating to a hypothetical company.

Table 5.1 ABC plc: Key Numbers

– Share Information			
	Shares in Issue		1000m
	Share price		200c
	Market Capitalisation		€2000m

– Excerpts from the Profit & Loss Account 2010	€m	Per Share
Sales	2000	200c
Operating Costs	(1650)	
Operating Profit	350	
Depreciation	(75)	7.5c
Interest Charge	(125)	
Pre-tax Profit	150	
Taxation	(30)	
After-tax Profits	120	12.0c
Dividend	(40)	4.0c
Retained Profits	80	

➡

– Excerpts from the Balance Sheet at end-December 2010

Fixed Assets	1300m
Net Current Assets	1400m
Total Assets	2700m
Less Net Debt	1500m
Shareholders Funds (Equity)	1200m

When analysing quoted companies a useful starting point is information on the company's capital structure, i.e. a list of the securities issued by the company and their market price. ABC has a simple structure with 1,000 million shares in issue and its share price of 200c results in a market capitalisation of €2,000 million (200c * 1,000m).

From the Profit and Loss Account it can be seen that sales in 2010 amounted to €2,000 million and, after various expenses, profit after tax (PAT) amounted to €120 million. Sales, depreciation, PAT, and dividends paid are also shown on a per-share basis, which is simply calculated by dividing each figure by the number of shares in issue (ABC has 1,000 million in issue).

For investors the two most important per-share statistics are the PAT per share, which is normally referred to by investment analysts as earnings per share (EPS), and the dividend per share (DPS). These are particularly important because they are the building blocks for three of the most commonly used valuation yardsticks, namely:

- the price earnings ratio (PER);
- the earnings yield;
- the dividend yield.

Price Earnings Ratio (PER)

ABC's PER is calculated as:

$$\frac{\text{Share Price}}{\text{EPS}} = \frac{200}{12} = 16.7$$

It is important to note that the PER is a ratio. In this example ABC's PER of 16.7 is often referred to as its historical PER, given that it is derived from ABC's last published EPS. Investment analysts generally also calculate the prospective PER, which is derived from a forecast of a company's EPS for the upcoming accounting period. Therefore if a company's earnings are forecast to grow, the prospective PER will be lower than the historical PER.

Earnings Yield

The earnings yield takes the same two pieces of information as the PER, but it is the inverse of it and is calculated as:

$$\frac{EPS}{Share\ price} \times 100 = \frac{12 \times 100}{200} = 6\%$$

Dividend Yield

ABC's dividend yield is calculated as:

$$\frac{Dividend\ Per\ Share}{Share\ Price} \times 100 = \frac{4}{200} \times 100 = 2\%$$

The dividend yield and earnings yield are closely related and the relationship between the two is expressed in terms of the pay-out ratio and the retention ratio. The pay-out ratio is defined as the proportion of earnings that are paid out in dividends to shareholders. ABC's pay-out ratio and retention ratio are:

$$Pay\text{-}out\ Ratio = \frac{Total\ Dividend}{PAT} = \frac{40m}{120m} = 0.33$$

This ratio tells us that ABC has paid out 33% of profits in dividends to its shareholders;

and

$$Retention\ Ratio = \frac{Retained\ Profits}{PAT} = \frac{80m}{120m} = 0.67$$

Therefore, we can see that the following holds:

$$Pay\text{-}out\ ratio = 1 - Retention\ ratio$$

Dividend Cover

Where an investor relies on the dividend yield as a valuation yardstick it will be necessary to establish what level of risk applies to future dividend payments. The dividend cover is a ratio that informs the investor in this respect, and is calculated as:

$$Dividend\ Cover = \frac{PAT}{Cost\ of\ Dividend} = \frac{120m}{40m} = 3$$

The dividend cover is a ratio, and in the case of ABC tells us that its dividend is covered three times by its earnings. This is quite a high cover ratio and indicates that even if ABC's profits were to fall sharply in the future, the company would still have sufficient earnings to afford to maintain its dividend payments to shareholders. A low number for dividend cover would raise questions about the sustainability of dividend payments. For example, a dividend cover of one means that the dividend cost equals all profits after tax for the period in question.

Cash Flow Per Share

Measures of cash flow have become increasingly important in recent years. In the case of ABC its cash flow may be defined as:

$$\text{Cash Flow} = \text{PAT} + \text{Depreciation} = €120m + €75 = €195m$$

and

$$\text{Cash Flow per Share} = \frac{€195m}{1,000m} = 19.5c$$

Analysts have become increasingly reliant on valuation yardsticks that are built on cash flows rather than accounting flows, although both are closely interrelated. These include the following:

Earnings Before Interest, Tax, Depreciation and Amortisation (EBITDA)

This is really a new name for operating profits, but it has the advantage of making explicit what is excluded from this number. In the case of ABC it can be seen that EBITDA equals €350m.

In recent years many analysts have given greater prominence to investment ratios derived from EBITDA for a number of reasons. First, globalisation of investment flows means that fund managers are increasingly investing on a global basis. Differences in accounting conventions create difficulties in interpreting traditional ratios such as price earnings ratios. Secondly, accounting scandals in the early years of the millennium highlighted the benefits of cash-flow-based measures, as they are more difficult to manipulate than accounting-based measures. A number of ratios have become popular based on enterprise value (EV).

Enterprise Value (EV)

This is the value of the total assets controlled by a business and it is usually defined as the sum of debt securities and equity securities issued by a company at their respective market values. The EV of ABC plc is:

$$EV = \text{Market Value of Debt} + \text{Market Value of Equity}$$
$$= \quad \text{€}1,500m \quad + \quad \text{€}2,000m \quad = \text{€}3,500m$$

Earnings Before Interest, Tax, Depreciation and Amortisation (EBITDA) is often expressed as a ratio to EV and for ABC we have:

$$EV/EBITDA = 3,500m\,/350m = 10$$

This ratio is akin to the PER. In businesses such as telecommunications, where capital investment is very high leading to high depreciation charges, this ratio is often preferable, given its focus on cash flows rather than accounting earnings, and on the market value of the total assets controlled by the company. Because of its focus on total assets it is useful in making comparisons of companies with different capital structures.

RATIOS BASED ON THE BALANCE SHEET

The ratios and valuation yardsticks set out so far are derived from the profit and loss account. We now turn to information that may be gleaned from the balance sheet. For investors and investment analysts the key information contained in the balance sheet relates to the net asset value or book value of a company, and various ratios that calibrate the strength of a company's balance sheet. Turning to the latter first, for ABC we have:

$$\text{Debt/Equity Ratio} = \frac{\text{Net Debt}}{\text{Shareholders' Funds}} = \frac{\text{€}1500m}{\text{€}1200m} * 100 = 125\%$$

$$\text{Debt/Capital Employed} = \frac{\text{Net Debt}}{\text{Capital Employed}} = \frac{\text{€}1500}{\text{€}2700} * 100 = 55.6\%$$

Note: Capital employed is equal to Fixed Assets + Net Current Assets, or Net Debt + Shareholders' Funds.

If these ratios are 'too high', then it indicates that the company is in a weak financial position. What constitutes 'too high' depends on the type of industry in question and on the overall economic climate. For example, in a climate of low interest rates and strong economic growth company balance sheets could sustain higher debt ratios than in a period of high interest rates and low growth.

Net Asset Value (NAV), Book Value and Shareholders' Funds

These amount to one and the same, and in ABC's case the number is €1200m. Again, investors like to express this number on a per-share basis to make it easy to compare one company with another and with averages for industry sectors and the overall market. ABC's NAV per share is:

$$\text{NAV per Share} = \frac{\text{Shareholders' Funds}}{\text{Number of Shares in Issue}} = \frac{\text{€}1200m}{1,000m} = 120c$$

This is sometimes referred to as the Book Value per Share, and is often related to the current market share price:

$$\text{Price/Book or Price/NAV} = \frac{\text{Share Price}}{\text{NAV per Share}} = \frac{200c}{120c} = 1.7$$

This ratio is not relied on to the same degree as those based on cash flows. It is useful in industry sectors such as property, where tangible assets are very important and where market values for those assets can be ascertained. In industries where human capital is the main asset this ratio is virtually useless.

MEASURING INVESTMENT RETURNS

Investment return typically consists of two components:

- income return
- capital return.

Assume that you purchased shares in Company A exactly one year ago and that you have just sold them on the stock market. The details of your transactions are set out in Table 5.2.

Table 5.2

Transaction	Number of Shares	Stock	Purchase or Sale Price	Consideration or Income
Bought on 2/01/2010	1	Company A	100c	100c
Sold on 2/01/2011	1	Company A	120c	120c
Dividend received on 2/01/2011				5c

The percentage capital gain (return) on this investment is:

$$\text{Capital Gain} = \frac{\text{Sale Price} - \text{Purchase Price}}{\text{Purchase Price}} * 100$$

$$= \frac{120c - 100c}{100c} * 100 = 20\%$$

and the total percentage return is:

$$\text{Total Return} = \frac{(\text{Sale Price} - \text{Purchase Price}) + \text{Income}}{\text{Purchase Price}} * 100$$

In the case of this transaction the total return is 25%, calculated as follows:

$$\frac{120c - 100c + 5c}{100c} * 100 = 25\%$$

This is usually referred to as the Holding Period Return.

Stock Market Indices

The performance of investment portfolios is normally assessed relative to an appropriate benchmark index. Analysis of historical market returns relies on time series of stock market indices to provide the raw data on overall market returns. Finally, investment strategists often try to quantify their expectations in terms of forecasting the levels of various stock market indices. Indeed, during the Christmas and New Year 'silly season' forecasting the coming year's index performance becomes a sport, as celebrities, fund managers and investment analysts are asked for their predictions.

Stock market indices are now published on a daily basis covering global equity markets and bond markets. Exhibit 5.1 shows information published daily in the *Financial Times* covering equity-market indices.

Construction of a Stock Market Index

Step one involves deciding which universe of stocks is to be covered by the index. In the case of the Irish market the obvious starting point is all companies publicly quoted and traded on the Irish Stock Exchange. However, the Irish exchange does have more than one market. It has the 'Official List', which includes the majority of quoted companies, but it also has the Enterprise Securities Market (ESM), which is geared to facilitate

Exhibit 5.1 Equity Market Indexes

STOCK MARKET - WORLD MARKETS AT A GLANCE

Country	Index	Feb 25	Feb 24
Argentina	Merval	3438.75	3382.71
Australia	ALL ORDINARIES	4924.91	4901.10
	S&P/ASX 200 Res	5906.05	5894.03
	S&P/ASX 200	4836.53	4809.35
Austria	ATX	2882.05	2862.60
Belgium	BEL 20	2692.41	2665.97
	BEL Mid	3827.21	3813.30
Brazil	Bovespa	66959.27	66948.99
Canada	S&P/TSX Met & Min	1424.29	1404.05
	S&P/TSX 60	807.06	798.44
	S&P/TSX Comp	14004.76	13867.31
Chile	IGPA Gen	20963.51	20679.86
China	Shanghai A	3014.01	3014.07
	Shanghai B	312.76	312.35
	Shanghai Comp	2878.57	2878.60
	Shenzhen A	1340.11	1339.23
	Shenzhen B	815.08	823.72
	FTSE/Xinhua A200	8574.65	8553.54
	FTSE/Xinhua B35	10748.06	10832.71
Colombia	CSE Index	14687.17	14587.73
Croatia	CROBEX	2250.38	2241.91
Cyprus	CSE M&P Gen	1156.60	1160.22
Czech Republic	PX	1241.20	1238.00
Denmark	OMXC Copenhagen 20	470.61	462.34
Egypt	EGX 30	(c)	(u)
Estonia	OMX Tallinn	764.41	(c)
Finland	OMX Helsinki General	7424.79	7345.42
France	CAC 40	4070.38	4009.64
	SBF 120	3040.74	2991.80
Germany	M-DAX	10182.38	10016.48
	XETRA Dax	7185.17	7130.50
	TecDAX	896.31	876.03
Greece	Athens Gen	1583.20	1599.97
	FTSE/ASE 20	741.26	749.16
Hong Kong	Hang Seng	23012.37	22601.04
	HS China Enterprise	12270.43	12059.75
	HSCC Red Chip	3961.44	3897.04
Hungary	Bux	23046.76	22537.64
India	BSE Sens	17700.91	17632.41
	S&P CNX 500	4226.75	4201.20
Indonesia	Jakarta Comp	3443.53	3439.13
Ireland	ISEQ Overall	2943.35	2900.78
Israel	Tel Aviv 100	(c)	1176.82
Italy	FTSE MIB	22349.71	21948.73
	FTSE Italia Mid Cap	24822.68	24451.10
	FTSE Italia All-Sh	22935.06	22530.12
Japan	Nikkei 225	10526.76	10452.71
	Topix	941.93	934.22
	S&P Topix 150	814.83	808.33
	2nd Section	2374.68	2367.21
Jordan	Amman SE	(c)	5078.71
Kenya	NSE 20	4269.51	4264.66
Latvia	OMX Riga	433.74	434.20
Lithuania	OMX Vilnius	412.40	410.92
Luxembourg	Luxembourg General	1165.57	1150.72
Malaysia	FTSE Bursa KLCI	1489.27	1489.87
Mexico	IPC	36667.92	36446.56
Morocco	MASI	12709.84	12514.98
Netherlands	AEX	366.77	363.73
	AEX All Share	575.11	570.31
New Zealand	NZX 50	3363.91	3368.35
Nigeria	SE All Share	26181.18	26217.28
Norway	Oslo All Share	495.19	490.27
Pakistan	KSE 100	11223.52	11539.26
Philippines	Manila Comp	3737.04	3730.84
Poland	Wig	46874.11	46547.75
Portugal	PSI General	2843.18	2827.50
	PSI 20	7978.06	7921.74
Romania	BET Index	5691.89	5607.32
Russia	RTS	1930.76	1901.14
	Micex Index	1747.72	1715.20
Singapore	FTSE Straits Times	3025.16	2973.08
Slovakia	SAX	252.63	239.71
Slovenia	SBI TOP	821.73	821.66
South Africa	FTSE/JSE All Share	31965.59	31706.47
	FTSE/JSE Top 40	28803.79	28571.23
	FTSE/JSE Res 20	58235.28	58171.55
South Korea	Kospi	1963.43	1949.88
	Kospi 200	259.28	257.69
Spain	Madrid SE	1108.41	1090.01
	IBEX 35	10822.70	10647.60
Sri Lanka	CSE All Share	7711.62	7583.42
Sweden	OMX Stockholm 30	1116.79	1102.30
	OMX Stockholm AS	354.70	350.44
Switzerland	SMI Index	6537.20	6515.97
Taiwan	Weighted Pr	8599.65	8541.64
Thailand	Bangkok SET	985.91	977.22
Turkey	ISE 100	61367.34	60760.82
UK	FTSE 100	6001.20	5919.98
	FT30	2232.30	2202.50
	FTSE All Share	3109.27	3066.32
	FTSE techMARK 100	2193.47	2148.93
	FTSE4Good UK	(u)	4917.01
USA	S&P 500	1316.91	1306.10
	FTSE Nasdaq 5000	7165.17	7070.89
	Nasdaq Cmp	2773.34	2737.90
	Nasdaq 100	2342.93	2313.31
	Russell 2000	815.61	804.18
	NYSE Comp.	8350.13	8276.29
	Wilshire 5000	(u)	13768.10
	DJ Industrial	12120.00	12068.50
	DJ composite	4128.11	4103.55
	DJ Transport	5064.56	5008.45
	DJ Utilities	410.35	408.32
Venezuela	IBC	67623.80	67721.50
Vietnam	VNI	466.96	461.29
Cross-Border	DJ Stoxx 50 €	2694.93	2667.52
	DJ Euro Stx 50 €	2985.02	2949.13
	DJ Global Titans $	185.20	184.19
	Euronext 100 ID	727.00	717.94
	FTSE Multinatls $	(u)	1188.96
	FTSE Global 100 $	1026.97	1019.63
	FTSE4Good Glob $	(u)	461.87
	FTSE E300	1159.60	1145.61
	FTSE eXT All Share €	187.45	184.47
	FTSEurofirst 80 €	3865.98	3817.91
	FTSEurofirst 100 €	3562.92	3518.72
	FTSE Latibex Top €	5285.00	5258.00
	FTSE Eurotop 100	2412.56	2386.15
	FTSE Gold Mn $	(u)	3716.58
	FTSE All World	(u)	222.78
	FTSE World $	(u)	389.08
	MSCI All World $	(u)	1327.06
	MSCI ACWI Fr$	(u)	338.53
	MSCI Europe €	(u)	1191.78
	MSCI Pacific $	2322.76	2297.01
	S&P Global 1200 $	1499.58	1486.14
	S&P Europe 350 €	1162.65	1149.11
	S&P Euro €	1224.32	1209.26

(c) Closed. (u) Unavailable.

smaller companies. Therefore a decision has to be made on whether to include all stocks, or to have different indices for the various 'sub-markets'. The normal solution is to construct different indices for the various markets. Therefore, in Ireland the ISEQ Overall Index does not include ESM-listed companies.

The stocks included in a stock market indicator must then be combined in certain proportions to construct the index or average. Therefore, each stock must be assigned some relative weight. Three possible approaches can be used:

i)   Weighting by the company's current market capitalisation.
ii)   Weighting by the price of one unit of the company's stock.
iii) Weighting each company equally regardless of its market price.

The vast majority of stock market indices are constructed using market capitalisations as weights. Once this is decided, it is then necessary to average the individual components. Two methods of averaging are possible: arithmetic or geometric. Virtually all indices are now constructed using arithmetic averaging.

BONDS: PRICING CONVENTIONS

In this section we detail conventions regarding bond price quotations, accrued interest and the treatment of ex-dividend dates.

Quoted Bond Prices

Quoted government bond prices nowadays are typically quoted as 'clean prices', i.e. they refer to the capital value of the bond only. They exclude the interest earned by the bond since its last coupon payment date.

Accrued Interest

Accrued interest is the interest earned by the bond since its last coupon payment date. The buyer of a bond will pay the seller the 'clean price' plus accrued interest.

Calculation of Accrued Interest

To calculate accrued interest, the number of days between the last coupon pay date and the settlement date of the transaction between buyer and seller is determined. There are different conventions ('day count') for determining the number of days accrued in different bond markets.

Ex-Dividend Dates

In the US (and indeed in Ireland for benchmark government bonds with a single annual coupon payment) if a bond is sold for settlement before the coupon date, the coupon is paid to the buyer. If settlement is on or after the coupon date, the coupon is paid to the seller. Ex-dividend dates and periods do not arise.

Ex-dividend dates arise for Irish government bonds that pay coupons semi-annually. For example, the 8.75% Capital Stock 2012 had ex-dividend and payment dates as follows:

Ex-dividend: 10 March 2010
Pay date: 30 March 2010

On 19 March 2010 this bond went 'ex-dividend' and traded in that form until 1 April 2010. The coupon payable on 30 March was paid to holders of the stock as at 18 March.

If an existing holder of the bond sells the stock on or after the ex-dividend date and before the payment date he or she must reimburse the buyer for interest which the seller will receive but that has properly accrued to the buyer. In this case accrued interest will be a negative amount and will be shown as a deduction from the 'clean price' on the transaction contract note (i.e. the invoice for the transaction) that will issue from the stockbroking firm involved.

The negative accrued interest amount is calculated as follows:

$$\frac{\text{Payment Date} - \text{Settlement Date} \times \text{Coupon } (\in)}{365}$$

In total, therefore, the seller receives:

the 'clean price' of the bond

plus the full six-month coupon payment

less the negative accrued interest earned by the bond when it was no longer owned by the seller,

whilst the buyer pays

the 'clean price' of the bond

less accrued interest for the period when the buyer owned the stock but the payment was made to the seller.

QUESTIONS

1. You are given the following information for the Balance Sheet of ABC plc:

	€ million
Fixed Assets	120
Net Current Assets	100
Total Assets	220
Less Net Debt	70
Shareholders' Funds (Equity)	150

   The Debt/Equity Ratio of ABC plc is:

   A. 31.8%
   B. 46.7%
   C. 70.0%
   D. 62.1%

2. You are further told that ABC plc has 100 million shares in issue and the shares are trading at a current market price of 100c. Earnings per share (EPS) for this year are expected to be 13c.

   What are the net asset value (NAV) per share: and the price earnings ratio (PER)?

   A. 150c : 12.9
   B. 220c : 7.69
   C. 150c : 7.69
   D. 70c : 13.0%

3. You are given the following information for XYZ plc:

	€ Million
Sales	100
Operating Profit	15
Profit after Tax	10
Dividend	5
Retained Profits	5

   XYZ has 150 million shares in issue and the current market price is 100c.

What are XYZ's Earnings Per Share (EPS), and Dividend Per Share (DPS)?

- A. 66.7c; 20c
- B. 100c; 10c
- C. 6.7c; 3.3c
- D. 10c; 6.7c

Case Study Exercise

Zoe SA is a top French ladies' and men's fashion retailer. Its leading design, strong supplier network and well-located stores have enabled the company to outperform its peers. This strong performance is expected to continue both against the peer group and against the market as a whole. The company's latest financial results are shown in summary form below. There are 200 million ordinary shares in issue.

Income Statement
Year to 31 January 2010

	€ million
Sales	2500
Cost of Goods Sold	2010
EBITDA	490
Depreciation	110
EBIT	380
Interest	60
Pre-tax Profits	320
Tax	100
Net Profit	220
Dividends	70
Retained	150

Balance Sheet
As at 31 January 2010

	€ million
Fixed Assets	1200
Net Current Assets	380
	1580
Net Debt	900
Shareholders' Funds	680

A. Based on the above financial statements, calculate the company's:
   1. Earnings per share
   2. Dividend per share
   3. Cash flow per share
   4. Net asset value per share.

Comment briefly on why each one of these ratios is considered to be useful in analysing a company.

B. The current market price of the company's shares is 1200c. Calculate:
   1. The company's market capitalisation
   2. Price earnings ratio
   3. Dividend yield
   4. Price to cash flow
   5. Price to book ratio.

Comment briefly on the general usefulness of items 2 to 5.

C. Current valuation metrics for the Eurozone market as a whole and for the company's peer group are shown below. Based on your results in Part B and this overall market information, state whether you think there is a good investment case for investing in Zoe, giving your reasons.

Eurozone:	PER	Dividend Yield	Price/Cash Flow	Price/Book
Equity Market	15.0	4.3%	8.0	1.8
Retail Peers	12.0	4.8%	9.0	2.6

Chapter six

Investment, Investors and Risk

This chapter distinguishes between the investor, the gambler and the speculator. It examines the different sources of investment return. The important concept of risk is introduced and what risk means to different investors is explored. The concept of risk as defined and measured by Markowitz is examined, and is extended to the implications for portfolio construction.

Learning Objectives

After reading this chapter, you will be able to:
- Define investment, investors, risk and return
- Recognise the characteristics and requirements of investors and their importance as a first step in determining investment policy
- List the various types of investment risk
- Explain Markowitz's important contribution to the definition and measurement of risk
- Calculate the return and risk of individual securities and of portfolios
- Explain the importance of correlation and covariance of assets in measuring a portfolio's risk
- Differentiate between naïve diversification and Markowitz diversification
- Describe Markowitz's efficient frontier and its role in the construction of optimal portfolios.

Investment is the process whereby consumption is deferred and resources are set aside to build a store of future value and to earn a return. Individuals invariably have short-, medium- and long-term financial commitments and goals. In the short term we must house, feed and clothe our family and ourselves. Our medium-term aspirations may be to educate our children, provide for family healthcare and generally improve our quality of life. In the long term we may need to repay a house mortgage or ensure a comfortable life in retirement. Organisations have a similar mix of financial objectives. A limited company, in the short term, must meet its obligations to its suppliers and workforce. Over the medium term it may be required to pay down debt and pay dividends to shareholders. Its long-term objective might be to generate growth and higher returns for its shareholders. A charity might, in the short term, require to generate steady or rising distributions to those who depend upon it for income whilst, in the medium to long term, preserving the value of its capital. A pension fund will be concerned with meeting its long-term obligation to provide pensions to existing and future pensioners, but will also be focused on its short-term statutory requirement to meet solvency standards. Prudent financial management, at the individual and organisational levels alike, requires that current and future needs are recognised, anticipated and provided for.

INVESTORS

An investor makes a commitment of resources now in anticipation of future reward. In effect, the investor will forgo current consumption in the expectation of generating a future increase in value. In attempting to generate this future increase in value the investor must live with uncertainty. The value he or she realises on the investment will depend on what someone else will pay for it in the future.

This uncertainty is evident in the frequently erratic path followed by the investment markets. The markets are subject to short-term fluctuations, to cyclical patterns that reflect the business or economic cycles and to secular, or long-term, trends that may be driven by changes in demographics, in inflationary expectations or in corporate profitability. In sharp contrast the biblical servant in the Parable of the Talents simply buried the talents (the money) in the ground and eventually returned them to his master. There was no expectation of return or reward. This was not investment. There are also important distinctions between the investor and the gambler:

i)   The gambler is prepared to lose all his stake in the pursuit of high and rapid rewards. The investor abhors the prospect of losing all his investment. For the investor it is essential to prevail and to meet his obligations or objectives.

ii)   Typically, when the gambler places his bet he is committed, unable to change his mind or withdraw. The investor will reserve the right to change his mind, to alter his position, perhaps withdraw his position altogether if economic, investment or business conditions change.

The speculator straddles the ground between the investor and the gambler. The speculator adopts a high-risk, short-term approach to investment in the pursuit of rapid gains. This appetite for risk and his short-term perspective distinguishes the speculator from the investor.

INVESTMENT RETURN

Components of Investment Return

There are three sources of investment return:

- investment income
- capital return
- currency return.

Investment Income

Investment income is the recurring payments receivable by an investor on his investment. Included in investment income are:

- interest on bank deposits
- interest on debt instruments (government securities, corporate bonds)
- dividends on ordinary shares (the annual payment made to shareholders out of profits by companies)
- rents on properties.

Investment income is the most reliable stream of investment return. It is recurring, forecastable and relatively stable. It normally grows over time as profits and dividends on ordinary shares and rents on property rise in response to rising economic activity. It is always positive, never negative.

Capital Return

The capital component of return refers to the appreciation or depreciation (rise or fall) in the value of the investment over time. The capital value of bank deposits is fixed. The capital value of the other investment assets – bonds, equities and property – fluctuates in response to changes in monetary, economic or business conditions. An improving investment environment – lower inflation, lower interest rates, better economic growth, better corporate profitability – will tend to boost capital growth and vice versa. The capital component of investment return is non-recurring, unreliable and difficult to predict and volatile. It may be positive or negative.

Currency Return

Where the investor invests only within his or her domestic country or currency bloc (e.g. an Irish investor who invests only in euro-denominated assets), he enjoys only the two streams of return discussed earlier – investment income and capital return. This investor is not exposed to currency gain or loss. Where the investor invests outside his domestic currency (e.g. an Irish investor who invests in sterling-denominated UK assets), he generates a third stream of return: currency gain or loss. The outcome here is dependent upon the performance of the external currency – in the example, sterling – against the domestic currency, the euro. If sterling rises against the euro, a currency gain results. The currency component of investment return is non-recurring, unreliable, difficult to predict and often volatile. It may be positive or negative.

Inflation

In providing a fund, through investment, to meet future obligations or liabilities the investor must account for inflation. Inflation means that the costs of education, healthcare and retirement will be higher in the future than they are today. The focus of the investor, therefore, is on generating a real return on his investment, i.e. an increase in the value of the investment after inflation has been allowed or accounted for.

Compound Interest

If inflation is the enemy of the investor, he or she has a powerful ally in compound interest. Compound interest generates a steady progression in the value of an investment over the long term. Assume an investor commits €1000 to an investment at a return of 4% per annum compound:

Table 6.1 The Power of Compound Interest

Opening Investment	€1000.00
After 1 year	€1040.00
After 2 years	€1081.60
After 5 years	€1216.65
After 10 years	€1480.24

The power of compound interest, of course, does not work on zero, reinforcing the investor's abhorrence of a permanent loss of capital, in contrast to the gambler's willingness to put all his bet at risk.

INVESTORS: DIFFERENT DRIVERS

Investors react in different ways to changes in the economic or investment environment. It is this difference in reaction that 'makes the market', with some investors wishing to buy and others wishing to sell in reaction to new information.

The reaction of investors to market developments is driven by:

i)   Their different liabilities
ii)   Their different time horizons
iii)   Their different requirements for income
iv)   Their different needs for protection against inflation
v)   Their different requirements to generate real returns above inflation
vi)   Their different base currencies
vii)   Their different requirements for liquidity
viii)   The different tax and regulatory regimes to which they are subject
ix)   Their different exposures to transaction costs
And, finally but importantly:
x)   Their different attitudes to risk.

INVESTORS: COMMON CHARACTERISTICS

Investors are not a unique species, highly logical and cold-bloodedly rational. Like the rest of us, they are human beings and they share our emotional and physiological characteristics. Amongst those common characteristics which have implications for the manner in which investors approach investment are:

i)   *A tendency to stick with existing beliefs*
        Beliefs tend to be based on the degree to which information is available – media mentions, rumour, chat. We tend to overvalue data which supports our beliefs and underweight contrary information.

ii)   *Conservatism*
        Investors tend to be fearful of the unknown or the new. They prefer the familiar to the unfamiliar. They seek protection in the herd.

iii)   *Myopia*
        Investors tend to use horizons which are over-focused on the short term. Specifically, their tendency to extrapolate recent events into the future is a particular weakness.

iv)   *Hindsight*
        Investors are inclined to remember the occasions when they beat the market, but not their unsuccessful transactions. Winners are attributed

to their own skill and expertise, losers to poor advice. Past events always look inevitable after the event.

v)   *Loss Aversion*

Investors, not unnaturally, hate to lose. They are heavily focused on book cost and will often defer for as long as possible the date of realisation of a loss. They sell winners too early, hold losers too long. Losses have a greater impact than gains of a similar magnitude.

vi) *Excessive Optimism*

Investors are inclined to be overconfident in their own or in analysts' forecasts. They often exaggerate their ability to control events and they tend to have excessively optimistic expectation of likely future long-term returns.

Investors, in their approach to investment, are complex. At times they may be contradictory and confusing. Their reactions to new information will depend on their different drivers, but also on their psychological characteristics. Their reactions are often unpredictable.

Risk Defined

The dictionary defines risk as 'hazard, danger, exposure to mischance or peril'.

Investment, as a forward-looking activity, is concerned with the uncertain future. The uncertain future will include the possibility that events that are damaging to the financial well-being of the investor may occur. Investors will attempt to account for these uncertainties and to protect themselves against them in the investment strategies they develop. In the mid-1970s, for example, Irish investors were concerned with protecting their investments from the risk of sustained high inflation. In the late 1970s and early 80s, the weak state of the national finances and fears of financial collapse were a major concern for investors. In the early 1990s the focus was on currency devaluations. More recently, in sharp contrast to the situation of the mid-1970s, investors have been concerned that persistent disinflation might lurch into deflation. For the current decade, the fall-out from the financial crash of 2008 and the ensuing recession has shifted the focus of concern to financial stability and the unsustainable build-up in sovereign debt.

Common Concepts of Risk

A survey of investors in the US showed that investors' attitudes to risk varied. The following concepts of risk emerged:

• Risk is the chance of losing some of my original investment.

- Risk is the chance that my investment will not keep pace with inflation.
- Risk is fluctuation in value.
- Risk is not having enough money to meet investment goals.

This last response is important, because it establishes a link between the riskiness of the investment and the consequences for the investor if investment objectives are not met.

The following definition of investment risk emerges:

> 'Investment risk is the likelihood of not having sufficient cash with which to make essential payments.'

Investor Attitudes to Risk

Risk is subjective. The investor's time horizons, requirements and objectives will be key influences on his or her attitude to risk. A strategy which is entirely prudent for a long-term investor may be totally inappropriate for an investor with short-term time horizons. Risk is multi-faceted. For example, within a single pension fund the attitudes to risk of the different participants will vary. The employee will be concerned that the pension fund is properly invested, so that it will be in a position to pay his pension or retirement in ten or twenty years' time. The employer may have the additional concern that the fund's investments perform well in the short term, thus reducing employer contributions into the fund. Meanwhile, the investment manager of the fund's portfolio will attempt to meet the requirements of both employee and employer, while at the same time attempting to generate competitive returns to manage the risk of losing the client.

Investors' attitudes to risk are inconsistent. Investors may be more tolerant of taking a risk when attempting to avoid a loss than when trying to make a profit. The investor's recent experience can be a factor in his or her attitude to risk. If the most recent experience was satisfactory, the investor may take on more risk because, in a sense, he or she is playing with 'house money'. An unsuccessful recent experience may cause the investor to adopt a very cautious attitude to risk subsequently. Risk is therefore complex. Not only does it vary from investor to investor, but even for one single investor it will vary as his or her time horizons and objectives change and according to his or her purpose and recent experience.

Types of Risk

Investors are concerned with the uncertain future. Risk, therefore, is an ever-present and unavoidable feature of the investment process. No listing of types of risk can be comprehensive. Risk by its very nature is unpredictable and surprising. It catches us unawares. Unexpected events outside the boundaries of our previous experience occur. The financial markets are surprised, unsettled and shocked. Risk takes many forms. The following listing simply illustrates various types of risk encountered by investors in recent years. By definition other risks, not currently anticipated or discounted by financial markets, will shock and confuse us at some point in the future.

Systemic Risk

This is the risk of system-wide collapse: for example, the Japanese financial system in the 1990s. The collapse of a huge hedge fund, LTCM, in 1998 threatened the collapse of the US Treasury Bond market, the world's most liquid and most transparent market. The collapse of Lehman Brothers in 2008 required unprecedented government and central bank intervention to prevent a complete collapse of the global financial system.

Specific Risk

This is overexposure to individual investments: for example, the unavoidable overexposure by Irish pension funds to leading Irish companies prior to the introduction of the euro. As soon as Ireland adopted the euro, pension funds moved to reduce this risk by diversifying their Irish equities across euro-denominated equity markets.

Currency Risk

This risk is that of exposure to currency loss, e.g. the sterling devaluation of 1992 and the Asian currency crisis of 1998.

Counterparty Risk

The risk of collapse of a counterparty, i.e. a bank or stockbroker. Even when the investor may be protected by government guarantee or compensation scheme from eventual loss, the inability to access cash or securities may cause financial difficulties.

Default Risk

The risk that the issuer of a bond may default on its obligation to pay interest or reply capital. For example, the default by Russia on its domestic debt in 1998.

Credit Risk

Credit risk is the additional risk taken on by the investor in the search for higher returns when investing in a corporate bond rather than a government bond. If the credit rating of the issuer disimproves, the bond value will suffer: for example, the downgrading of General Motors' debt in 2005.

Market Risk

This is the unavoidable exposure to the uncertainty of the market, and is the uncertainty that the investor must embrace in the search for higher returns. The other types of risk may be diversified away. The investor has to live with market risk.

Risk Measurement: Volatility

The discussion so far has emphasised the multi-faceted nature of investment risk. It may therefore come as a surprise to learn that nowadays investment theory and practice focus on quite a narrow, albeit all-embracing, concept of risk. This concept of risk is built upon work carried out by a statistician, Dr Harry Markowitz, in the 1950s. Markowitz defined risk as volatility or fluctuation in prices, as indeed did some of the respondents to the survey discussed above. He further concluded that, by using normal distributions and standard deviations, the spread of returns on an asset around their average could be measured and quantified.

Therefore, for the first time, there were now available hard numbers to measure the two elements of investment: return numbers, which had long been available, and now risk numbers based on volatility. Investors could address both risk and return in a quantified way and examine the trade-offs between them. Markowitz's insights, together with the availability of greatly improved computing power, enabled us to prove some of the basic concepts which heretofore we had instinctively understood:

- Diversification controls risk.
- The higher the expected return, the higher the risk.

Markowitz's insights were key building blocks in the development of a more scientific and sophisticated approach to investment management. Volatility as a measure of risk has the attraction that we instinctively feel that uncertainty should be associated with something whose value jumps around a lot over a wide range. However, volatility has some inherent limitations; it is not a comprehensive measure of risk. Using data from the past can be dangerous; forecasting the future is unreliable. Importantly, volatility is an asset-based measure. It tells us nothing about the consequences for the investor of fluctuations in values.

Nevertheless, despite these limitations, volatility has become the standard measure of risk in the investment business today and has wide application in portfolio construction.

INVESTMENT OBJECTIVES AND RISK

It is clear from the discussion so far that risk is an integral part of investment. Investment is a two-handed process; it is about risk and return. Investment objectives, therefore, must embrace both the risk and return dimensions of investment. A single-minded focus on return alone is insufficient. Investment is not about the maximisation of returns, getting the best possible return. Investment, rather, is about the optimisation of returns, the maximisation of returns subject to an acceptable or appropriate level of risk.

In the next section we set out the key building blocks of the Markowitz approach to measuring risk and to constructing diversified investment portfolios.

Before doing this we are going to digress to set out some technical, but very important, issues regarding the measurement of investment returns.

DIGRESSION: TOTAL RETURNS, TOTAL WEALTH AND MEASURING RISK

Measuring Returns: As discussed earlier, the total return on a security for a given holding period consists of two components: income yield and price change. The total return (TR), sometimes referred to as the holding period return (HPR), is straightforward to calculate:

$$\frac{(\text{Sale Price} - \text{Purchase Price}) + \text{Investment Income}}{\text{Purchase Price}}$$

Example 6.1 Calculating the TR

You purchase shares in Kerry Group for €21 per share. You hold them for one year during which period you receive dividends of €1. At the end of the year you sell the shares for €22. What is your TR?

$$TR = \frac{(22 - 21) + 1}{21} = \frac{2}{21} = 0.095$$

Therefore TR is 9.5% expressed as a percentage.

Calculating Total Returns on an Index: When calculating historical returns on an index, the total returns are normally based on end-of-year index values. Example 6.2 gives three years' data for a notional equity index.

Example 6.2 Equity Index ABC

	Index Value	Dividend Received
Year 0	100	
Year 1	110	2.75
Year 2	105	2.95

The TRs are:

Year 1: $\dfrac{(110 - 100) + 2.75}{100} = 0.1275$ or 12.75%

Year 2: $\dfrac{(105 - 110) + 2.95}{110} = -0.0186$ or -1.86%

Therefore, expressed as percentages, Equity Index ABC produced returns of 12.75% and −1.86% in years 1 and 2 respectively.

Return Relative, Cumulative Wealth, Arithmetic Mean and Geometric Mean

It is often necessary to measure returns on a slightly different basis from total returns. This is particularly true when calculating either a cumulative wealth index or a geometric mean, because negative returns cannot be used in the calculation. The return relative (RR) eliminates negative numbers by adding 1.0 to the total return:

$$\text{Relative Return (RR)} = \text{TR in decimal form} + 1.0$$

The RR is particularly appropriate when measuring an investor's cumulative wealth over time. Measuring cumulative wealth involves compounding returns over an investor's total holding period, which usually lasts for several years or even decades. Assume an investor invested €10,000 in Equity Index ABC at year 0, what would that investor's cumulative wealth (CU) be at end of year 2?

$$CW_2 = W_0 *(1 + TR_1)(1 + TR_2)$$

where CW_2 = cumulative wealth at end of year 2
W_0 = initial wealth
TR_1 = periodic total returns in decimal form.

Therefore, the investor's wealth will have grown to the following at end of year 2:

$$CW_2 = €10,000 * (1 + 0.1275)(1 - 0.0186) = €10,000 * 1.1065 = €11,065$$

Cumulative wealth reflects the effects of compounding returns over any chosen period of time.

Summary Statistics for Returns

When someone refers to the average or mean return they are usually referring to the arithmetic mean, as that is the best-known statistic. If we have n values, the arithmetic mean is calculated as the sum of these values divided by n. Based on the return data for Equity Index ABC, the arithmetic mean is calculated as:

$$X = \frac{12.75\% - 1.86\%}{2} = 5.45\%$$

The geometric mean is defined as the nth root of the product resulting from multiplying a series of return relatives together:

$$G = [(1 + TR_1)(1 + TR_2) \ldots (1 + TR_n)]^{\frac{1}{n}} - 1$$

Staying with our Equity Index ABC example, the geometric mean is calculated as:

$$G = [(1 + (0.1275)(1 - 0.0186)]^{\frac{1}{2}} - 1 = (1.1065)^{\frac{1}{2}} - 1 = 1.0519 - 1 = 0.0519$$

or 5.19% expressed as a percentage.

Note that the geometric mean in this example is much lower than the arithmetic mean. In fact the geometric mean will always be lower than the arithmetic mean unless the values being considered are identical. The spread between them depends on the dispersion of the distribution: the greater the dispersion, the greater the spread between the two means.

What mean should we use when describing the returns from financial assets? The answer depends on your objective. If the objective is to estimate the expected return over a single period (say for next year), then the arithmetic mean is appropriate. This is because the arithmetic mean can be interpreted as providing an estimate of the return for a 'typical' year. On the other hand, if the objective is to measure the realised compounded return over a number of periods, then the geometric mean is the appropriate statistic.

Measuring Risk and the Consequences of Risk

In the next section we will discuss Markowitz's portfolio theory. At the heart of this theory is the view that risk can be precisely measured using some simple statistical measures. However, it is important to remind ourselves constantly that these statistical measures are just proxies for risk. To grasp this point, when a risky decision is being contemplated, it is useful to distinguish between the size of the risk being taken on and the consequences if a bad outcome materialises. For example, when crossing the road we take great care because even though the probability of being hit by a vehicle is low, the consequences of being hit are catastrophic. In contrast, if we place a wager on the horses or the lotto, we know that we are highly likely to lose, but we know that the consequences are simply that we lose our wager. Therefore, risky decisions are not just about measuring the probabilities of various outcomes, they also involve assessing the consequences when those potential 'bad' outcomes materialise.

CALCULATING EXPECTED RETURNS AND RISK

In analysing investment opportunities investors need to think explicitly about a security's distribution of probable returns. By assuming that the distribution of these potential returns is a normal distribution, investors can benefit from the statistical properties of the normal distribution. The normal distribution is a cornerstone of modern portfolio theory, although it is important to recognise that the actual distribution of a security's returns may not be normal. Active institutional investors and hedge fund managers who use sophisticated mathematical models carry out ongoing analysis of the pattern of security returns. Such studies have shown that it is often the case that the pattern of returns is not normal. For example, the one-day fall on 19 October 1987 in the US stock market was an event that supposedly had a tiny statistical probability of occurring. Statistical models simply could not cope with the extreme events that occurred during the 2008 global financial crash. The statistical models would have predicted that such an event should occur only once in several hundred years. There have in fact been many more instances of these extreme events in investment markets than would be predicted by the normal distribution.

While there are some caveats, the key advantage of the normal distribution is that it is a two-parameter distribution that is fully described by the mean and the variance (or standard deviation). For any security we can calculate its average or expected return, which is the single most likely outcome for its particular distribution. While the average return is probably the most important piece of information to an investor, it tells us only the centre of the data. It does not tell us anything about the spread of the data. If we define risk as the chance that the actual outcome of an investment will differ from the expected outcome, then we can associate risk with the dispersion of the likely outcomes. If we can assume that the distribution of returns from financial assets is normal, or close to normal, then we can measure risk using variance or standard deviation.

We can rely on extensive historical data to calculate average returns and standard deviations. However, it is extremely difficult to predict the future probability distributions of returns for securities. In practice we rely on the historical data to provide us with an estimate of these future probability distributions.

Table 6.2 Calculation of Expected Return and Standard Deviation for ABC plc

Observations	Returns (R_i)	Probability (one in five for each) (PR_i)	Weighted Returns $(2*3)$	(R_i-ER)	$(R_i-ER)^2$	$(R_i-ER)^2 pr_i$
(1)	(2)	(3)	(4)	(5)	(6)	(7)
20%	.20	.2	.04	.116	.01346	.002692
−2%	−.02	.2	−.004	−.104	.01082	.002164
10%	.10	.2	.02	.016	.00026	.000052
8%	.08	.2	.016	−.004	.00002	.000004
6%	.06	.2	.012	−.024	.00058	.000116
		= 1.0	=.084(ER)			=.009724 (Variance)

Standard Deviation = $(.009724)^{1/2}$
=.0986

Table 6.2 gives a detailed example of the mechanics of calculating the expected return and variance/standard deviation based on historical data. We are given return information for ABC plc for the past five years and from these we can readily calculate the average annual return by summing each return and dividing by the number of years. This gives an average annual return of 8.4%. We can also consider the data in terms of a probability distribution, which enables us to calculate the expected return as well as other statistical measures such as variance and standard deviation. In this example we have in effect assumed that each annual return has an equal probability of occurring in the future. Columns 2–4 calculate the expected return based on this probability distribution using the formula:

$$E(R) = \sum_{i=1}^{n} R_i \, pr_i$$

where:

$E(R)$	=	the expected return on a security
R_i	=	the return in period i
pr_i	=	the probability of ith return
n	=	number of possible (or historical) returns.

We can see that the probabilities sum to 1.0 and the expected return is .084 or 8.4%. Columns 5–7 calculate the variance of returns, from which we can calculate the standard deviation which computes to .0986 or 9.86% based on the formulae:

$$\text{Variance of returns} = \sigma^2 = \sum_{i=1}^{n} [R_i - E(R)]^2 \, pr_i$$

$$\text{Standard Deviation} \quad \sigma = \sqrt{\sigma^2}$$

We can now use this information to generate a picture of the range of likely future returns. In doing this we are assuming that the patterns of the past, as represented by these statistical measures, will be repeated in the future. Using the statistical information that we have calculated for ABC plc, Figure 6.1 shows how we can use the standard deviation (SD) of returns to generate a picture of what we can say about the future.

Figure 6.1 Expected Returns for ABC plc

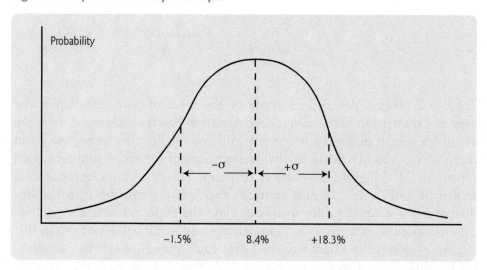

Now we see that two-thirds of the time we can expect the annual return from ABC plc to lie within a range of –1.5% to +18.3%, which is given by the E(R) +/– 1SD. If we expand the range of returns to E(R) +/– 2SD, we can be confident that returns will lie within this range 95% of the time. Even at one SD, the range of returns is wide and highlights how difficult it is to forecast point estimates of security returns with any degree of accuracy. However, the key application of this statistical approach is not in predicting future returns, but in creating a framework for making rational investment decisions.

Figure 6.2 The Risk-Averse Investor

Figure 6.2 illustrates a key assumption that underlies portfolio theory, namely that investors are risk-averse. On the basis of the historical return information available for another stock – XYZ plc – we now have return/risk information for two stocks. The same analysis as applied to ABC results in finding that XYZ has an E(R) of 8.4%, the same as ABC's, but it has a lower SD of 5.9%. Armed with this information we can forecast next year's return for XYZ as lying within a range of +2.5% to +14.3%, with a 66% chance of being correct. This is a much narrower range than that for ABC, as illustrated in Figure 6.2. Both companies have the same E(R) but XYZ is the lower-risk investment. Investment theory states that investors are risk-averse and therefore they will always choose XYZ over ABC. In a rational investment world investors will take on the higher-risk ABC only if its expected return is greater than XYZ's. In a well-functioning market investors

would sell ABC's shares, thus driving down the price and increasing its E(R) to the point where it offers a return that compensates investors for its higher risk level.

Portfolio Return and Risk

The approach described above for assessing individual securities can also be applied to portfolios. The E(R) and SD may be calculated for any portfolio of securities, and this information can then be used to compare the relative investment merits of various portfolios. The E(R) of a portfolio is the weighted average of the E(R) of the portfolio constituents.

Table 6.3 Calculation of Portfolio Expected Return and Standard Deviation

	Investment €	Portfolio Weights	E(R)	Standard Deviation	Weighted Portfolio Return
	(1)	(2)	(3)	(4)	(2)*(3)
CRH	5,000	.5	.11 (11%)	.12	.055
DCC	2,500	.25	.10 (10%)	.10	.025
Ryanair	2,500	.25	.12 (12%)	.15	.030
	10,000	1.00			=.110 (11%)

Imagine that you have invested €10,000 in three companies as set out in Table 6.3 and the expected portfolio return is 11%. Algebraically, the E(R) for any portfolio is:

$$E(Rp) = \sum_{i=1}^{n} W_i \, E(R_i)$$

where:
$E(Rp)$ = expected return of the portfolio
W_i = portfolio weight of ith security
$\sum W_i$ = 1.0
$E(R_i)$ = expected return of ith security
n = number of securities in the portfolio.

The calculation of portfolio return is therefore relatively straightforward and, irrespective of the number of securities and their respective weights, it is calculated as the weighted average of those security expected returns.

Calculating Portfolio Risk

In Table 6.3 we are also given information about the SD of Ryanair, CRH and DCC. We could try to estimate the SD of the portfolio as the weighted average of the portfolio constituents, but this would in fact be incorrect. This is because there is another dimension that must be taken into account when calculating portfolio variance or standard deviation. This dimension revolves around the extent to which the individual stock returns move in tandem with one another, or otherwise. For example, if we find that Ryanair performs well when CRH and DCC perform poorly, we would expect this to dampen down the volatility of the portfolio. On the other hand, if the patterns of returns for the three companies were exactly the same, then the volatility of the portfolio would be equal to the weighted average of the SDs of the three stocks. Therefore, the interrelationships between the stocks that make up a portfolio can reduce portfolio volatility.

Random Diversification

Investors have intuitively known for years that spreading investments across a range of securities reduces risk. Random or naive diversification refers to the act of randomly diversifying without regard to investment characteristics such as expected return and risk. An investor adds to his portfolio by simply randomly adding stocks to it. The good news is that in fact this will substantially reduce portfolio risk with a relatively small number of holdings. Figure 6.3 illustrates how portfolio risk declines very rapidly as the portfolio expands from one stock to several stocks.

Figure 6.3 Random Diversification

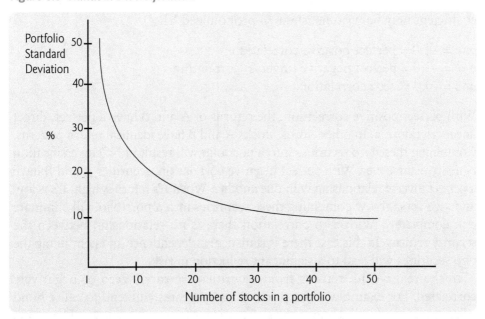

Studies of large equity markets, such as that in the US, have shown that approximately 50% of portfolio standard deviation is eliminated with as few as ten stocks, randomly selected. However, as more stocks are added the marginal portfolio risk reduction becomes smaller and smaller. In fact most of the diversification benefits are achieved when a portfolio consists of approximately 30 stocks. Such a portfolio will then have a level of risk that is quite close to that of the overall equity market. Studies of the US equity market have shown that this risk level equates to an annual standard deviation of approximately 20%.

Efficient Diversification

Markowitz's statistical analysis enabled investment theory, and eventually investment practice, to move forward by advancing our understanding of the true nature of portfolio risk. As we saw earlier, Markowitz's analysis distilled the key investment characteristics of any security into two variables – expected return and SD (a measure of risk). The investment characteristics of portfolios may also be described by these two variables. However, to calculate portfolio SD one additional piece of statistical information needs to be gathered. This additional variable measures the interrelationship between the securities that make up a portfolio. The covariance between two securities is a statistical measure that quantifies this interrelationship. An adjustment is often made to this to give the correlation coefficient between two securities, which is a statistical measure of the relative co-movements between security returns. It is bounded by +1.0 and –1.0, making it relatively easy to interpret. If we have two securities A and B, the correlation coefficient may be written as ρ_{AB} (ρ pronounced 'rho').

ρ_{AB} = +1.0 = perfect positive correlation
ρ_{AB} = –1.0 = perfect negative (inverse) correlation
ρ_{AB} = 0.0 = zero correlation.

With perfect positive correlation, the returns of A and B have a perfect, direct linear relationship. In other words, stocks A and B have identical return patterns. Combining these two securities into a portfolio will result in NO diversification benefits whatsoever. With perfect negative correlation, securities A and B have a perfect inverse relationship with one another. When A's return is high, B's is low and vice versa. Now combining these securities into a portfolio will eliminate risk completely. With zero correlation there is no relationship between the security returns. In this case there is statistical independence and combining the two securities will lead to a significant reduction in risk.

In the real world, returns from securities are rarely zero or negatively correlated. For example, a sharp rise in interest rates will tend to cause bond prices to fall and will dampen the share prices of most companies. Therefore, the correlation coefficient between two equities quoted on the same stock exchange will usually be much higher than zero. In fact, studies have shown that the value of the correlation coefficient between pairs of stocks quoted on the same market has a value of approximately 0.5. This is sufficiently far away from a value of 1.0 to deliver diversification benefits to equity portfolios. The correlation coefficient between stocks in the same sector would be higher again. For example, in the Irish market we would expect Bank of Ireland and Irish Life and Permanent to have a higher correlation coefficient than Bank of Ireland and Ryanair. However, in all cases we would expect the correlation coefficients to be significantly less than 1.0. The calculation of portfolio risk must take account of the interrelationship between each pair of securities. In the case of a two-security portfolio the formula for measuring portfolio risk is:

$$\text{Portfolio Risk} = \sigma p = \left[W_A^2 \sigma_A^2 + W_B^2 \sigma_B^2 + 2(W_A)(W_B)(P_{A,B})\sigma_A\sigma_B \right]^{1/2}$$

where W_A = weight of stock A in portfolio and $P_{A,B}$ = correlation coefficient between A and B.

When we are dealing with a small number of securities Markowitz mean-variance analysis can be applied with relative ease, always remembering that usually the values are based on the assumption that the historical data provides a good guide to the future. However, the model becomes very complex for a large number of securities because of the large number of covariances that have to be calculated. If the model has to deal with 250 securities, the number of unique covariances will be 31,115! Irrespective of the availability of computing power, analysts are unlikely to be able to directly estimate such a large number of correlations. To get over this problem Markowitz suggested using an index to which securities are related as a means of reducing the number of covariances required.

One of Markowitz's key contributions to portfolio theory is his insight about the relative importance of the variances and covariances. If the number of securities in a portfolio is large, the contribution of each security's own risk to total portfolio risk will be small. In fact the covariances between securities will have a greater impact on portfolio risk. —r/ships between Shares more imp than Share risk itself.

Efficient Portfolios

Markowitz's approach led investors to focus on the trade-off betweeen risk and return and led to the concept of the *efficient portfolio*, which is defined as that portfolio that has the smallest risk for a given level of expected return, or the largest expected return for a given level of risk. First we need to list the possible portfolios that can be derived from a given set of securities. Figure 6.4 illustrates the opportunities available, which we can see are very numerous.

Figure 6.4 The Efficient Frontier

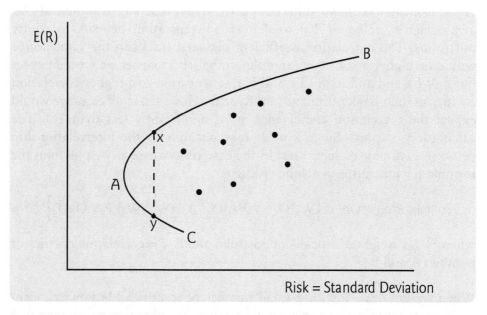

Risk = Standard Deviation

Only those portfolios that lie on the line segment AB – the efficient frontier – need to be considered. The reason for this may be illustrated by examining the portfolio at point X compared with point Y. Investors will *always* choose X over Y because X offers a higher expected return for the same amount of risk as Y. This is true for every portfolio on the curve AB. We can say that any portfolio on the curve segment AB is preferable to any portfolio below the curve. Portfolios above this curve are unattainable.

Plotting the efficient set or efficient frontier of portfolios provides us with the set of available efficient portfolios. It does not tell us what actual portfolio will be chosen by an investor. In order to do this we first assume that investors are risk-averse. If we think in terms of utility, for most investors the disutility of losing €1 is greater than the utility of gaining €1. The greater the disutility from potential loss, the greater the degree of risk aversion.

An investor's personal preferences can be represented by indifference curves (see Figure 6.5). Each indifference curve represents the combinations of risk and expected return that are equally desirable to that particular investor. Investors will seek to get onto the highest attainable indifference curve, so that the actual portfolio chosen will be where the indifference curve is tangential to the efficient frontier.

Figure 6.5 Indifference Curves

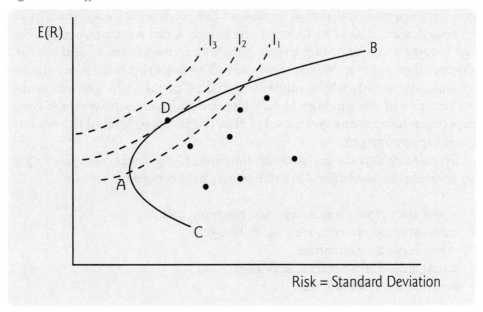

Using the Markowitz Model for Asset Allocation

The Markowitz model is typically thought of in terms of selecting portfolios of individual securities, which is how Markowitz expected his model to be used. However, it is very cumbersome to use in this way because of the enormous number of covariance estimates needed when dealing with a large number of individual securities. The single-index model (discussed in Chapter 7) offers a refinement that is easier to calculate. However, if the available investments are small in number, then the basic Markowitz model can be employed to select an investor's optimal portfolio. For example, an Irish-based investor may limit his or her investment choice to the following assets: Eurozone equities, MSCI world equities (ex Eurozone), Eurozone government bonds, commodities and euro cash. Historical data on returns and variances is readily available for proxy indices for each of these asset classes, and with only five different assets the number of covariances required is manageable. Portfolio optimisation tools are readily downloadable from the Internet and can be used to create the efficient set of efficient portfolios for the chosen assets. Given a limited number of assets, the output from such optimisation tools can be readily understood and interpreted.

CONCLUDING COMMENTS

Markowitz's contribution to investment theory and portfolio management is enormous. As a result of his insights the business of asset management has become more quantitative and scientific. The importance of the conceptual link between risk and return is now at the forefront of even the novice investor's mind. Risk is no longer a fate before which we are powerless, but has become a choice, rather than a fate. We can manage risk, deal with it, shape and engineer it. We can now use risk to construct portfolios, aiming to maximise return whilst minimising risk. Central to investment is the construction of efficient portfolios, which are designed to deliver the highest expected return for any given level of risk, or the lowest level of risk for any given expected return.

Diversification is the key to controlling risk. Granny was right: 'Don't put all your eggs in one basket.' Portfolios may be diversified:

- across asset types (bonds, equities, property, cash)
- across currencies (euro, sterling, dollar, yen)
- across regions or countries
- across industrial or market sectors
- across a range of securities.

Markowitz, with his hard numbers, confirmed our instinctive understanding that diversification reduces risk. He went further: by establishing that investors can achieve an optimum position by efficiently diversifying their investments.

The next chapter provides a more detailed analysis of Markowitz's portfolio theory, and also presents the best-known capital market theory, namely the capital asset pricing model (CAPM).

SUMMARY

- An investor makes a commitment of resources in expectation of future reward.
- Understanding the requirements and characteristics of investors is the first step in formulating investment strategy.
- Investment is a two-handed process; it is about risk and returns.
- Investment risk is the likelihood of not having sufficient cash with which to make essential payments.
- Markowitz defined risk as volatility and measured it in hard numbers using normal distributions and standard deviations.
- The return of a portfolio is the weighted average of the expected return of the securities in the portfolio.
- Markowitz demonstrated that the risk of a portfolio is not, however, the weighted average of the risk of the securities in the portfolio, but is

➡

affected by the covariance or the correlation between the securities in the portfolio. The lower the correlation, the lower the risk.
- Markowitz demonstrated that diversification controls risk.
- Markowitz led investors to the concept of the efficient portfolio, that portfolio which has the smallest risk for a given level of expected return or the largest expected return for a given level of risk.
- Efficient portfolios sit on Markowitz's efficient frontier.

QUESTIONS

1. With regard to total risk, which of the following statement(s) is/are TRUE?

   A. Market risk is part of total risk.
   B. Market risk is not diversifiable.
   C. Systematic risk is also called market risk.

   1. All of the above
   2. None of the above
   3. A & B only
   4. A & C only

2. Please select the TRUE statement(s):

   A. Realised returns help investors form expected future returns.
   B. Realised returns help investors assess the performance of their portfolios.
   C. A probability distribution contains a set of likely outcomes and their associated probabilities.
   D. The sum of these probabilities equals 1.

   1. A, B & C only
   2. All of the above
   3. B, C & D only
   4. C & D only

3. Which statement(s) is/are FALSE regarding diversification?

   A. Random diversification chooses only securities with positive dividend yields.
   B. Random diversification can completely eliminate market risk.
   C. As the number of securities held in a portfolio increases, the marginal benefit of diversification significantly decreases.

➡

D. A large number of securities (at least 100) are required to achieve substantial diversification benefits.

    1. None of the above
    2. A, B & C
    3. A, B & D
    4. B & D

4. **Which statement(s) is/are TRUE regarding portfolio risk?**

    A. Portfolio risk takes only individual security risk into consideration.
    B. Portfolio risk takes only covariance between securities into consideration.
    C. Portfolio risk takes both individual security risk and covariance between securities into consideration.
    D. Portfolio risk is totally independent from the investment weight of the securities held in a portfolio.

5. **Markowitz defines an efficient portfolio as one that:**

    A. Has the smallest risk for a given level of expected return.
    B. Has the smallest expected return for all levels of risk.
    C. Has the largest expected return for a given level of risk.
    D. Has the largest expected return and zero risk.

    1. A & B only
    2. A & C only
    3. A, B & C only
    4. A only

6. **When the arithmetic mean is compared to the geometric mean, which of the following statement(s) is/are TRUE?**

    A. Arithmetic mean is an appropriate measure of the return over multiple periods.
    B. Geometric mean is an appropriate measure of the return for a particular time period.
    C. Geometric mean is always larger than arithmetic mean.
    D. Arithmetic mean is the nth root of the product derived from the multiplication of a series of return relatives.
    E. None of the above statements are true statements.

7. **You have been seconded to your bank's Argentine office for two years. You have 100,000 pesos to invest, which you plan to**

➡

put on deposit at a fixed annual effective interest rate of 9.5%. Argentine inflation is forecast at a cumulative 16% over the two years. Which of the following is closest to the real effective annual rate of interest?

A. 1.80%
B. 1.59%
C. 1.67%
D. 3.37%

8. Mr Wilson bought stock A for $35 per share two years ago. At the end of the first year, stock A moved to $47 per share, but at the end of the second year, stock A declined slightly to $40. So, what is the arithmetic mean of Mr Wilson's investment return in stock A over two years?

A. 8.39%
B. 9.70%
C. 14.28%
D. 34.28%

9. Based on the previous question, what is the geometric mean of Mr Wilson's investment in stock A over two years?

A. 6.90%
B. 9.70%
C. 16.82%
D. 34.29%

10. Regarding standard deviation, please select the TRUE statement(s):

A. Ex post standard deviation is always equal to ex ante standard deviation.
B. Standard deviations of well-diversified portfolios are reasonably steady across time.
C. Ex post standard deviation is calculated from realised returns.
D. Both A and B are true statements.
E. Both B and C are true statements.

Chapter seven

Portfolio Theory

In Chapter 6 we discussed investment risk, and the important concept of Markowitz diversification was introduced. This chapter explores Markowitz diversification further and shows how a concept such as the correlation coefficient can be used to construct portfolios. The concept of the efficient frontier is discussed and the impact on the efficient frontier of introducing a risk-free asset is explored. The separation theorem is also discussed. Building on this analysis, the capital asset pricing model (CAPM) is introduced. The capital market line and the security market line are described and discussed.

Learning Objectives

After reading this chapter you will:

- Understand the Markowitz approach to portfolio construction
- Understand how portfolio return and risk are calculated
- Be aware of the importance to portfolio risk of the covariance or correlation between pairs of securities
- Understand the concept of the efficient frontier
- Be aware of how indifference curve analysis can be applied to show how individual investor preferences interact with the efficient frontier
- Understand the concept of the optimal portfolio
- Be aware of how the single-index model offers a simpler way of establishing the efficient frontier
- Be able to distinguish between market risk and unique risk
- Have developed an understanding of how the introduction of the risk-free asset expands the efficient frontier
- Understand how capital market theory builds on Markowitz portfolio theory to explain how share prices are set in equilibrium.

The final chapter in the book presents information on the historical returns delivered by the various asset categories. These realised returns provide the historical data on which measures of risk such as standard deviation can be calculated. However, when constructing portfolios our concern is with expected returns – in an uncertain world we know that future returns are subject to a wide range of possible outcomes. In Chapter 6 the basic principles underlying the analysis of portfolio risk and return were explored. There we saw that for the purpose of portfolio construction all investment assets can be characterised by just two variables – expected returns and estimated standard deviations of returns.

Before moving on to the selection of optimal portfolios we first recap and extend our analysis of the Markowitz equations first introduced in Chapter 6.

The expected return on any portfolio E(Rp) can be calculated as:

$$E(Rp) = \sum_{i=1}^{n} W_i E(R_i)$$

[Equation 7.1]

where: E(Rp)   = expected portfolio return
         W_i = portfolio weight for i^{th} security
         $W(R_i)$ = expected return on i^{th} security
         n   = number of securities in the portfolio.

Note: $$\sum_{i=1}^{n} W_i = 1.0$$

Calculating portfolio risk is not quite so straightforward and we find that portfolio risk does not simply equal the sum of each security's variance (risk) weighted by its percentage weight in the portfolio:

$$\sigma p^2 \neq \sum_{i=1}^{n} W_i \, \sigma_i^2$$

[Equation 7.2]

where: σp^2 = portfolio variance
        σ_i^2 = variance of ith security
        W_i = portfolio weight for i^{th} security.

We saw above that the calculation of portfolio return is determined by two variables:

i)   The expected return of each security.
ii)   The weight of each security within the portfolio.

To calculate portfolio risk we need to add one more variable: namely the interrelationship between each pair of securities within the portfolio. This is measured by the covariance or the correlation coefficient. These concepts were introduced in Chapter 6 and here we explore them in more detail.

Covariance and Correlation Coefficient

The covariance is an absolute measure of the degree of association between returns for a pair of securities, and we will express it as:

$$COV_{AB} = \text{the covariance between the securities A and B.}$$

The actual absolute value of the covariance is not easy to interpret and hence the correlation coefficient (ρ_{AB}) is usually used to assess how interdependent the returns are between two securities. The correlation coefficient and covariance are related as follows:

$$\text{Correlation Coefficient} = \rho_{AB} = \frac{COV_{AB}}{\sigma_A\, \sigma_B}$$

[Equation 7.3]

where σ_A, σ_B are the standard deviations of securities A and B, respectively.

This states that the correlation coefficient is the covariance standardised by dividing it by the product of the standard deviations of A and B respectively. The correlation coefficient is a relative measure of association that lies between +1 (perfect positive correlation) and –1 (perfect negative correlation). If we could find pairs of securities that are negatively correlated, it would enable us to reduce portfolio risk to extremely low levels. In the real world this rarely occurs and we normally find that the correlation coefficients among securities usually lies between 0 and +1. For example, if I decide to invest in just two quoted Irish companies, I would ideally like to find two companies with a very low (or negative) correlation coefficient. What I will find is that the typical value of the correlation coefficient between pairs of securities quoted on the same stock exchange will be approximately 0.5. This is because all stocks on (say) the Irish exchange are affected by many of the same variables such as interest rates, the performance of the Irish economy, the impact of the monetary policy of the European Central Bank, etc. Nevertheless, a correlation coefficient of +0.5 is still far enough below a value of +1.0 to deliver significant diversification benefits. In other words, it should in general be possible to combine stocks in such a way as to reduce risk without adversely affecting expected returns.

Calculating Portfolio Risk

Applying the basic Markowitz approach to portfolio construction is complex, and where many securities are involved it is extremely cumbersome. First, let's consider the case of just two securities, A and B. The risk of the portfolio consisting of these two securities is given by the equation:

$$\sigma_p = \left[W_A^2\, \sigma_A^2 + W_B^2\, \sigma_B^2 + 2\,(W_A)(W_B)(COV_{AB})\, \sigma_A \sigma_B \right]^{1/2}$$

[Equation 7.4]

This equation states that the risk of the portfolio is determined by the sum of the variances of A and B multiplied by their respective portfolio weights (squared), plus a second term consisting of the covariance between A and B, and the portfolio weights and standard deviations of A and B respectively. The risk of the portfolio, as measured by its standard deviation, will be lowered as the covariance reduces or as the correlation coefficient moves downward from +1.0. Therefore, in this simplified two-security case, portfolio risk depends upon the interplay of:

* the risk of each security
* the portfolio weights assigned to each security
* the covariance or correlation between the two securities.

Extending the Analysis to Many Securities

This two-security case can be generalised to many securities and the same mathematical principles will apply. Therefore, portfolio risk can be reduced by combining assets with correlations of less than +1.0, and the smaller the positive correlation the better. The big problem in applying this technique is the exponential rate of increase in the number of covariances as the number of securities is extended. In the case of two securities there are just three variance–covariance numbers, the variances of A and B and the COV_{AB} plus the COV_{BA}. The number of covariances grows quickly based on the calculation that there are:

$$[n(n-1)]\,/\,2$$

unique covariances.

With four securities, the number of unique covariances jumps to six. With ten securities, the number jumps to 45. An investment analyst with a list of 100 securities to choose from must estimate 4,950 unique covariances. As well as the sheer computing power required to calculate these covariances, analysts must decide on what raw data to use. Historical returns are usually used to estimate expected returns, variance, etc., but appropriate data may not be available for all the securities being considered.

Efficient Portfolios

Setting aside the practical issues of estimation and calculation, Markowitz's approach to portfolio selection assumes that all investors evaluate portfolios based on their expected return and risk. Markowitz portfolio theory is based on a small set of assumptions that include:

- a single investment period, usually a year
- no transactions costs and no taxes
- investors base their preferences only on a portfolio's return and risk, as measured by variance or standard deviation.

In Chapter 6 we discussed the concept of efficient portfolios, and, assuming that we have calculated the efficient set of portfolios (the efficient frontier), we must then select the portfolio most appropriate to us from the efficient frontier. Markowitz's model does not select this optimal portfolio; rather, it produces a range of optimal portfolios from which investors make their

Figure 7.1 Indifference Curves

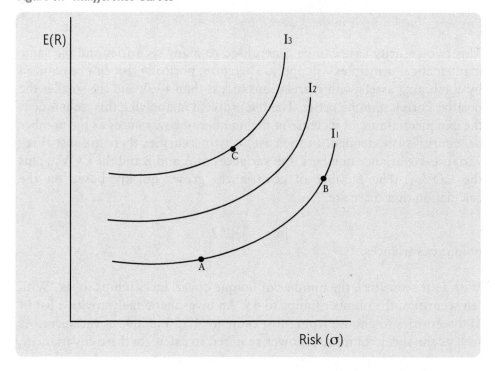

choice. The key assumption that investors are risk-averse provides a mechanism for choosing each individual investor's optimal portfolio. Investors have different attitudes to risk and these preferences can be expressed in the form of indifference curves, which should be familiar to students of economics. A set of indifference curves is shown in Figure 7.1 and each curve represents the set of portfolios that are equally desirable to an investor.

If we think of an investment portfolio in terms of delivering a certain amount of 'wealth satisfaction', then each of portfolios A and B delivers the same amount of satisfaction to this particular investor. Portfolio B has a higher return and higher risk than A, but the investor is indifferent between the two. Portfolio C is preferable to both A and B because it is on a higher indifference curve. For risk-averse investors the curve will always be upward sloping, but the shape will vary depending on the differing risk preferences of investors. An investor will choose the portfolio that places him on the highest attainable indifference curve. This occurs at point P in Figure 7.2, which is the portfolio that enables the investor to reach indifference curve I_2.

Figure 7.2 Indifference Curves and the Efficient Frontier

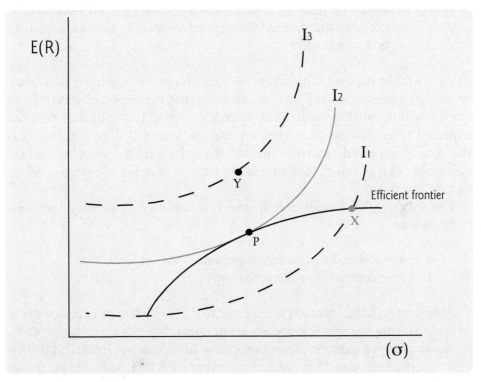

Portfolio X on the efficient frontier is inferior to P, as it leaves the investor on the lower indifference curve I_1. Portfolio Y on I_3 is superior to both P and X, but is unattainable as it is above the efficient frontier.

The Single-Index Model

An alternative and simpler method of obtaining the efficient frontier was developed by William Sharpe. This single-index model relates returns on each security to the returns on a common index. In America this common index may be the S&P 500 index. In Ireland it may be the ISEQ Overall index or a broader European index that includes stocks across Europe, such as the FTSE E300 index. The key advantage of the single-index model is that it reduces dramatically the number of calculations required, because we do not need to calculate the relationship between all pairs of securities being considered. Instead we define each security in terms of its relationship with the market (as measured by the relevant index). The equation for the single-index model is:

$$R_i = \alpha_i + \beta_i R_m + e_i$$

[Equation 7.5]

where: R_i =   return on security i
R_m =   return on the market index
α_i =   that part of security i's return that is independent of market performance
β_i =   a constant that measures the expected change in R_i, given a change in R_m
e_i =   random residual error.

The β (beta) term is very important as it measures the sensitivity of a stock to market movements. If $\beta_i = 1$, it indicates that the expected return from stock i will equal that of the market index. If $\beta_i < 1$, it indicates that the expected return is less than that for the market; and $\beta_i > 1$ means that the stock's expected return is greater than the expected market return. Remember that in this model returns are framed in terms of a single period, usually one year.

The single-index model divides the returns from a security into two components:

i)   a market-related component represented by $\beta_i R_m$
ii)   a unique component represented by α_i.

The third term in the equation is the error term, which has an expected value of zero. The unique or stock-specific component depends on factors specific to the company in question. Such factors would include the successful launch of a new product, a sudden unexpected event such as a crash for an airline company, etc. For example, the share price of the oil company BP fell sharply in 2010 owing to the catastrophic oil spill in the Gulf of Mexico. This was an event that was clearly unique to BP, affecting only its share price. Market-related events are ones that affect all businesses and would include a change in interest rates, a change in the rate of corporation tax, or a sudden unexpected event such as a terrorist attack. As well as splitting the expected return into two components, the single-index model also splits risk into the same two components. The total risk for a security thus splits into market risk and stock-specific or unique risk:

$$\sigma_i^2 \;=\; \beta_i^2 \left[\sigma_m^2\right] + \sigma_{ei}^2$$

[Equation 7.6]

Stock Risk = Market Risk + Unique Risk

Unique risk can be eliminated through the construction of a diversified portfolio – leaving market risk, which cannot be reduced. The single-index model makes two important simplifying assumptions:

i)   It assumes that the market index (R_m) is unrelated to the residual error (e_i).

ii)   It assumes that the residual errors between pairs of securities are unrelated to one another. More formally, this is expressed as $Cov(e_i, e_j) = 0$, for securities i and j.

The upshot of these simplifying assumptions is that the only common influence on each security is the market index. All other factors are random. This now means that the covariance between any two securities (i and j) can now be calculated from their respective betas and the variance of the market:

$$COV_{i,j} \;=\; \beta_i\, \beta_j\, \sigma_m^2$$

[Equation 7.7]

This greatly simplifies the task of calculating risk values for securities and portfolios.

Using the Markowitz Model

For the selection of portfolios consisting of individual securities, the basic Markowitz model is very cumbersome. The single-index model is far more practical when applying the model to the selection of portfolios of individual securities. However, the basic model can be applied more readily to the task of asset allocation, where investors are choosing from a limited set of asset categories. For an Irish-based investor such a list could include:

- Eurozone equities
- Eurozone government bonds

- US equities
- Emerging-markets equities
- US Treasuries
- Japanese bonds.

The first step is to decide on an appropriate index for each asset class. Historical data on each of these asset classes is readily available, so that the return and risk parameters for each index can be calculated. Given the relatively small number of assets, a variance/covariance matrix can be generated and the efficient frontier can be calculated. An investor can then decide on the weights for each category depending on their own risk preferences.

Introducing the Risk-Free Asset

The Markowitz analysis involves establishing the efficient frontier based on risky assets. However, investors in most markets have the option of investing in risk-free assets such as short-term government bonds or bills. Introducing the risk-free asset into the Markowitz world leads to some very interesting developments. First, we can define the risk-free asset in terms of expected return and variance. There is certainty about its expected return and consequently the variance of this return is zero. More interestingly, the risk-free asset will have a correlation coefficient of zero with all risky assets. Intuitively, most investors know that cash or near-cash instruments are a good way to protect a portfolio in falling markets. More formally we can see this from the equation that describes the relationship between the covariance and correlation coefficient:

$$COV_{RF, i} = \rho_{RF, i}\, \sigma_i\, \sigma_{RF}$$

$$= \rho_{RF, i}\, (0) = 0$$

[Equation 7.8]

where: $COV_{RF, i}$ = covariance between the risk-free asset and security i
$\rho_{RF, i}$ = correlation coefficient between the risk-free asset and security i
σ_i = standard deviation of i
σ_{RF} = standard deviation of risk-free asset = 0.

One of the key insights of Markowitz portfolio theory was the identification of the relative importance of the covariances (or correlations) between securities. Applying the theory to the practicalities of portfolio construction means that investors seek pairs of securities with correlation coefficients of well below one. The correlations between the securities that make up the portfolio will have a greater impact on portfolio risk than will the size of the variance (or standard deviation) of each individual security. Therefore, a portfolio consisting of mainly very high-risk securities could have a relatively low portfolio risk, as long as the correlations between the securities were very low or negative.

As we noted earlier, the correlation coefficients between stocks will often be approximately 0.5. Yet the risk-free asset has the very desirable attribute of a correlation coefficient of zero with all risky assets! Viewed in this light it is perhaps not surprising to find that introducing the risk-free asset to the Markowitz efficient frontier radically alters that efficient frontier. In effect it expands the frontier as illustrated in Figure 7.3.

Figure 7.3 The Risk-Free Asset Expands the Efficient Frontier

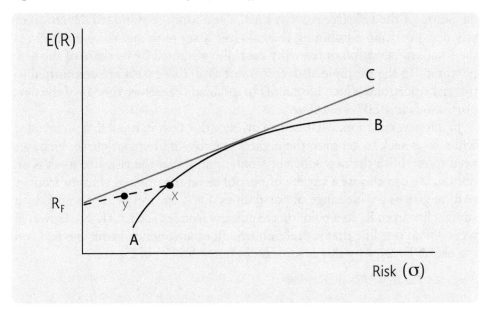

Remember that the efficient frontier consists of those portfolios that deliver the highest E(R) for a particular risk level, or the lowest risk level for a given E(R). The curve AB is the efficient frontier calculated on the basis of Markowitz covariance/variance analysis. R_F has a SD = 0 and a certain E(R) and is therefore represented at point R_F on the chart. Investors can now combine this risk-free asset with any risky portfolio on the efficient frontier. Let's assume that an investor picks portfolio X on the efficient frontier and creates a new portfolio with (say) 90% in portfolio X and 10% in R_F. The new portfolio is represented by Y on the chart. As usual, the E(R) for the new portfolio will be the weighted average return of R_F and portfolio X. If we are given values for the relevant variables, we can calculate the E(R) and standard deviation for the portfolio:

Given: $R_F = 3\%$; $ER(P_X) = 20\%$; $\sigma_X = 20\%$

[Equation 7.9]

$$ER(P_y) = W_{RF}\,R_F + (1 - W_{RF})\,ER(P_X)$$
$$= (.1)(.03) + (.9)(.20) = .183 \text{ or } 18.3\%$$

Because there is zero correlation between R_F and P_X, the calculation for the standard deviation of the new portfolio simplifies to:

$$\sigma_y = (1 - W_{RF})\,\sigma_X$$
$$= (.9)(.20) = .18 \text{ or } 18\%$$

[Equation 7.10]

In this case the covariance term becomes zero, because the standard deviation of the risk-free asset is zero. Therefore the standard deviation of any new portfolio combining the risk-free asset with any risky portfolio is the standard deviation of the risky portfolio weighted by its share of the new portfolio. In the example above, 90% of available assets are committed to this risky portfolio which has an SD of 20% and therefore the SD of the new portfolio is (.9)(20%) = 18%.

In this new situation, what will an investor do? Bear in mind that an investor will always seek to get onto the highest possible indifference curve. First, we need to establish the new efficient frontier, now that the risk-free asset is an option. We can choose a variety of portfolios on the original efficient frontier (AB) to give us a wide range of possibilities. Each one can be represented by a straight line from R_F to a point on the efficient frontier, such as (R_FX). However, we will find one line that is preferable to all others, which is the line R_F C on the chart. To see why this is so, look at portfolio (Y) in Figure 7.4.

Figure 7.4 The New Efficient Frontier

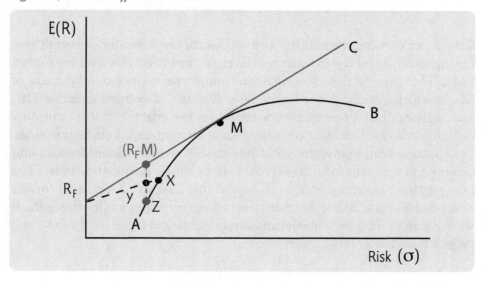

This portfolio is better than portfolio (Z) on the efficient frontier because it delivers a higher return for the same level of risk. However, it in turn is not as good as portfolio ($R_F M$) on the line $R_F C$, because this portfolio delivers a higher E(R) than Y, but with the same level of risk. What we find is that the line that is tangential to the curve AB becomes the new efficient frontier. The implication of this is that all investors will choose just one risky portfolio (M), which we will refer to as the market portfolio, and combine that with varying proportions of the risk-free asset. Therefore, an investor with indifference curves I_1, I_2 (Figure 7.5) will choose portfolio ($R_F M$).

Figure 7.5 The Market Portfolio and the Risk-Free Asset

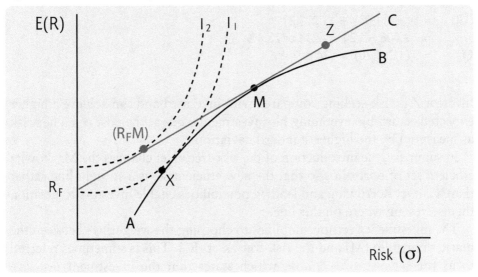

Without the risk-free asset this investor would choose portfolio (X) on the original efficient frontier AB, which is on a lower indifference curve I_1. The line $R_F M$ now replaces AM as the new efficient frontier, where every point is preferable to every point on AM. In this model investors now have only one decision to make – how to split their assets between M, the market portfolio, and the risk-free asset. In theory the market portfolio should consist of all available risky assets. In practice we can think of it as a broad-based index of risky assets. For example, an Irish-based equity investor may consider the FTSE Eurofirst 300 index as his relevant market index. According to this analysis the investor should invest a portion of his assets in a fund that tracks this index, and the balance in short-term Eurozone government bonds. A cautious investor would allocate a high proportion of available assets to government bonds, whereas an aggressive investor will invest a much higher proportion of assets in M.

Borrowing Possibilities

Allowing for borrowing possibilities leads to the efficient frontier extending from M to C (Figure 7.5). An investor seeking a high-return/high-risk portfolio might choose a portfolio represented by Z. This portfolio lies on the efficient frontier $R_F C$ and is reached by borrowing at the risk-free rate of interest and investing those funds in the market portfolio. Assume that investor Z has borrowed 20% of his investable assets and invested the borrowed funds (on top of available funds) in M. If $R_F = 3\%$, $R_M = 20\%$ and the standard deviation of the market portfolio (σ_M) is 20%, we can calculate the expected return and risk of portfolio Z as:

$$
\begin{aligned}
E(R) &= (-.2)(.03) + (1.2)(.2) \\
&= -.006 + .24 = .234 \text{ or } 23.4\% \\
\sigma_Z &= (1.2)(.20) = .24 \text{ or } 24\%
\end{aligned}
$$

[*Equation 7.11*]

Investor Z is risk-seeking compared with investor I and can achieve a higher expected return by leveraging his investments, but at the cost of higher risk as measured by the higher standard deviation.

In summary, the introduction of the risk-free asset changes the Markowitz efficient set of portfolios so that the new efficient set is a straight line rather than a curve. Borrowing and lending possibilities enable investors to position themselves anywhere on this line.

The investment decision simplifies to choosing the weightings between the market portfolio (M) and the risk-free asset (R_F). This is sometimes referred to as the separation theorem, which states that the investment decision (which portfolio of risky assets to invest in) is separate from the financing decision (what proportion of investable assets to invest in the market portfolio and the risk-free asset, respectively).

CAPITAL MARKET THEORY

The Capital Asset Pricing Model (CAPM)

Markowitz portfolio theory is normative in the sense that it describes how investors should go about the task of selecting portfolios of risky securities. If everyone adopted this approach, then all portfolios would consist of some combination of the market portfolio and the risk-free asset. Portfolios would differ only in terms of the weighting applied to each. Capital market theory tries to explain how security prices would behave under these idealised conditions. The most widely known model is the capital asset pricing model (CAPM). The CAPM is attractive as an equilibrium model, because it can be applied to the job of portfolio construction relatively easily. It does have a number of weaknesses and alternative theories have been developed, the most important of which is arbitrage pricing theory (APT).

The CAPM was originally developed independently by W. Sharpe, and Lintner and Mossin, in the mid-1960s. The model assumes that each investor diversifies his portfolio according to the Markowitz model including the risk-free asset. The following additional assumptions are made:

- All investors have identical probability distributions for future rates of return. Therefore, investors use the same information to generate the efficient frontier.
- All investors have the same one-period time horizon.
- All investors can borrow or lend at the risk-free rate.
- There are no transaction costs and no taxes.
- Investors are price-takers, capital markets are in equilibrium and there is no inflation.

While these assumptions may appear highly unrealistic, they can be relaxed without causing too much damage to the CAPM's predictions. We take as our starting point Figure 7.6, which replicates Figure 7.4.

Figure 7.6 The New Efficient Frontier

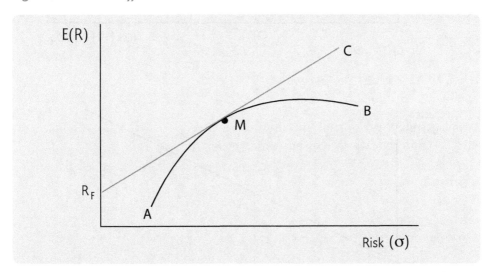

The market portfolio M is a portfolio of all risky assets and is determined by the Markowitz variance/covariance analysis. Because all investors are basing their decisions on the same information, and have identical time horizons, they will all choose the same portfolio of risky assets. In theory this market portfolio should include all risky assets worldwide, with the weight of each determined by its market value. All risk other than market risk is thus diversified away and market risk is quantified by the standard deviation of this market portfolio.

The Capital Market Line and the Security Market Line

The CAPM encompasses two important relationships that are represented graphically in Figures 7.7 and 7.8.

Figure 7.7 The Capital Market Line

Figure 7.8 The Security Market Line

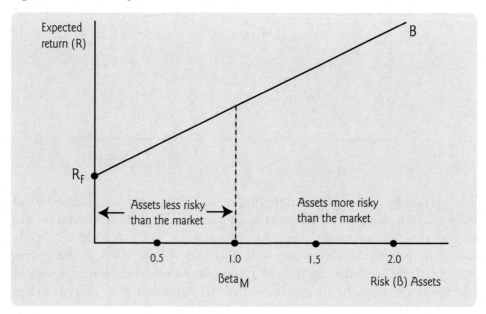

The capital market line plots the equilibrium relationship between expected portfolio return and the total risk, measured by standard deviation, of efficiently diversified portfolios. This plots the familiar trade-off between risk and return for efficient portfolios. All combinations of portfolios consisting of the risk-free asset and the risky market portfolio are bounded by the line R_F–C. In equilibrium all investors will end up on the capital market line. This line R_F–C is upward sloping and the slope of the line quantifies the risk/return trade-off. The vertical distance between the risk-free rate and R_F–C at point M in Figure 7.7 equals the excess return above the risk-free rate. If M is proxied by a broad-based equity index, then this distance equals the familiar equity risk premium.

The capital market line plots the risk/return trade-off only for efficient portfolios. It cannot be used to assess the equilibrium expected return from an individual security, because under the CAPM all investors will hold the market portfolio. How does an individual security contribute to the risk of the market portfolio? We can reformulate the expected return/risk trade off with beta, as a measure of risk, rather than standard deviation. This is achieved by relating each individual security's risk to the overall market risk through its covariance with the market portfolio. By using beta rather than standard deviation as a measure of risk, we recognise that the contribution of a security to the total risk of a diversified portfolio is its systematic risk. The security market line (SML) graphically depicts the CAPM taking into account the risk/return trade-off for individual securities (and inefficient portfolios).

Beta

Beta is a measure of the systematic risk of a security that cannot be avoided through diversification. It is a *relative* measure of risk that measures the risk of an individual stock relative to the market portfolio of all stocks. A security whose returns move in line with the overall market will have a beta of 1.0. A security that is more risky than the market will have a beta of greater than 1.0, indicating that it moves by more than the market. For example, a stock with a beta of 1.5 would be expected to rise by 15% when the market excess return is 10%. A stock that is less risky than the market will have a beta of less than 1.0, indicating that it will move by less than the market. In practice stocks can be ranked by their betas, and because the variance of the market is a constant across all securities for a particular period, ranking stocks by beta is the same as ranking them by their absolute systematic risk.

The CAPM formally relates the expected rate of return for any security or portfolio through the expected return–beta relationship. This relationship states that the expected rate of return on an asset is a function of the two components of the required rate of return – the risk-free rate and the risk premium. Thus we have:

$$E(R_i) = R_F + \beta_i [E(R_m) - R_F]$$

[Equation 7.12]

where: $E(R_i)$ =   expected return on asset i
        $E(R_m)$ =   expected return on the market portfolio
        β_i =   beta coefficient for asset i
        R_F =   risk-free rate of return.

This is the equation that underlies the security market line in Figure 7.8. This graphical representation of the CAPM risk/return trade-off illustrates how the theory posits a positive linear relationship between an asset's risk and its required rate of return. The security market line plots risk as measured by beta on the horizontal axis and required rate of return on the vertical axis.

Estimating Beta

Analysis of historical return data is usually the approach taken to estimate beta values for stocks. Once betas for stocks have been estimated, it is relatively straightforward to calculate the beta of portfolios. Historical returns from a stock are plotted against the historical returns from the relevant market index, and the line of best fit is called the characteristic line.

Figure 7.9 Hypothetical Characteristic Line

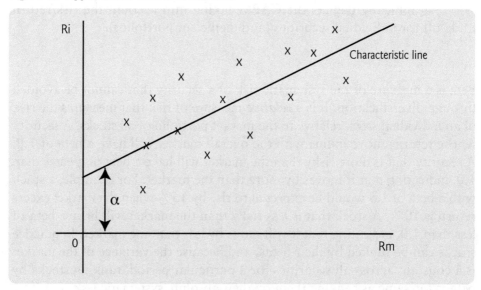

Figure 7.9 shows the characteristic line for a hypothetical stock. In this case annual returns are available for the past 15 years for the stock and the market index, and the returns for each year are plotted on the chart. The characteristic line can be plotted visually or more usually regression analysis

is used to produce the line of best fit. The slope of this line provides an estimate of beta and the intercept on the vertical axis should equate to the alpha of the stock. In equilibrium the alpha of all stocks should equal the risk-free rate of return. Often the characteristic line is calculated using excess returns. The excess return is calculated by subtracting the risk-free rate from both the market returns and the stock returns. In this form the intercept with the vertical axis again represents the alpha for a stock and the slope of the line will be the same in both cases. In equilibrium the alpha should now equal zero.

The big problem with beta estimates is that the betas of individual stocks change over time. Unfortunately it is impossible to predict such changes, making beta estimates for individual stocks unreliable. Researchers have found that forecast betas *on average* turn out to be closer to 1.0 than the models predict. This information can be used to adjust beta estimates to make them somewhat more reliable. When it comes to estimating beta for large portfolios the news is somewhat better. In a portfolio of (say) 40 or more stocks the betas of some stocks may be rising while the betas of others may be falling. This averaging effect means that estimates of portfolio betas tend to be more robust than beta estimates of individual stocks.

Empirical Evidence

The key conclusions of the CAPM are quite straightforward:

i)   Investors are rewarded for taking extra risk and there is a positive linear relationship between risk and reward.
ii)   The relevant risk for a security is its impact on portfolio risk.

Although the assumptions underlying the CAPM are very restrictive, empirical studies in general support the main predictions of the CAPM. The security market line appears to be linear, indicating that the trade-off between expected return and risk is an upward-sloping straight line. Also, it appears that unsystematic risk does not command a risk premium and therefore the evidence supports the prediction that investors are rewarded only for assuming systematic risk.

The CAPM has proved itself to be a very useful practical tool in the world of investment. It has flaws, such as the fact that the theoretical market portfolio that it is based on cannot be observed. Researchers have developed another model called arbitrage pricing theory (APT), which some argue as being superior to the CAPM.

Arbitrage Pricing Theory (APT)

APT has emerged as an alternative theory of asset pricing to the CAPM. Its appeal is that it is more general than the CAPM, with less restrictive assumptions. A key difference is that APT is not critically dependent on an underlying market portfolio. CAPM predicts that only market risk influences expected returns, whereas APT recognises that several types of risk may affect security returns.

The Law of One Price

APT is based on the law of one price, which states that two otherwise identical assets cannot sell at different prices. APT assumes that asset returns are linearly related to a set of indexes, where each index represents a factor that influences the return on an asset. Under APT, assets can be described by the factors that affect them. Risk is defined in terms of a stock's sensitivity to these factors, and expected return is directly related to this sensitivity. As always, expected return increases with risk.

Comparing CAPM and APT

APT does not make the following CAPM assumptions:

- Investors choose portfolios on the basis of expected return and risk only.
- There is a single holding period that is the same for all investors.
- There is a riskless security and all investors can borrow and lend at this risk-free rate.

APT does assume that:

- Investors are risk-averse and seek to maximise utility.
- All investors are in full agreement with regard to expectations of future outcomes.
- Factors such as transaction costs are ignored.

The expected return–risk relationship for the CAPM is:

$$E(R_i) = RF + B_i [E(R_M) - RF]$$

The CAPM assumes that the only required measure of risk is the sensitivity to the market. In contrast, the expected return–risk relationship for APT can be described as:

$$E(R_i) = RF + b_{i\,1}(\text{risk premium for factor 1}) + b_{i\,2}(\text{risk premium for factor 2}) + \ldots b_{i\,n}(\text{risk premium for factor n})$$

The sensitivity measure for the CAPM (B_I) and for APT (b_i) have similar interpretations. They are measures of relative sensitivity of a security's return to a particular risk premium.

Identifying the Factors

The CAPM can be thought of as a factor model, with just one factor, which is the market portfolio. APT is more general in that it creates a theoretical framework that includes all the factors that affect a security's returns. Unfortunately there is a catch: it does not tell us what those factors are. In contrast, the CAPM tells us what the important factor is: the market portfolio, which is something that is well understood conceptually. Under APT, the factors need to be determined empirically. Early empirical work by Roll and Ross ('An Empirical Investigation of the Arbitrage Pricing Theory', *Journal of Finance* 35, December 1980) suggested that three to five factors influence security returns and are priced in the market. A later study by Michael A. Berry *et al.* ('Sorting Out Risks Using Known APT Factors', *Financial Analysts Journal*, March–April 1988) argues that an APT model that incorporates unanticipated changes in five macroeconomic variables is superior to the CAPM. These are:

i)   Default risk.
ii)   The term structure of interest rates.
iii)   Inflation or deflation.
iv)   The expected long-run growth rate of profits in the economy.
v)   Residual market risk.

The proponents of APT argue that it offers an approach to strategic portfolio planning. The idea is to recognise that a few systematic factors affect long-term average returns such as those listed above. Investors should identify those few factors that influence most asset returns and seek to quantify the impact that unanticipated changes in each factor will have on portfolio returns.

CONCLUDING COMMENTS

While APT can be viewed as an alternative to the CAPM, the two models are not mutually exclusive. Indeed, if, in the APT world, we were to conclude that the only one factor that mattered was the market portfolio, then the APT risk–return equation would be exactly the same as the CAPM security market line. Both theories try to provide a framework for answering the question of how security prices and equilibrium returns are established. Both models provide a useful input to the job of portfolio management. Both have their flaws. The CAPM relies on observation of the market portfolio, which cannot be observed. APT creates an intuitively appealing factor equation, yet it offers no clue as to what those factors might be. Both models rely on expectations that are not directly observable. They are, however, the best models that we have and as such they are indispensable tools for all portfolio managers.

SUMMARY

- For the purpose of portfolio construction all investment assets can be characterised by just two variables – expected returns and estimated standard deviations of returns.
- The calculation of portfolio return is determined by the expected return of each security and the weight of each security within the portfolio.
- The covariance is an absolute measure of the degree of association between returns for a pair of securities.
- The correlation coefficient is a relative measure of association that lies between +1 (perfect positive correlation) and –1 (perfect negative correlation).
- In general it should be possible to combine stocks in such a way as to reduce risk without adversely affecting expected returns.
- In the simplified two-security case, portfolio risk depends upon the interplay of the risk of each security, the portfolio weights assigned to each security, and the covariance or correlation between the two securities.
- Applying the basic Markowitz approach to portfolio construction is complex, and where many securities are involved it is extremely cumbersome.
- The key advantage of the single-index model is that it reduces dramatically the number of calculations required, because we do not need to calculate the relationship between all pairs of securities being considered.
- Introducing the risk-free asset to the Markowitz efficient frontier radically alters that efficient frontier and in fact it expands the frontier.
- Introduction of the risk-free asset has the result that *all* investors will choose just one risky portfolio (M), which we refer to as the market portfolio, and combine that with varying proportions of the risk-free asset.
- The separation theorem states that the investment decision (which portfolio of risky assets to invest in) is separate from the financing decision (what proportion of investable assets to invest in the market portfolio and in the risk-free asset, respectively).

➡

- The CAPM assumes that each investor diversifies his portfolio according to the Markowitz model, including the risk-free asset.
- The **capital market line** plots the equilibrium relationship between expected portfolio return and the total risk, measured by standard deviation, of efficiently diversified portfolios.
- By using beta as a measure of risk rather than standard deviation, we recognise that the contribution of a security to the total risk of a diversified portfolio is its systematic risk.
- The **security market line (SML)** graphically depicts the CAPM taking into account the risk–return trade-off for individual securities (and inefficient portfolios).
- Beta is a measure of the systematic risk of a security that cannot be avoided through diversification.
- The equation for the security market line states that the expected rate of return on an asset is a function of the two components of the required rate of return – the risk-free rate and the risk premium.

QUESTIONS

1. **Which statement(s) is/are TRUE regarding the Markowitz model?**

   A. The relative importance of variance of each security increases when more securities are included in a portfolio.
   B. If 100 securities are included in a portfolio, 100 covariances are needed to estimate the risk of a portfolio.
   C. Adding two securities with a –1 correlation coefficient, with all other things remaining constant, will reduce the risk of a portfolio.
   D. In a large portfolio, the covariance terms become less important than the covariance terms in a small portfolio.

   1. All of the above
   2. C only
   3. None of the above
   4. A, B and C only

2. **Which statement(s) is/are TRUE regarding covariance and correlation coefficients?**

   A. Covariance measures the relationship between two securities in relative terms.
   B. The correlation coefficient ranges in value from –1 to +1.

C. Negative covariance means the returns of two securities move in opposite directions.

D. A correlation coefficient value of 0 indicates there is positive relationship between the returns of two securities.

    1. B and C only
    2. A and B only
    3. A, B and C only
    4. None of the above

3. **Which of the following statement(s) is/are TRUE?**

A. By combining securities with perfect positive correlation with each other, the portfolio's expected return is maximised and risk is minimised.

B. By combining securities with perfect positive correlation with each other, the portfolio's expected return is minimised and risk is minimised.

C. By combining securities with perfect negative correlation with each other, the portfolio's expected return is minimised and risk is minimised.

D. By combining securities with perfect negative correlation with each other, the portfolio's expected return is maximised and risk is minimised.

    1. All of the above
    2. None of the above
    3. A and B only
    4. A and D only

4. **Which statement(s) is/are TRUE regarding portfolio risk?**

A. Portfolio risk takes only individual security risk into consideration.

B. Portfolio risk takes only covariance between securities into consideration.

C. Portfolio risk takes both individual security risk and covariance between securities into consideration.

D. Portfolio risk is totally independent from the investment weight of the securities held in a portfolio.

5. **Markowitz defines an efficient portfolio as one that:**

A. Has the smallest risk for a given level of expected return.

B. Has the smallest expected return for all levels of risk.

C. Has the largest expected return for a given level of risk.

D. Has the largest expected return and zero risk.

1. All of the above
2. A & C only
3. A & D only
4. B & D only

6. Which of the following is/are considered input variables for the Markowitz model?

A. Weights

B. Expected returns

C. Standard deviations

D. Correlation coefficients.

1. None of the above
2. A, B & C only
3. All of the above
4. B, C & D only

7. Regarding risk, which of the following statement(s) is/are TRUE?

A. Systematic risk affects only stocks but not bonds.

B. Through a well-diversified portfolio, non-systematic risk can be eliminated.

C. In the best case, total risk for a portfolio approaches the systematic risk after diversification.

1. All of the above
2. None of the above
3. A & C only
4. B & C only

8. Which is the TRUE statement about 'beta'?

A. Beta is a measure of total risk, including market risk and issuer risk.

B. An efficient portfolio has the smallest beta of any other portfolios.

C. Beta is the slope of the SML (Security Market Line).

D. A security with a beta of 2 is considered to be less risky than the risk of the benchmark market index.

➡

9. Which statement(s) about CAPM is/are TRUE?

   A. CAPM relates the expected return of securities to their relative risk measure, i.e., their beta.
   B. Market risk premium is equal to expected return on the market portfolio less the risk-free rate.
   C. Stocks with higher beta tend to have a higher risk premium than stocks with lower beta.
      1. A & B only
      2. All of the above
      3. B & C only
      4. A only

10. Assume the market expected return and the risk-free rate for the next period are 12% and 4% respectively. What is the required rate of return for a stock with a beta of 1.8?

    A. 15.8%
    B. 11.2%
    C. 18.4%
    D. 17.6%

11. Stock A has a required rate of return of 18%. If the risk-free rate is 4% and the market risk premium is 11%, what is the beta of stock A?

    A. 0.79
    B. 1.27
    C. 1.96
    D. 2.12

Chapter eight

Derivatives

This chapter analyses derivative contracts, which are now an intrinsic part of the financial fabric. Derivatives first emerged in a significant way in agricultural commodities markets in Chicago in the mid-nineteenth century. Although financial derivatives made their appearance quite early in the history of stock markets, they have really come to prominence only since the early 1980s. Today financial derivatives play a central role in all developed financial markets. This chapter focuses on describing basic futures and options contracts and analysing how they can be used either to manage risk, or to speculate on the price movements of underlying securities.

Learning Objectives

After reading this chapter you will:

- Be familiar with the characteristics of a basic futures contract
- Be familiar with the characteristics of a call option and a put option
- Understand how futures and options contracts can be used to alter the risk/reward profile of investment exposures
- Understand the principles underlying option valuation
- Be aware of the existence of over-the-counter derivative markets.

Financial derivatives are essentially instruments that call for money to change hands at some future date, with the amount to be determined by one or more reference items, such as interest rates, stock prices or currency values. The main economic function of derivative contracts is to provide a means of hedging. Companies such as Ryanair and Irish Continental Group may use derivative contracts to protect themselves against the fluctuating price of oil. A company such as CRH, which generates substantial revenues in dollars, may use derivative contracts to hedge itself against the fluctuating €/$ exchange rate. Over the past decade financial institutions have developed innovative retail products such as tracker bonds and other structural products, which are generally backed by derivative contracts, in order to enable millions of small investors to benefit from the risk-reduction benefits offered by derivative contracts.

Derivatives were primarily invented to reduce risk and not to fuel speculative activity. They developed in order to enable buyers and sellers of commodities to avoid the uncertainty associated with price fluctuations. Physical commodities and financial instruments are typically traded in cash markets. A cash contract calls for immediate delivery and is used by those who need a commodity now or who have cash to invest. There are two types of cash market: spot markets and forward markets. Spot markets are for immediate delivery and forward markets are for deferred delivery. The forward price is the price of an item for forward delivery. Forward contracts are centuries old, whereas the story of futures contracts begins in the Chicago futures exchanges of the mid-nineteenth century.

At that time Chicago had become the biggest agricultural trading centre in the US. Forward contracts in agricultural commodities such as wheat and other grains quickly developed. The American Civil War gave a huge boost to the volumes traded on the Chicago exchanges. At the time of the American Civil War the horse was the key mode of transport, so that any planned military campaign required a large supply of oats to feed the horses. Therefore, if this is spring and the generals are planning a big offensive in the autumn, the quartermaster knows that there will be a large requirement for oats in the autumn. By purchasing September futures contracts today, the quartermaster can secure a supply of the required quantity of oats at the current price of the relevant contract. On the other side of the bargain, a farmer will have entered into a futures contract to deliver oats in September at the same fixed price. In this example both parties have hedged their exposure to fluctuations in the price of oats. Both parties have averted the risk of prices going against them. Of course both parties have also given up the potential for windfall profit, but that is a price they are willing to pay.

Taking a more modern example, an airline such as Ryanair knows that summer is its busiest season. In January it could enter into a forward contract with Shell Oil to purchase jet fuel to be delivered in June. The price of the transaction would be agreed between the parties in January and, come June, Shell would deliver oil to Ryanair in exchange for cash. In this case the parties must negotiate the terms of the forward contract with one another. A futures contract is exactly the same as a forward contract, except that the futures contract will be standardised in terms of quality of commodity, expiry date, etc. and as a result it can normally be traded on a futures exchange.

Going back to the mid-nineteenth century, it was not long before organised futures exchanges developed in Chicago, where forward contracts became standardised in terms of contract size, delivery dates, and the condition of the items that could be delivered. Therefore, only the price and number of contracts were left for futures traders to negotiate. In effect, futures contracts are organised and standardised forward contracts. From around the 1970s the potential offered by futures contracts on financial instruments began to be recognised, and since then there has been an explosion in the range of financial derivative contracts available and in the volumes traded.

FINANCIAL FUTURES

A financial future is a contractual notional commitment to buy or sell a standard quantity of a financial instrument at some point in the future, at a price determined today. The risk profile of a futures contract is identical to the risk profile of an equivalent quantity of the relevant underlying security. The profit or loss on a futures contract is determined by the movement in the price of the underlying security. Today, standardised futures contracts are traded in large volumes on a wide variety of stock market indices and government bonds over a range of maturities. Futures contracts are also available on all the key currency exchange rates. Indeed, there are also futures contracts on specific sectors of the equity market and on some individual securities.

Expiry

On the expiry date of any futures contract one of the following must occur:

i)   The seller of the contract must deliver the appropriate physical amount of the underlying commodity or security (so many bushels of wheat or barrels of oil, so much of a government bond). The buyer of the contract must take delivery and pay the appropriate settlement amount as determined by the price of the futures contract.

ii) For most financial futures contracts, physical delivery does not take place. Instead the difference between the futures contract strike price and the price of the underlying asset at the futures expiry date is used to calculate the profit (loss) of the buyer/seller of the contract. A cash settlement amount is thus calculated and one party pays the other.

Role of the Clearing House

Futures contracts that are traded on exchanges are normally settled through a Clearing House. The Clearing House guarantees the fulfilment of each contract and becomes the formal counterparty for both buyer and seller. The key functions of a Clearing House are twofold:

i)   It establishes the credibility of the market and participants in the
        market have only one counterparty (the Clearing House) to vet
        regarding counterparty risk.
ii)   It improves the liquidity of the contracts traded in the relevant market.

In order to ensure that the market operates smoothly the Clearing House
normally sets out the margin requirements of each contract that must be paid
to it by participants. Normally, the margin required will be a relatively small
percentage of the face value of the contract and will have two components:

i)   Initial Margin: this must be paid to the Clearing House on the day the
        futures contract is entered into. It will usually be calculated with refer-
        ence to the likely maximum daily loss associated with the contract.

ii)   Variation Margin: each day the profit (loss) of the futures position is
        calculated. If it moves to a loss the Clearing House receives the cash,
        and if there is a profit the Clearing House credits the holder's account.
        For each contract the Clearing House has two open positions: one with
        the buyer of the contract and the other with the seller of the contract.

Figure 8.1 Gain/Loss from Buying a Futures Contract

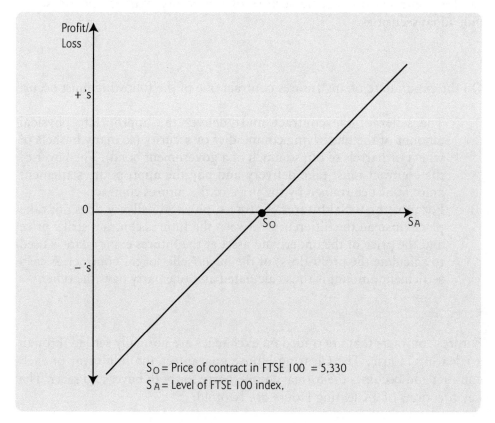

S_O = Price of contract in FTSE 100 = 5,330
S_A = Level of FTSE 100 index,

The margining system should therefore act to limit the likelihood of participants being unable to meet their obligations.

Figure 8.1 illustrates the profit/loss profile associated with the purchase of a futures contract.

The line S_A plots the prices of the underlying commodity, security or index. The point S_0 represents the price paid for the futures contract.

Let's assume that I am bullish regarding the UK equity market and I decide to use the futures contract on the FTSE100 index to gain exposure to UK shares. It's late March and the FTSE100 is trading at 5,310. I buy (go long of) the FTSE June contract at a price of 5,330. I am paying a small premium to today's index level (price) because I will not have to put up cash (except for a small margin requirement) until June. The potential profit (loss) profile that I am exposed to is illustrated in Figure 8.1.

An FTSE100 futures contract relates to a value of stock equal to the futures index multiplied by £10. So if I buy one futures contract at 5,330 (S_0 on chart) it equates to $5,330 * £10 = £53,330$ worth of shares. If the index rises to 6,000 I will make a profit of $6,000 - 5,330 = 670 * £10 = £6,700$ (ignoring transaction costs and taxes). This is the same profit I would make if I had invested £53,300 in the FTSE100 index (for example, through investing it in a fund that tracks the index).

Likewise, if the index falls to 5,000 I will make a loss of $5,000 - 5,330 = -330 * £10 = -£3,300$.

This example highlights the key features of a futures contract, which is that the buyer is fully exposed to both the upside and downside caused by fluctuations in the price of the relevant underlying security. The seller of a futures contract is exposed to a profit (loss) profile that would be identical to going short of the underlying index. In this example, selling one futures contract at 5,330 would expose me to the same risk/reward profile as if I had borrowed £53,300 worth of the constituents of the index and sold them in the market.

Therefore, if the index falls to 5,000 and I am short the contract, I will make a profit of: $5,330 - 5,000 = +330 * £10 = +£3,300$.

Advantages of Financial Futures

Trading volumes in financial futures have exploded over the past two decades in tandem with a huge increase in the range of instruments available. Now, it is often the case that the liquidity of a futures contract is greater than the liquidity of the respective underlying market. Futures contracts are a cash-efficient way of taking a position and can be used to hedge exposures to the underlying securities and/or to take speculative positions. Effectively, market participants can use futures contracts to take a leveraged exposure to the underlying securities. Traders can also use futures contracts to take a short position to the underlying security. Finally, transactions costs are often lower in the futures markets as compared with the relevant markets in the underlying securities.

Pricing of Futures Contracts

The pricing of futures contracts can be viewed as being based on the alternative of borrowing funds to invest in a market. The futures price should be such that there is no arbitrage profit from buying stock (with borrowed money) and simultaneously selling futures contracts. Staying with the FTSE100 index of the top 100 UK-quoted companies we can readily estimate the fair price of a futures contract on the index.

Assume that it is end-March and the FTSE100 is trading at 5,000. I wish to purchase a futures contract expiring at end-June, i.e. in exactly three months. I could borrow funds at a 5% annual rate of interest and invest in a FTSE100 Index fund that has an expected annual dividend yield of 2% over the next three months. The difference between my borrowing rate of 5% and divided yield of 2% represents a 'cost-of-carry' of 3%. Ignoring margin requirements and transactions costs, I can calculate the price of a futures contract where I will be indifferent as to which alternative I use as:

Fair Futures Price (FP) = Spot Index Level *multiplied by* (Interest Cost *less* Dividend Yield) *multiplied by* Time (expressed as a fraction of a year)

$$FP = 5,000 * (.05 - .02) * 0.25 = 25$$

Therefore the fair value premium is 25, so that the fair price of the FTSE100 June futures contract will be 5,025. Arbitrageurs will ensure that futures contracts will normally trade at or very close to the 'Fair Price' as calculated here. Transactions costs, uncertainty regarding the exact expected dividend yield on the market, etc. mean that the 'no-arbitrage fair price' will be a range rather than an exact premium. However, this range will normally be very narrow, although it can at times be significant. At expiry the price of any futures contract must converge on the spot price of the relevant index. Hedgers and speculators will naturally endeavour to purchase futures contracts when they are below fair value (and of course sell contracts when they are above fair value). This is known as basis trading and if the position is held to maturity an additional small profit will accrue.

The No-Arbitrage Principle

The example above illustrates the key underlying principle that determines the values (and hence market prices) of all derivative instruments. This states that in efficient markets there should not be a riskless profit to be gained by combining a forward contract position with positions in the relevant related assets. Remember that futures contracts are essentially forward contracts with standardised terms and conditions.

SWAPS

The swaps market is a huge component of the overall derivatives market and has an estimated face value outstanding of $300 trillion. Swaps may be defined as multi-period extensions of forward contracts. The two largest markets for swaps are the foreign exchange markets and the interest rate markets. For example, rather than agreeing to exchange euros for dollars at an agreed upon forward price at a single date, a foreign exchange swap would call for an exchange of currencies on several future dates. The parties might exchange $1.3 million for €1 million in each of the next five years. Similarly, interest rate swaps call for the exchange of a series of cash flows based on a notional principal amount, with one series of cash flows determined by a floating interest rate and the other set of cash flows determined by a fixed interest rate. An example is the best way to understand the dynamics of a swap contract.

Let's take the example of, say, Ryanair, which has €100 million nominal value issued in a variable rate bond linked to one-year Euribor, maturing in five years on its balance sheet. The corporate treasurer takes the view that short-term interest rates could rise sharply from next year onwards. It is too expensive to retire the bond so Ryanair enters into a swap agreement with a bank to swap variable interest payments into fixed interest payments.

Figure 8.2 Swap Flows from Ryanair Perspective

Figure 8.2 plots the cash flows of the underlying bond and of the swap agreement amongst the three parties involved: Ryanair, the Bank and the Investors. There is no change to the Investors' cash flows over the five-year period – they continue to receive cash flows determined by the relevant variable interest rate and, of course, Ryanair continues to be the payer of

these cash flows. However, Ryanair now has two other sets of cash flows determined by its swap agreement with the Bank. It pays the Bank interest determined by a five-year fixed rate of interest, and it receives from the Bank cash flows determined by one-year variable interest rates.

To illustrate what happens over the life of this contract, let's assume that the variable interest rate is currently 2% and that interest rates rise by 1% each year over the lifetime of the bond. The terms of the swap are that Ryanair agrees to pay a five-year fixed rate of interest of 4% and in return receives one-year variable or floating interest.

For the floating-rate bond, the cash flows paid out by Ryanair and received by the Investors are set out in Table 8.1.

Table 8.1 €100m Floating-Rate Bond

Year	1	2	3	4	5
Interest Rate	2%	3%	4%	5%	6%
Interest Payment (End Year)	€2m	€3m	€4m	€5m	€6m

For the swap agreement (combined with the underlying bond) the cash flows are set out in Table 8.2.

Table 8.2 Swap Bond Cash Flows

Year	1	2	3	4	5
Ryanair Pays Bank – Fixed	€4m	€4m	€4m	€4m	€4m
Bank Pays Ryanair – Floating	€2m	€3m	€4m	€5m	€6m
Ryanair Pays Investors – Floating	€2m	€3m	€4m	€5m	€6m

Effectively Ryanair has ended up with the equivalent of five forward rate agreements to receive a variable interest payment in exchange for a fixed interest payment. It has protected itself against rises in variable rates of interest over the life of the bond. In this particular example the net impact on Ryanair's interest costs is neutral over the five years. Note that interest is based on the nominal €100 million and no principal changes hands.

Credit risk is an important issue for the swaps market since there is an enormous interdependence between the various counterparties involved. The collapse of Lehman Brothers threw into stark relief the systemic risk inherent in the very large market place for OTC swap contracts. It is expected to take years for the liquidators of Lehman to unravel the web of interrelated transactions. Regulators and banks continue to work hard to bring more and more transactions into centralised market exchanges.

Credit Default Swaps

Despite the similarity in name, a credit default swap (CDS) is not the same type of instrument as interest rate or currency swaps. Payment on a CDS is tied to the financial status of one or more reference firms, or sovereign issuers of bonds. The CDS allows two counterparties to take positions on the credit risk of the issuers of particular securities. The CDS market has grown enormously and has enabled participants to take positions on the credit-worthiness of bonds issued by companies throughout the world as well as bonds issued by governments. Unlike interest rate swaps, credit default swaps do not entail periodic netting of one reference rate against another. They are more like insurance policies written on particular credit events. In the event of a default on a bond or a failure to meet an interest payment, the seller (writer) of the CDS will be obliged to make good the loss incurred by the credit event to the buyer of the CDS.

OPTIONS

In this section we are going to discuss options relating to company shares or a group of shares represented by market or sector indices. However, option contracts are available on an enormous range of securities and commodities. Options represent claims on an underlying ordinary share and are created by investors and sold to other investors. The company whose stock underlies these claims has no direct interest in the transactions. There are two basic types of option:

- A call option gives the holder the right to buy (or 'call away') 1,000 shares of a particular company, at a specified price, at any time up to a specified expiration date.
- A put option gives the buyer the right to sell (or 'put away') 1,000 shares of a particular company, at a specified price, at any time up to a specified expiration date.

Investors purchase call options if they expect the price of the underlying share to rise and purchase put options if they expect the price of the underlying share to fall.

Why Options Markets?

i)   Puts and calls expand the range of opportunities available to investors, making available a wider range of risk/return opportunities.
ii)   Options provide leverage.
iii)   Put options, in particular, allow the buyer to hedge underlying positions in stocks.
iv)   Institutional investors that actively sell (or write) options can generate extra income on their portfolios.

Pay-off Profiles of Options

Pay-off Profile of a Call Option

Figure 8.3 illustrates the pay-off profile at expiry of the buyer and seller, respectively, of a call option.

Figure 8.3 Profit and Loss Profiles of Buyer and Seller of a Call Option in ABC plc

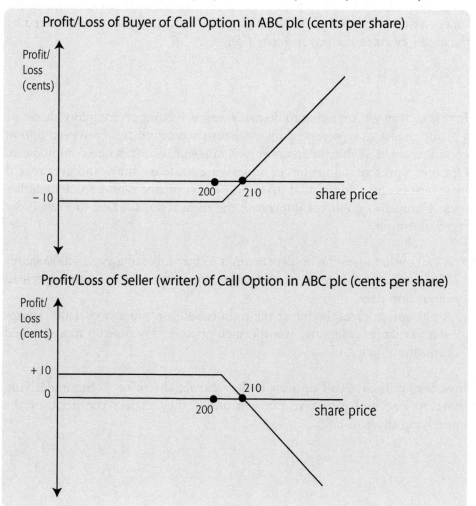

In the example the call option details are:

> Option premium: 10 cents per share
> Strike price: €2.00

If the share price rises above €2.00, the call option is said to be 'in the money'. However, the share price needs to rise above €2.10 (strike price plus premium) before the buyer moves into profit. The buyer can benefit from all the potential upside in the stock, whilst at the same time his potential loss is limited to the premium paid (10 cents per share in this example).

The risk/reward profile of the seller (or writer) of the call option is the mirror image of the buyer's profile.

Effectively, the writer of a call option is going short of the stock. As the share price rises ever higher, the seller is exposed to ever-greater losses. In this example the seller of the call option will suffer a loss once the share price moves above €2.10 (strike price plus premium received). In the case of the seller his potential profit is capped at the premium received, but his potential losses are unlimited.

Pay-off Profile of a Put Option

The buyer of a put option benefits when the price of the underlying share falls. In the example illustrated in Figure 8.4 the put option details are:

> Option premium: 12 cents per share
> Strike price: €2.00

If the share price falls below €2.00 the buyer of the option is in the money, but starts making a profit only when the share price goes below €1.88 (strike price minus premium).

The exact reverse is the case for the seller (writer) of the put option. As the price falls below the 'break-even' level of €1.88, the seller is exposed to ever-greater losses. If the company were to go bankrupt, the seller would suffer the full loss of €1.88 per share. The seller's maximum profit is the premium received of 12 cents per share.

Some Investment Strategies Using Options

There are many situations where options may be used to efficiently implement a desired investment strategy. Often the desired risk/reward profile may be achieved only through the employment of derivative contracts. Because of the small initial cash outlay required and the potentially large pay-off,

Figure 8.4 Profit and Loss Profiles of a Buyer and Seller of a Put Option in ABC plc

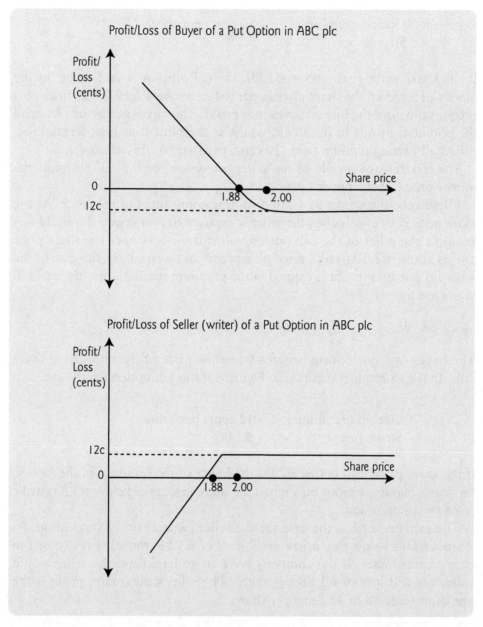

purchasing options will often appeal to those who wish to speculate on share price movements. For the sellers (or writers) of options, a policy of continuously writing options may be adopted to earn a small additional income for an equity portfolio. Studies have shown that the odds favour the sellers of options in a somewhat similar fashion to where the odds over time favour the bookies rather than the punters.

Figure 8.5 Pay-off Profile for a Covered Call Position

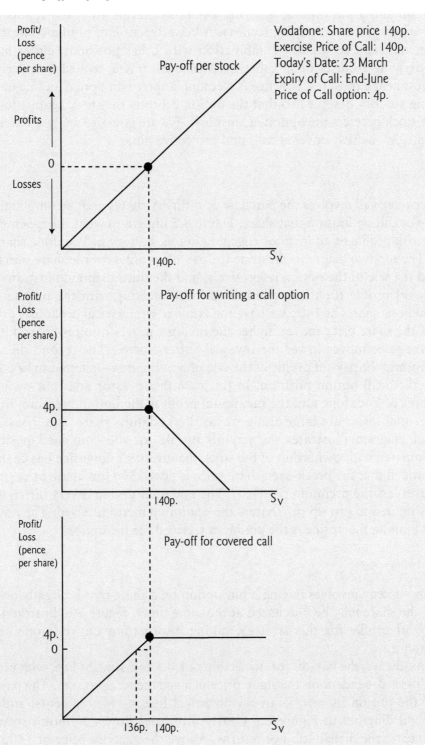

Profit/
Loss
(pence
per share)

Pay-off per stock

Vodafone: Share price 140p.
Exercise Price of Call: 140p.
Today's Date: 23 March
Expiry of Call: End-June
Price of Call option: 4p.

Profits

0

Losses

S_V

140p.

Profit/
Loss
(pence
per share)

Pay-off for writing a call option

4p.
0

140p.

S_V

Profit/
Loss
(pence
per share)

Pay-off for covered call

4p.
0

136p. 140p.

S_V

Above we illustrated the profit/loss profiles of the buyers/sellers of a call option and a put option, ignoring any position that the participants may have had in the underlying security. A key attraction of option contracts is that they can be used in combination with other positions, either in the underlying security or in other derivative contracts, to hedge underlying investment exposures. A hedge is a combination of an option and its underlying security designed so that the option protects the stock against loss or the stock protects the option against loss. We are going to analyse two such strategies, namely covered calls and protective puts.

Covered Calls

A covered call involves the purchase of ordinary shares and the simultaneous sale of call options on that share. Figure 8.5 illustrates what is happening to the risk profile of an investor engaging in this strategy in Vodafone shares.

The top two diagrams illustrate the pay-off profiles for the share purchase and the sale of the option respectively, and the third diagram illustrates the pay-off profile for the combined position. Starting with the purchase of Vodafone shares at 140p we have the familiar symmetrical profit/loss profile – if the share price moves higher the investor moves into profit, and if the share price moves lower the investor suffers losses. The second diagram illustrates the pay-off profile of the sale of a call option – referred to as taking a naked call option position. In this case the investor does not own any shares in Vodafone and the maximum profit is the option premium of 4p. Potential losses are large and grow as the Vodafone share price rises. The final diagram illustrates the pay-off profile for the combined position. Compared with ownership of the stock the investor's downside has changed a little in that the break-even share price is now 136p (purchase price of the shares less the premium received). The potential upside is very different as it is limited to just 4p per share – the option premium received. The reward for limiting the upside is the premium received for the option.

Protective Puts

This strategy involves buying a put option on a share that is already owned (or the share may be purchased at the same time). Figure 8.6 illustrates the pay-off profile for this strategy, taking information on Vodafone as an example.

As always, the pay-off for ownership of stock is a straight line, with profits or losses dependent on the share price in a symmetrical fashion. The pay-off for the put on its own is an asymmetrical line in two segments, and the second diagram in Figure 8.6 clearly illustrates how the option strategy truncates the distribution of returns. Above the exercise price of 140p the

Figure 8.6 Pay-off Profile for a Protective Put Position

pay-off line is horizontal and reflects the fact that loss is limited to the 3p cost of the put. The position moves into profit as the share price falls below the exercise price less the premium, which is 137p in this example. The third diagram plots the pay-off profile for the combined position. The break-even point occurs at 143p – the exercise price plus the option premium. Above 143p ownership of the stock ensures that the investor participates fully in the upside. Below 140p the stock position moves into loss but the put position offsets the losses penny for penny. If the share price falls to 139p there will obviously be a loss of a penny per share, whilst the put option will have an intrinsic value of 1p. The impact on the investor's P&L of the combined position for a number of selected share prices may be summarised as:

Share Price of:	139p	137p	130p	150p
Stock Position	−1p	−3p	−10p	+10p
Option Value	+1p	+3p	+10p	0
Option Premium	−3p	−3p	−3p	−3p
Net Position	−3p	−3p	−3p	+7p

Above the break-even point of 143p, ownership of the stock ensures that the protective put strategy (simultaneous purchase of stock and put option) fully participates in the gains as the share price rises. Clearly, the key attraction of a protective put strategy is that it provides a relatively simple and easily executed method to limit the downside of investing in shares.

It is beyond the scope of this text to provide more detail on the wide range of strategies that can be created using derivative contracts.

The protective put strategy and the covered call strategy illustrated here highlight how the combination of a position in an underlying security with option contracts alters an investor's risk/reward profile. A variety of derivative securities may also be combined to create an almost limitless array of alternative risk/reward profiles. It is this variety and flexibility regarding risk/reward profiles offered by derivative contracts that enables the financial services industry to innovate so extensively to provide new products and services.

EVERYDAY USE OF DERIVATIVES

Today derivative contracts play a big role across a vast range of industries. The participants in these markets fall into two broad categories:

i)   Hedgers will normally hold risky positions in the underlying securities or markets, and will use options or futures to offset or limit some of this risk. By taking a position opposite to one already held in the physical market, hedgers plan to reduce the risk of adverse price fluctuations. Essentially, a hedger is prepared to forgo some profit potential in exchange for having someone else assume part of the risk. Hedging therefore reduces the risk of loss, at the cost of reducing the return possibilities compared with the unhedged position.

ii)   Speculators will buy or sell futures or options contracts with the sole object of profit and will be attracted by the leverage offered by options and the ability to go short of the underlying securities. Unlike hedgers, speculators do not normally transact in the physical commodity or financial security underlying the futures contract. Speculators are essential to the functioning of derivatives markets, absorbing the excess demand or supply generated by hedgers and assuming the risk of price fluctuations that hedgers wish to avoid. Speculators add to the overall liquidity of the market and their trading activity should reduce the variability of prices over time.

An individual or an institution may of course take out some positions in a hedging capacity, but at the same time may take speculative positions in a different segment of their business. Derivatives are most widely used in the financial sectors of banking and insurance and indeed trading in derivative contracts forms a separate business unit in many financial institutions. The explosive growth in both the variety of derivative contracts traded, and the value of transactions, are due to both the hedging options offered and the speculative opportunities.

In some quarters derivative contracts have a bad name, due to several very high-profile financial scandals and disasters. John Rusnack racked up losses from trading currency contracts totalling close to $800m before his superiors in AIB's Allfirst subsidiary discovered the fraud. Baring's Bank was not so lucky when rogue trader Nick Leeson was allowed to run amok in Singapore. The derivative contracts that he entered into were so large that they led to the collapse of the long-established and respected bank.

Another high-profile collapse was Long Term Capital Management in 1998. This was an enormous hedge fund whose founding partners included Robert Merton and Myron Scholes, Nobel laureates in economics, who between them all but invented modern finance through their theory on pricing options. At its peak LTCM commanded funds of $130 billion and a derivatives portfolio with a notional value of $1.25 trillion. A financial crisis precipitated by the failure of Russia to honour its debts led to the near-collapse of the Fund, which was saved only by a rescue package organised by the banks as the US Federal Reserve worried that it could damage the entire financial system.

In the aftermath of the near collapse of the financial system in 2008, derivatives and financial structures built on complicated and opaque financial instruments have been identified as a key culprit in the debacle. It is beyond the scope of this book to explore the very complicated issues involved. Suffice it to say that some changes to derivative markets in terms of their structures and regulation are inevitable. Nevertheless, derivative instruments and markets will continue to play a hugely important role in financial markets.

Irrespective of these failures it is generally accepted that the development of derivatives markets radically improves the risk-sharing capacity and innovative ability of the financial system.

Valuing Options

In thinking about the value (or price) of an option, it is useful to analyse it in terms of two factors. This discussion will cover a call option, but the principles are the same for a put option. First, if a call option is 'in the money' (share price is above the strike price), the option has an immediate value that is the difference between the two prices (share price *minus* strike price). In other words, the buyer of the call option could exercise the option and immediately sell the stock on the market at a profit. This is referred to as the intrinsic value of the option and is the difference between the current market price of the underlying share and the strike price. If the market price of the share is at or below the strike price, the intrinsic value of the option is nil.

Even if the intrinsic value of a call option is nil, it can still have a positive value. This is because there is a second source of value, commonly referred to as 'time value'. In general, the longer the time to the option expiry date, the greater will be the time value of the option. This time value is influenced by the interest rate over the relevant period and the volatility of the underlying share. The higher (more risky) the volatility, the higher will be the time value of the option. Also, given that ownership of the underlying asset is deferred until the expiry date, higher interest rates will be reflected in a higher premium. However, in a low interest rate environment the time value of an option is primarily determined by the volatility of the underlying security.

Assume that the current share price of CRH is €21 and that a 3-month call option is available at an exercise price of €20. This option is 'in-the-money' because the share price is greater than the exercise price.

$$\text{Intrinsic value of call option} = €21 - €20 = €1$$

Puts work in reverse. A 3-month put option with a strike price of €20, with the shares trading at €21, has an intrinsic value of nil.

$$\text{Intrinsic value of put option} = €20 - €21 = -€1$$

However, a put option (or a call option) cannot have a negative value. Therefore, the formula for estimating the intrinsic values of calls and puts may be written as:

$$\text{Intrinsic value of a call} = \text{Maximum } (S_0 - E), 0$$
$$\text{Intrinsic value of a put} = \text{Maximum } (E - S_0), 0$$
$$\text{where:} \quad S_0 = \text{price of underlying security}$$
$$E = \text{exercise price}$$

In plain English, the formula states that the intrinsic value of a call option is equal to the share price less the exercise price, as long as the result is positive. If the result is negative, then the intrinsic value is zero. For a put option the intrinsic value is the exercise price less the share price, again as long as this value is positive. Otherwise the intrinsic value of the put option is zero. On the expiry date the intrinsic value of the option will equate to the price or value of that option. Prior to the expiry date the price of the option will equal the intrinsic value plus the time value of the option. As we saw above, the call option in CRH with an exercise price of €20 has an intrinsic value of €1 if the shares are trading at €21. The price of this option in the market will be €1 if today is the expiry date. However, if the option has a significant amount of time to run to expiry, it will be worth more than €1. It should be intuitively clear that if we have two call options that are identical in every respect except with regard to time to expiry, the option with more time to expiry will be more valuable.

Estimating the Time Value of Options

This is much more difficult than estimating the intrinsic value. The three variables that determine time value are:

- the time remaining to the expiration of the option
- the interest rate
- the volatility (as measured by standard deviation) of the underlying security.

The Black–Scholes (B/S) Model is a widely used model, developed by Fischer Black and Myron Scholes for the valuation of call options. The model itself is mathematically complex and beyond the scope of this text. However, the model can be easily accessed and is widely used to estimate the fair value of call options. The B/S Model uses the following five variables to value the call option of a non-dividend paying share:

- the price of the underlying security
- the exercise price of the option

- the time remaining to the expiration of the option
- the interest rate
- the volatility of the underlying share.

As discussed earlier, the first two variables determine the intrinsic value of the option, i.e. whether it is 'in-the-money' or 'out-of-the-money'. If the option is 'out-of-the-money', the option has only time value. Time remaining to expiration (measured as a fraction of a year) is relevant because value generally increases with maturity. The interest rate affects option values because of the opportunity cost involved. Buying a call option is an alternative to purchasing shares using borrowed funds, on which interest must be paid. The higher interest costs are, the more interest is saved by buying options, and therefore higher interest rates add to the value of call options.

The first four variables are all observable in the market, and it is only the last one, the stock's volatility, that has to be estimated. Volatility is normally estimated from historical price data. The greater the volatility, the higher the price of a call option, because of the increased potential for the share price to move up. Strictly speaking, the B/S Model applies to non-dividend-paying stocks. The payment of a dividend will cause the price of a share to fall and will lead to a reduction in the price of call options on that share (and a rise in the price of put options). Taking into account shares that pay dividends, the relationship between the price of call options and the factors that determine such prices is summarised below:

Effects of Variables on Prices of Call Options

Variable	Impact on Value of Call Option
Share Price	Positive
Exercise Price	Negative
Time to Expiration	Positive
Volatility of Underlying Share	Positive
Interest Rates	Positive
Cash Dividends	Negative

So if the share price rises, it will have a positive impact on the price of a call option. A higher exercise price will mean a lower price for the call option, etc. It is clear from this table that at any point in time the only variable that will cause differences in the estimate of the fair value of a call option is the volatility of the underlying security. Whilst such estimates rely heavily on historical data, most market participants take into account potential events that may impact on a share's volatility. Therefore, the announcement of an unexpected item of news concerning a company can lead to an almost instantaneous change in the price of options as market participants 'price in' higher expected volatility in the relevant share price.

Market participants often use the B/S Model to estimate the level of volatility in the marketplace implied by the price of traded options. The market prices of traded options are plugged into the model, together with the other variables with the exception of volatility. If the model shows that implied volatility is high (compared with a benchmark level, which may be some historical average), then it suggests that option prices are high compared with historical norms. An institution that holds a large equity portfolio may use this information to increase its sales of options to take advantage of the higher premium available. A private investor who is considering the purchase of put options to hedge their investments in the equity market may decide to hold off until implied volatility declines.

Pricing Put Options

The B/S Model applies initially to call options, but the existence of the principle of put–call parity means that it can also be used to price put options. The put–call parity expresses the relationship between the prices of puts and calls on the same stock that must hold if arbitrage is to be ruled out. It can be expressed as:

Price of a Put = Exercise Price/e^{rt} – Share Price + Price Call Option

where: e = the base of natural logarithms
           r = riskless rate of interest
           t = time to expiry of the option expressed as a fraction of a year.

If this relationship does not hold between a put and a call, then arbitrageurs will be able to make risk-free profits. In efficient markets such a situation cannot persist, and therefore the put–call parity means that the B/S Model can be used to price both calls and puts.

FUTURES AND OPTIONS EXCHANGES

Futures contracts are essentially forward contracts with standardised terms and conditions. It is worth enumerating the similarities and what differentiates them.

In general, both forward and futures contracts:

i)   Obligate the buyer to buy and the seller to sell a certain quantity of an asset at a price determined today at a specified future date.

ii)   Can be settled through cash settlement based on the value of the
        relevant contract at the expiry date.
iii)   Have prices determined by the No-Arbitrage Principle, so that at the
        initiation of the contract it has zero value.

The differences include:

i)   Forward contracts are private contracts negotiated between the
        relevant parties and usually are not tradable. Futures contracts trade
        on organised exchanges.
ii)   Forward contracts are customised contracts satisfying the needs of the
        parties involved and this is an attraction over futures contracts, which
        are highly standardised.
iii)   Counterparty risk is a factor to be taken into account with forward
        contracts. For futures contracts the clearing house is the single
        counterparty for all transactions.
iv)   Futures contracts are marked to market every day and variation
        margin has to be paid to (received from) the clearing house. As they
        are not traded, forward contracts are not marked to market each day.
v)   Futures exchanges are normally regulated by the respective financial
        regulators.

A similar situation exists regarding options contracts. Contracts that are
entered into privately are customised to the needs of the parties concerned.
Such contracts will usually not be traded and there will normally be a cash
settlement between the parties on the expiry date. Options traded on exchanges
are standardised, but the valuation principles are exactly the same for both.
Standardised futures and options contracts now trade in large volumes on
various exchanges such as Euronext.liffe. Information on these contracts is
readily available in the financial pages. Exhibit 8.1 shows the information
provided in the *Financial Times* on equity options on a daily basis.

This lists call and put options in FTSE100 stocks. For example, it can be
seen that on 26 February 2011 BP shares were trading at 494p. Calls
exercisable at end-May with a strike price of 490p traded at a premium of
21.5p. The call option with a strike price of 500p traded at a premium of
16.75p. The May 490 put option had a premium of 19.5p and the May 500
put option had a premium of 25p.

Accessing the respective websites of the various futures and options
exchanges will reveal extensive information regarding the contracts traded,
latest traded prices, open positions, etc. The advantages of exchange-traded
standardised contracts are numerous and include:

Exhibit 8.1 Equity Options

(Panel 1 — Calls Mar/Apr/May · Puts Mar/Apr/May)

Option	Calls Mar	Apr	May	Puts Mar	Apr	May
AstraZeneca (*2960) 2900	89	115	142	29	51	75.5
3000	34.5	60.5	86.5	74	97	120
Aviva (*462.200) 460	14	14	17.25		24	29.25
470	9	9.5	12.75	16	30.75	34.75
BAE Systems (*327.600) 320	12.75	16.75	17.25	5	8.75	16.5
330	7	11.25	12	9.25	13.5	22.5
Barclays (*313.300) 310	11.75	16.25	21	9	13.75	18.5
320	6.75	11.25	15.5	14	18.75	23.75
BG Group (*1497) 1450	70.5	90.5	106.5	24.5	45.5	63
1500	43	63	80	46	69	87.5
BHP Billiton (*2432.5) 2400	79.5	111.5	144	68.5	104	135
2500	35.5	66	98	128	159.5	188
BP (*494.75) 490	13	17.5	21.5	8	13	19.5
500	7.75	12.25	16.75	12.75	18	25
BAT (*2466.5) 2400	71.5	77.5	87	47.5	68	88.5
2500	13	23	38	120	133.5	149
BT Group (*178.700) 175	6.5	8.25	10.75	2.5	4.75	7
180	3.5	5.5	8	4.25	6.75	9.25
Diageo (*1205) 1200	18	27	38.5	28	38.5	47
1250	4.5	11.5	19	66	71	78.5
GlaxoSmKl (*1180) 1150	41.5	50	56.5	9.5	19.5	34.5
1200	13	23	29	32.5	42	60
HSBC (*711.100) 700	20.5	25.75	32.5	14.5	21.5	31
720	10.5	16.25	22.75	25.75	32.25	42.25
Int Consolidated Airlines SA 220 (*224.600) 220	11.25	15.25	19.25	6.75	11.75	14.5
225	8.5	13	15.75	9	14.25	15.75
Kingfisher (*256.900) 250	10.5	14	15.5	3.5	7	11.25
260	4.5	8.5	10.25	8	11.5	16.25

(Panel 2 — Calls Mar/Apr/May · Puts Mar/Apr/May)

Option	Calls Mar	Apr	May	Puts Mar	Apr	May
Land Sec Gp (*749) 740	17	21.5	26.5	10.5	17.5	21.75
760	6.5	11	16.75	22	27.5	31.5
Legal & Gen (*117.600) 115	4.25	6.25	6.75	2.25	3.5	6
120	1.75	3.5	4.25	4.25	5.75	8.75
Lloyds Bkg (*62.850) 60	4.25	5.25	6	1.25	2.25	2.5
64	1.75	2.75	3.75	3	4	4.75
Man Group (*288.700) 280	14	19	21.5	5	9.5	12.5
290	8	13.25	16.5	9	14	17.25
Marks & S (*351) 350	10	15.75	19.25	9	14.25	17.5
360	6.25	11.5	15	15	20	23.25
Morrison (Wm) (*282.800) 280	7	9.25	10	4	6.5	11.5
290	3	4.5	5.5	9.75	11.5	18
Rio Tinto (*4265.5) 4200	144.5	217	275	118.5	190	242
4300	96.5	168.5	—	169.5	240.5	—
Royal Bk Scot (*45.650) 44	2.5	3.25	4	0.75	1.5	2.25
46	1.25	2.25	3	1.75	2	3.25
Royal Dutch Shell 'B' (*2202.5) 2200	43.5	63.5	78.5	40	58	88
2300	11.5	24.5	36	108.5	119	151
RSA Ins Gp (*141.200) 140	2.25	2.75	4	5.25	7	8.25
145	0.75	1.25	2	9.5	10.75	11.75
Sainsbury (*374.700) 370	11	15	17.75	5.5	9.75	17
380	6.5	10	13	10.75	14.5	23.75
Std Chartd (*1627) 1600	51.5	65	82.5	45	62	80.5
1638	31.5	—	—	67.5	—	—
Tesco (*406.050) 400	10.5	14.25	16	4.25	8	16
410	4.75	9	11.25	8.75	12.75	22
Vodafone (*174.700) 170	6.5	8.25	9.75	1.75	3.5	5
175	3.5	5	7	3.75	5.25	7

(Panel 3 — Xstrata: Mar/Apr/May; remaining stocks: Mar/Jun/Sep)

Option	Calls 1	2	3	Puts 1	2	3
Xstrata (*1383) 1350	69	94.5	110.5	35	57	80
1400	43.5	67	84.5	58	81	105.5
3i Group (*310.900) 300	12.5	21.5	27.75	2.25	10.25	15.25
310	6.25	—	—	5.5	—	—
Carnival (*2766) 2700	112.5	—	—	45.5	—	—
2800	57	133.5	187.5	87.5	172	229.5
Compass (*553.5) 540	18.5	—	—	5.25	—	—
560	7.5	23	31.75	13.5	28	39.25
Experian (*770.5) 760	23.75	44.25	53.75	12.75	32.25	48.5
780	12.75	—	—	21.5	—	—
Impl Tobacco (*1996) 1950	72	—	—	24.5	—	—
2000	43.5	98.5	129.5	46.5	96	146.5
IntCont Hotels (*1355) 1350	39.5	—	—	34.5	—	—
1400	18.5	53.5	82.5	62.5	117	148.5
Intl Power (*332.300) 328	9.25	15.5	19.5	5	16	20.5
336	5	—	—	8.75	—	—
Lon Stk Exchg (*892.5) 880	31	63.5	74.5	18	44.5	71
900	21.25	—	—	27.75	—	—
ITV (*86.150) 84	3.75	—	—	1.5	—	—
88	1.5	5	7	3.5	6.5	8
Natl Grid (*570.5) 560	16.25	26.25	29.5	5.5	28.25	35.25
580	5.25	—	—	14.5	—	—
Next (*2024) 2000	65.5	121.5	152.5	38.5	125.5	165
2100	24.5	—	—	95	—	—
Pearson (*1041) 1000	52.75	60.5	72.25	11.75	37.5	56.75
1050	22	—	—	31.25	—	—
Rekitt Bncksr Gp (*3163) 3100	103.5	—	—	38.5	—	—
3200	46.5	133	172.5	83.5	157.5	231

(Panel 4 — Calls Mar/Jun/Sep · Puts Mar/Jun/Sep)

Option	Calls Mar	Jun	Sep	Puts Mar	Jun	Sep
Reed Elsevier (*547.5) 540	14.75	22.75	—	7.25	25.75	—
560	5	13.25	20	17.5	38.25	48
Rentokil Init (*90.900) 88	4.5	7.75	9.5	1.25	4.5	6.75
92	2.25	—	—	3	—	—
Rolls-Royce (*612) 600	21	32.5	43.75	8.5	27	37
620	10.25	—	—	17.75	—	—
SAB Miller (*2053) 2000	80	138	164.5	25	78	124
2100	27	86	—	72.5	126	—
Sage (*283) 280	7.75	14.25	19.75	4.75	12.5	17.5
290	3	—	—	10	—	—
Scot & Sthn Energy (*1219) 1200	34.5	60.5	69	14	38.5	79.5
1250	11.5	37	—	40.5	65	—
Shire (*1742) 1700	57	101.5	134	17.5	59.5	88
1750	28	—	—	39.5	—	—
Sm & Nephew (*717.5) 700	32	—	—	13.75	—	—
720	21.75	45	57	23	50.5	58.5
Standard Life (*240.5) 235	7.75	—	—	6.5	—	—
240	4.5	8.5	12.25	9.75	15.25	22
Unilever (*1837) 1800	51.5	87	112	14	58	93
1850	23.5	61.5	—	36.5	82	—
Utd Utilities (*590) 580	15.75	28	31.25	5	16	33
600	5.25	17	21	15	25.5	44.25
Whitbread (*1800) 1750	73.5	—	—	25.5	—	—
1800	43.5	87	120.5	41	108	142
Wolseley (*2150) 2100	82.5	—	—	29	—	—
2200	28.5	92.5	145.5	82.5	142.5	188
WPP (*834) 820	28.25	—	—	14.75	—	—
840	17.25	40	56.25	23.75	50.75	66.5

* Underlying security price. Premiums shown are based on settlement prices. Source: Euronext.liffe

February 25 Total contracts, Equity & Index options:
119,968 Calls: 56,292 Puts: 60,804

- Counterparty risk resides with the respective exchange's clearing house for both buyers and sellers of derivative contracts.
- The existence of the clearing house also ensures anonymity for participants.
- Standardised contracts ensure that interest in each market is concentrated into a relatively small number of contracts. This improves liquidity in each contract, as volumes traded are limited to the available contracts. This can create a virtuous circle where high volumes in a contract generate low bid/offer spreads and high liquidity, which in turn generates even more activity.
- Transparency is a key feature of these markets. Traded prices and open interest are available virtually on a real-time basis. As well as providing timely information to market participants on specific contracts, the information available can also reveal important information concerning the associated underlying securities/markets.
- Regulation: the transparency of derivative exchanges is very appealing to the respective regulatory authorities. Also, the existence of a clearing house allows regulators to easily monitor the adequacy of the capital that is committed to the various markets.

Over-the-Counter (OTC) Derivative Markets

The diversity of derivative contracts that are traded on exchanges, and the enormous volumes traded, do not represent the full picture of derivative activity. There is an extensive market in derivative contracts that are not traded on regulated exchanges. These are contracts where the buyer and seller come together directly and agree the terms of the contract between themselves. Therefore, such contracts can be tailored to meet the specific requirements of the parties involved. The explosion in the so-called OTC market has been driven by a number of factors:

- Most contracts that are traded on exchanges have expiry dates of less than one year. Demand for longer-dated contracts has grown exponentially and can be fulfilled only on the OTC market.
- OTC markets enable participants to tailor contracts to their specific requirements.

With regard to pricing and valuation, the same principles apply to OTC derivatives as to those traded on exchanges. Counterparty risk, however, is a key aspect of OTC markets and one that all participants must carefully manage. From the perspective of market regulators the counterparty risk of each individual entity is not of any particular concern. However, regulators are concerned about the systematic risk posed by the explosion in the scale and diversity of OTC derivative contracts. Respected market participants and observers have been pointing out the potential dangers posed by these markets.

- The volumes of outstanding positions are impossible to quantify, but are now sufficiently large to pose a risk to the entire financial system if there were a wide-scale crisis.
- The variety of contracts is extensive and could be creating unknown risks to the financial system.
- Because these contracts do not trade on regulated exchanges they may fall outside the scope of financial regulators.

Events in 2008, and in particular the collapse of Lehman Brothers, brought painfully to the fore the systemic risks posed by the unfettered growth of OTC derivative markets. The response of governments and regulators has been to put in place a process of bringing as much as possible of OTC derivative markets into formal exchanges. This would reduce counterparty risks, increase trans - parency and allow more of the market to be effectively regulated.

SUMMARY

- Financial derivatives are essentially instruments that call for money to change hands at some future date, with the amount to be determined by one or more reference items, such as interest rates, stock prices or currency values.
- Derivatives were primarily invented to reduce risk and not to fuel speculative activity.
- The risk profile of a futures contract is identical to the risk profile of an equivalent quantity of the relevant underlying security.
- On the expiry date of most financial futures contracts the difference between the futures contract strike price and the price of the underlying asset at the futures expiry date is used to calculate the profit (loss) of the buyer/seller of the contract. A cash settlement amount is thus calculated and one party pays the other.
- Futures contracts that are traded on exchanges are normally settled through a Clearing House. The Clearing House guarantees the fulfil - ment of each contract and becomes the formal counterparty for both buyer and seller.
- Initial Margin must be paid to the Clearing House by both the buyer and seller of a futures contract on the day the futures contract is entered into.
- Each day the profit (loss) of the futures position is calculated. If it moves to a loss the Clearing House receives the cash, and if there is a profit the Clearing House credits the holder's account.

➡

- The No-Arbitrage Principle states that in efficient markets there should not be a riskless profit to be gained by combining a forward contract position with positions in the relevant underlying assets.
- A call option gives the holder the right to buy (or 'call away') 1,000 shares of a particular company, at a specified price, at any time up to a specified expiration date.
- A put option gives the buyer the right to sell (or 'put away') 1,000 shares of a particular company, at a specified price, at any time up to a specified expiration date.
- Puts and calls expand the range of opportunities available to investors, making available a wider range of risk/return opportunities.
- Options provide leverage.
- Put options, in particular, allow the buyer to hedge underlying positions in stocks.
- Institutional investors that actively sell (or write) options can generate extra income on their portfolios.
- Hedgers will normally hold risky positions in the underlying securities or markets, and will use options or futures to offset or limit some of this risk.
- Speculators will buy or sell futures or options contracts with the sole object of profit and will be attracted by the leverage offered by options and the ability to go short of the underlying securities.
- The intrinsic value of an option is the difference between the current market price of the underlying share and the strike price. More precisely, the intrinsic value of a call option is equal to the share price less the exercise price, as long as the result is positive. For a put option the intrinsic value is the exercise price less the share price, again as long as this value is positive.
- The three variables that determine time value are the time remaining to the expiration of the option; the interest rate and the volatility (as measured by standard deviation) of the underlying security.
- The advantages of exchange-traded standardised contracts include counterparty risk limited to the clearing house; standardised contracts improve liquidity in each contract, as volumes traded are limited to the available contracts; transparency is a key feature of these markets.
- Over-the-Counter (OTC) derivatives are contracts where the buyer and seller come together directly and agree the terms of the contract between themselves.
- OTC contracts have gained in popularity because most contracts that are traded on exchanges have expiry dates of less than one year, and demand for longer-dated contracts has grown exponentially.
- OTC markets enable participants to tailor contracts to their specific requirements.

QUESTIONS

1. Which of the following statements is FALSE?

    A. Futures contracts originated in the agricultural trading markets in Chicago in the mid-eighteenth century.
    B. The activities of speculators benefit the marketplace by increasing the liquidity of the contracts traded.
    C. Too much speculative activity can generate additional volatility in the prices of underlying assets.
    D. An American-style option can be exercised only at the expiry date and not before.

2. If you had €100,000 invested in CRH shares, which of the following option strategies would be most appropriate to hedge your investment?

    A. Buy call options.
    B. Buy put options.
    C. Write/sell call options.
    D. Write/sell put options.

3. Which of the following is the correct definition of a traded call option in ABC company shares?

    A. The right to buy shares in ABC at a fixed price with a fixed expiry date.
    B. The right to sell shares in ABC at a fixed price with a fixed expiry date.
    C. The right to buy or sell shares in ABC.
    D. The right to buy shares in ABC at a fixed price with a variable expiry date.

4. The _____ is the price paid by the option buyer to the writer of either a call or a put option.

    A. exercise price
    B. option premium
    C. current stock price plus liquidity premium
    D. call (put) risk premium

5. A call option contains the following information, EXCEPT:

    A. expiration date of call contract
    B. number of shares that can be bought
    C. current market price of a stock
    D. exercise price at which investor can buy the stock

6. Regarding call options, which of the following statement(s) is/are TRUE?

    A. Trading in call options is a zero-sum game; that is, the gain for a call buyer is the same as the gain for a call writer, ignoring expenses.
    B. The break-even price for a call buyer is the sum of the option premium and exercise price plus expenses such as commissions.
    C. A call option could be unprofitable for both the buyer and writer, ignoring expenses.
    D. The pay-off of the call option is the same as the net profit of the call option.

        1. A & B only
        2. All the above
        3. A, B & C only
        4. B, C & D only

7. A call option written on a stock that is not owned by the writer is called a _____:

    A. naked call
    B. risky call
    C. covered call
    D. volatile call

8. A call option is said to be _____ if the exercise price is higher than the current stock-market price.

    A. at the money (ATM)
    B. out of the money (OTM)
    C. in the money (ITM)
    D. zero money (ZM)

➡

9. Define each of the following derivative contracts:

   A. A forward contract
   B. A futures contract
   C. A call option
   D. A put option
   E. A warrant

From the perspective of the buyer, explain why options contracts limit the downside, but futures contracts do not. Illustrate with examples.

10. Comment on the suitability for a 50-year-old personal investor whose protection, income and emergency funding needs have been met, and who has surplus funds of €250,000, for long-term investment in a tracker bond with the following features:

    - 100% capital guaranteed.
    - Plus return equal to 130% of return on Eurostoxx 50 over five years.
    - No early withdrawal.
    - Gain taxed as deposit interest but at 3% higher rate.

Chapter nine

Alternative Assets

THE NEED FOR DIVERSITY

Diversification lies at the heart of all long-term investment strategies. Before the advent of what we now call modern portfolio theory, most investors understood that spreading their funds amongst a diverse range of opportunities was the only way to cope with risk. This involved investing in different types of investments. In the early days such investments ranged from fixed-interest bonds sold by governments, often to fund colonial expansion, to investing in private transportation companies involved in railroads and shipping, to commodities such as gold bullion. As stock markets developed, the range of opportunities available to investors broadened considerably. Companies involved in most areas of economic activity listed their shares on stock markets. By investing in as few as fifteen to twenty different companies across a range of sectors, investors could substantially reduce the risk of their portfolios.

As portfolio management grew and evolved, portfolio management techniques became ever more sophisticated. Creating optimal portfolios involves finding that portfolio that offers the highest expected return for a given level of risk, or that offers the lowest risk for a particular target expected return. While sophisticated models have been developed and are widely available to 'optimise' portfolios, the process of diversification can be more simply characterised, as shown in Table 9.1.

Whether we look at large institutional funds such as pension funds, or small retail investors, we find that the vast bulk of assets are invested in the so-called traditional assets: equities, bonds and property. However, some investors have a long history of investing a substantial part of their portfolios in what we now refer to as alternative assets. From as early as the 1970s a minority of investors – such as high net worth individuals and family offices, and US university endowments – had begun to invest outside the traditional asset classes. These alternative asset classes included private equity,

Table 9.1 The Process of Diversification

	Choices Available
Broad Asset Allocation – Core Assets	Equities or bonds
Broad Asset Allocation – Other Assets	Property, forestry, infrastructure, private equity, hedge funds, commodities
Geographic/Currency Diversification	Emerging markets' equities and bonds, corporate bonds, non-domestic currency assets
Allocation within Asset Classes/Strategies	Stock selection within equity and bond portfolios, currency selection, property selection, passive or active strategies

commodities and hedge funds. However, after the telecom and technology stock market bubble burst in 2001/2, a much larger and more diverse range of investors began to invest significant parts of their portfolios in alternative assets.

What Stimulated the Interest in Alternatives?

In part this heightened interest in alternatives was a direct result of the 2001/2 equity bear market. Of course, bear markets are part and parcel of stock market investing. However, through the 1980s and 1990s investors had bought into the idea of globalisation and believed that by diversifying their portfolios across different markets they would enjoy much lower levels of risk. Put simply, the theory was that when, for example, the US equity market was falling, emerging equity markets might rise, and vice versa. The reality has turned out to be quite different. Globalisation has led to capital markets that are closely intertwined, with the end result that bear and bull markets across the globe have become increasingly synchronised.

In the aftermath of the bear market in the early 2000s many investors took the view that they needed to invest across a much broader range of assets than heretofore. High-quality government bonds would continue to play a part in reducing portfolio risk. However, the rates of return on offer from such bonds are too low for many investors.

At the core of the growth in popularity of alternative assets over the past decade is the age-old drive to achieve higher expected returns at acceptable levels of risk. In the world of modern portfolio theory, the introduction of additional asset categories offers the prospect of expanding the efficient frontier.

ALTERNATIVE ASSETS: INVESTMENT CHARACTERISTICS

In assessing alternative assets the following characteristics are vital:

i)   expected returns
ii)   volatility
iii) correlation with equity returns.

Issues such as the liquidity of the various asset classes/investment strategies and the expected timing of cash flows are also relevant. First, we will describe each of the main assets that are commonly included under the alternative assets umbrella. The categories that we discuss here are private equity, hedge funds, commodities, currencies, and other assets such as forestry and infrastructural projects.

Private Equity

Private equity investment, and venture capital in particular, is concerned with the commitment of monies to unquoted, developing and immature companies. Private equity may be divided into venture capital and buyouts. Venture capital refers to the provision of capital for growth and expansion to companies with underdeveloped or developing products and revenues at an early stage of their corporate life cycle. Typically, investee companies are unquoted small to medium-sized enterprises. A buyout refers to the investment, through the use of leverage, in mature, cash-generative companies with established business models, to finance expansion, consolidation, turnaround and disposal.

Because of its nature, private equity is expected to generate returns that are higher than those available from the quoted equity markets. Buyouts generate relatively high returns by gearing up returns on equity through the use of leverage (debt), while venture capital generates relatively high returns by accessing the superior growth rates of smaller, unquoted, immature, developing companies. By providing access to unquoted companies, private equity enhances the diversification of the overall equity portfolio.

Clearly, by comparison with quoted stock market investment, the investor approaching private equity investment must adopt longer time horizons and expect relatively poor liquidity. However, liquidity is perhaps less constrained than is generally supposed. Liquidity is facilitated by the cash flow characteristics of the private equity fund and by the generally improving availability of exit mechanisms.

Exit Mechanisms

Strategic or Trade Sales: These are the most common forms of exit and result in a 100% exit in contrast to the partial exit that results from IPOs. Balance sheet strength and strong corporate cash flows underpin demand for such trade sales.

Development of a Secondary Market: A market has developed in interests in existing private equity funds, referred to as 'secondaries'. Buyers may include specialist purchasers of secondaries or private equity funds wishing to construct a diversified fund of funds portfolio.

Accessing Private Equity

The institutional investor may adopt one or more of the following approaches to private equity investment.

Direct Investment: The investment institutions may invest directly in individual unquoted companies and projects. However, experience in Ireland and elsewhere suggests that this is a difficult and relatively high-risk approach. Attrition at the individual investee company level is high and without the benefit of diversification risk is unacceptably high. The investment institutions, accustomed to the flexibility of the quoted markets, typically do not have the specialist skill set critical to success in private equity investment, in particular the skills of hands-on intervention at underperforming investments and of arranging and implementing exit strategies.

Pooled Investment in Fixed-Term Funds: Typically these funds are constituted as limited partnerships, usually for fixed periods of ten years. The institutional investors are limited or passive partners. The private equity specialist, as general (or managing) partner, will select investments, structure deals, monitor progress and devise exit strategies. The fund will typically invest in fifteen to thirty portfolio companies, ensuring diversification and risk control. The pooled fund structure offers the institutional investor access to the private equity investors' deal flow and skill set. The institution may further diversify its risk by investing in a number of funds, perhaps with different sectoral (buyout or venture capital) or regional specialisations.

Fund of Funds: A fund of funds is a pooled vehicle that invests in private equity funds selected by a specialist fund of funds manager. Diversification is high, with perhaps up to twenty funds selected. Access to deal flow and specialist skill set is offered with the benefit of enhanced diversification. These advantages must be weighed against the additional layer of fees and costs payable to the fund of funds manager.

Publicly Quoted Private Equity Funds: These are listed companies whose core business is private equity and specially structured investment vehicles. These vehicles are typically 'evergreen' funds, where capital is raised from the public markets and proceeds from exits are reinvested in the fund rather than distributed to shareholders. A key attraction is the liquidity or marketability of a quoted vehicle, though typically they trade at a discount to net asset value. Perhaps the best known of these companies is 3i in the UK.

The Venture Capital General Partner

By comparison with the management of quoted equity portfolios, venture capital investment is a hands-on and intensively active process. The unique characteristics of private equity discussed earlier demand a distinct skill set on the part of the general partner and one that is quite different from that of the fund manager or research analyst involved with quoted equities.

The skill set of the general partner includes:

- The ability to access a high level of deal flow.
- A high degree of selectivity in determining which deals to participate in.
- The ability to develop strong shareholders' agreements that align management objectives with those of shareholders.
- The ability to add strategic business planning to investee company management.
- A portfolio construction skill to provide diversification and to control cash flows.
- The ability to devise exit strategies.

Management fees of venture capital limited partnerships are high. The typical fund has an annual management fee of 1.5% to 2.5% of committed capital and a 'carried interest' (or participation) of 20% of total gains. This carried interest may be subject to the fund exceeding a certain hurdle rate on drawn-down monies. Venture capital fees are much more closely aligned with those arising on hedge funds, international property funds and other specialised investment products.

Hedge Funds

Calling hedge funds an asset category is in fact a misnomer. This is not an asset class in the sense that, for example, fixed-interest bonds are, with characteristics that are common to all securities that are categorised as bonds. Hedge funds are in fact a particular type of pooled investment vehicle. Mutual funds are also a particular type of investment vehicle, yet they are not categorised as a separate asset class, but hedge funds are. It is logical that mutual funds are not considered to be a separate asset class because they offer investors the same risk–return characteristics as if they invested directly in the underlying assets. For example, a fund that invests in the US equity market offers investors a pooled vehicle that will have the same investment characteristics as a direct portfolio of US stocks. Hedge funds offer something that is completely different to long only mutual funds, or indeed portfolios that consist of direct investment in stocks and bonds.

Several characteristics are common to what are considered to be hedge funds. The key characteristics are:

- Unconstrained trading strategies.
- The ability to take both long and short positions in the chosen securities.
- Extensive use of leverage.

A definition of hedge funds is that they are strategies for investing in securities and derivatives with the ability to use leverage and take both long and short positions. Therefore, assessing a hedge fund involves understanding what trading strategies are being employed by the managers. We can identify three core aspects that characterise a hedge fund:

- The markets that it operates in: commodities, equities, interest rate securities, currencies, etc.
- The types of trading strategies that it adopts: outright long or short positions; arbitrage positions between different types of securities.
- The scale of the leverage that it employs: usually hedge funds take leveraged positions using derivative securities.

Another distinguishing characteristic of hedge funds is that they target absolute rates of return compared with the relative return targets that characterise the long only pooled fund industry. Hedge funds are generally categorised according to various types of identifiable trading strategies. A selection of some of the main trading strategies employed by hedge fund managers are described below:

Equity Hedged: Managers strive for alpha (excess return) through superior sector allocation and stock selection.

Event Driven: Corporate events such as mergers, restructurings and bankruptcies are catalysts for performance.

Relative Value: Pursue arbitrage opportunities by buying securities and selling related issues short.

Trading Funds: Seek to profit from discretionary or systematic trading techniques, e.g. Global Macro, Emerging Markets.

The performance of hedge funds is tracked by a number of performance measurement services and data. Those funds participating in these surveys are usually categorised into one of a variety of trading strategy categories. The summary performance data produced by Hedge Fund Research (HFR) to end-December 2009 is shown in Table 9.2 for selected investment strategies.

Table 9.2 Summary Performance Data to End-2009

HFR Indices	Total Return 2009 (%)	Three-Year Annualised Return to December 2009 (%)
HFRI Fund Weighted Composite Index	20.0	2.2
HFRI Equity Hedge (Total) Index	25.1	0.5
HFRI Event Driven (Total) Index	25.9	1.6
HFRI Macro: Systematic Diversified Index	−2.5	8.3
HFRI Relative Value (Total) Index	25.8	4.0
HFRI Emerging Markets (Total) Index	40.3	3.2
HFRI Fund of Funds Composite Index	11.1	−1.2

Hedge Fund Caveats

As we have seen, hedge funds cover an array of diverse investment strategies, are characterised by leverage and high levels of trading activity, and focus on absolute returns. They cover a wide risk spectrum and most strategies aim to produce returns that are uncorrelated with equity markets. Management fees are generally high, typically 2% p.a., with performance fees equal to 20% of fund performance.

It is very difficult to assess accurately whether hedge funds have lived up to their objectives. During the 2008 financial crash all risk assets and funds fell, including most hedge funds. Judged against their absolute return objectives, they failed miserably. However, most hedge funds fell by a lot less than stock markets, so on a relative basis they did deliver some diversification benefits. Arguably, given the extraordinary circumstances of the financial crash, this could be viewed as some type of success.

However, academic studies of hedge fund performance statistics indicate that such data is far less robust than that published for the traditional asset categories. These studies argue that hedge fund indices generally overstate the true return from the hedge fund universe. A key factor that causes this is 'survivorship bias'. Weaker hedge funds tend to drop out of indices before all of their negative impact is captured in the performance statistics. Also, sensibly, hedge funds need to be trading for a reasonable period of time to be included in an index, often about three years. Some new hedge funds fail before they reach this hurdle and are not captured in the performance statistics. The core problem is that the very nature of hedge funds creates a universe of funds where there is a high amount of formation and destruction of funds. The industry is also characterised by a lack of transparency. It is an inherently unstable universe and consequently measures of overall industry performance will be unreliable. This contrasts with the highly regulated mutual fund industry in the US and the UCITS regime in Europe.

Funds of Hedge Funds

Most hedge funds are reliant upon a small number of key managers, who typically focus on a narrow range of trading strategies. As a result, many investors in hedge funds do so through 'fund of funds' vehicles. As the name suggests, these funds invest in other hedge funds in order to gain a diversified exposure to the industry. Fund of funds managers devote considerable resources to assessing the risk characteristics of the underlying funds. The types of trading strategy employed, the types of securities and derivatives used to execute such strategies and the amount of leverage employed are all scrutinised. Just as important, the operational risks of each underlying business are analysed in detail, given that most hedge funds are incorporated in offshore locations and operate in a lightly regulated environment. There are much fewer protections for investors in hedge funds compared with investors in onshore pooled funds such as mutual funds in the US and UCITS in Europe.

Commodities

Commodity markets have long attracted speculative investors. Until recently the participants in commodity markets, and the many derivative markets based on commodities, tended to be limited to the 'real' commodity players – producers, trading companies and the final buyers – and a small group of specialised speculators. In the late 1990s some mainstream investors began to view commodities as an asset class worthy of long-term investment. Gold has for a long time been viewed as an asset class in its own right. Many high net worth individual investors have for many years invested some of their assets in gold as the ultimate safe haven.

Following the 2001/2 equity bear market some analysts and investors began to take notice of the fact that commodity markets exhibited very low correlation with stock markets. On its own, low correlation with equities is probably not a sufficient reason to include commodities in a long-term portfolio. However, by the early 2000s investors were beginning to wake up to the rapid rate of economic growth occurring in the emerging world. In particular, rapid growth in China and India was creating enormous additional demand for many raw materials. If these economies continue to grow over the medium term, then commodity prices may be in a long-term secular bull market. Therefore, commodities could deliver effective diversification and high long-run returns.

Practicalities of Investing in Commodities

Compared with hedge funds and private equity, investing in commodities is relatively straightforward and low cost. This is because large and liquid derivative markets have evolved for most commodities over centuries. Various pooled vehicles such as exchange-traded funds have been launched and are being actively marketed by major investment banks.

Currency/Currency Funds

Investing globally involves making decisions with regard to the currency exposure associated with investing in assets that are denominated in foreign currency. Therefore, some element of currency management is part and parcel of investing. However, some investors view currency or currency funds as offering characteristics similar to alternative assets. For example, managed currency funds offer investors the benefit of diversification when held with a portfolio of bonds and equities, as currencies typically behave differently from bonds and equities.

Forestry and Infrastructural Projects

There are several other investment categories that are now viewed as forming part of alternative assets. Some investors have long invested in these assets. One example is forestry and another is infrastructural projects such as toll roads and bridges. Illiquidity and very long-term time horizons characterise these investment categories. In return for accepting such illiquidity, investors look to get a relatively high return from such investments, and of course they are effective at improving the diversification characteristics of an overall portfolio. An example of investment institutions that invest in these asset types are large university endowments in the US. Such funds have extremely long time horizons and can 'afford' to lock away a significant part of their portfolios in such illiquid and long-term investments.

Alternative Assets Compared

Table 9.3 summarises how the various categories of alternative assets compare with equities on those investment characteristics that are of interest to investors.

Table 9.3 Investment Characteristics of Alternative Assets Compared with Equities

	Private Equity	Commodities	Hedge Funds – Absolute Return Strategies	Currency/ Currency Funds	Forestry and Infrastructure
Expected Long-Term Returns	Higher	Similar	Lower	Lower	Higher
Volatility/Risk	Higher	Similar	Lower	Lower	Lower
Event/Tail Risk	Higher	Similar	Higher	Lower	Higher
Correlation with Quoted Equities	Medium correlation	Low correlation	Low correlation	Low correlation	Low correlation
Liquidity	Much lower	Lower	Lower	Higher	Extremely low
Transaction Costs and Management Fees	Much higher	Higher	Much higher	Lower	Much higher
Cash Flows	Less predictable	No cash flows	Less predictable	Trading income only	More predictable

Different commentators may make somewhat different assessments than those in Table 9.3. In this table we distinguish between volatility risk and other risks that we term event risk or tail risk. In Chapter 6 we discussed how the investment industry has come to rely almost exclusively on standard deviation as a measure of risk. We pointed out the weaknesses of this measure and investors have become increasingly aware of the risks that may not be captured by volatility measures of risk. For example, the risk posed by a system-wide collapse is unlikely to be captured by volatility measures of risk. In general our assessment is that event risk is a bigger risk for most alternative asset categories compared with quoted equities.

Case Study 9.1 Venture Capital and the J-Curve

Private equity investment, and venture capital in particular, is concerned with the commitment of monies to unquoted, developing and immature companies. In comparison with quoted stock-market investment, the investor approaching venture capital investment must adopt longer time horizons and expect relatively poor liquidity.

Cash Flow Characteristics

Venture capital funds typically have a ten-year life. The amount committed by the institutional investor is normally a maximum commitment that is rarely drawn down in full. The investor is typically required to fund only a small proportion of the total commitment at the outset. This initial funding will be followed by subsequent draw-downs as underlying investments are made. Normally, all of the funds to be drawn down are invested by the general partner in underlying investments by the end of year 4. In the fund's early years investors should expect low or negative returns due to establishment costs, management fees and running expenses.

As investee companies mature and exits occur, the fund distributes proceeds to investors. Net cash flows typically turn positive by year 5, with payback of monies committed achieved by year 8, according to research undertaken by the London Business School. Inflows then continue up to year 10 and typically for longer because a small number of investments may not be exited within the intended ten-year life of the fund. When all investments are fully divested the fund is terminated.

This pattern of cash flows results in a 'J-Curve', as illustrated in Figure 9.1. As distributions normally commence before the total committed has been drawn, it is unusual for the investor ever to have the full commitment actually managed by the manager.

Figure 9.1 J-Curve: Ireland 1994 Fund

Source: F. O'Brien and B. O'Loughlin, *Developing Pension Fund Investment Strategy*, IFI, 2006.

This pattern of cash flows means that the effective life of the investment in the fund is significantly shorter than the ten-year lifespan of the fund itself.

QUESTIONS

1. Over the past decade alternative assets have begun to play a
   significant role in asset allocation strategies. Set out how each
   of the asset categories listed below rates in terms of its key characteristics (i.e. how does it rate in terms of liquidity, expected
   return, etc.). In particular, identify the features of each of these
   assets that differentiate it from the 'traditional' assets of cash,
   government bonds and high-quality corporate bonds, property
   and equities.

   A. Private equity
   B. Hedge funds
   C. High-yield corporate bonds
   D. Commodities

2. Possibly the key argument in favour of alternative assets is that
   they have a low correlation with equities. For the above list,
   examine how these assets behaved compared with equities and
   government bonds during the period 1 January 2007 to 31
   December 2009.

Chapter ten

The Retail Investor's Choices

This chapter discusses the alternative of indirect investing used by many investors. With indirect investing the investor pools his assets with those of others to create a single pool of money, which is then managed by professional investment managers in accordance with a well-defined investment strategy. A key point about indirect investing is that the investor is not directly responsible for the asset, although he is exposed to the same market risk as if he did hold the asset directly; he also reaps whatever investment return those assets generate (less management fees and expenses). In Ireland the life assurance unit-linked funds offered by life assurance companies form the backbone of the industry. Latterly, the emergence of mutual funds – called open-ended investment companies or OEICs – has occurred as a result of EU Investment Services Directives. Once an OEIC is regulated in one EU country it can be sold throughout the EU. More recently, the term 'investment company with variable capital' (ICVC) has begun to replace the term OEIC. ICVC and OEIC are often used interchangeably, in general and in this text. The basics of how these collective investment schemes (CIS) are priced is discussed.

Learning Objectives

After reading this chapter you will:
- Understand the basic mechanics of pooled investment funds or collective investment schemes (CIS)
- Be aware of the advantages of indirect investing
- Be able to distinguish between unit-linked funds, OEICs, unit trusts and investment trusts
- Have a broad understanding of how the price of unit-linked funds and unit trusts is calculated, and how the price of shares in OEICs is calculated
- Understand exchange-traded funds
- Have an awareness of structured products that offer capital guarantees
- Understand the difficulties faced by investors in matching individual investment objectives with appropriate investment products.

The role of investment advice and ensuring that individual investors are sold investment funds appropriate to their particular circumstances is a key issue that is addressed in this chapter.

In most economies the dominant form of investment is indirect, and Ireland is no exception in this respect. Direct investing involves purchasing securities in the stock market and holding the title to these securities as share certificates or through a nominee account with a financial institution. Indirect investing usually involves placing money with a financial institution that then invests that money on a collective basis on behalf of all of its clients. The essential elements of indirect investing are the same irrespective of any particular jurisdiction and may be summarised as:

- Regulated financial institutions such as banks, insurance companies, investment management companies develop suites of investment products for sale to individuals, companies, pension funds, charitable trusts, etc.
- Each product (or suite of products) is normally structured as a separate entity that allows the institution to collect assets from a large number of clients and to create a clearly identifiable pool of money for investment.
- The investment strategy applied to this 'pool of money' is normally clearly set out in the relevant prospectus or trust deed, depending on the precise legal structure. In addition, a key function of any promotional literature and advertising will be to communicate that investment strategy clearly to potential investors.
- Clients who invest money on this 'pooled basis' will receive a 'pro rata' interest in the investment returns achieved by the relevant investment manager. If the relevant fund produces an investment return of 10%, each and every investor will enjoy the same 10% return (after management charges). Likewise if the value of the fund falls by (say) 5%, every investor will suffer the same decline in the value of their particular investment.
- The legal and regulatory structure varies across different product types and across jurisdictions. However, the essential elements are the same, i.e. a large number of investors commit differing amounts of funds to collective investment vehicles. The sponsoring financial institution then invests the entire pool of funds in line with the relevant investment strategy.

ADVANTAGES OF INDIRECT INVESTING

- Diversification: Indirect investing will nearly always achieve much greater diversification than can be achieved through investing directly in the markets. Such pooled portfolios should therefore be more efficient than portfolios created by individual investors. In other words they should achieve similar or superior returns but with much lower levels of risk.

- Access to a much wider range of markets and asset classes: For example, a single commercial property investment may involve an investment of millions of euro, which is way beyond the scope of most investors including smaller financial institutions. A pooled fund that invests in property provides even the smaller investor with the opportunity to gain exposure to property markets. Other examples include specialist emerging market funds and funds that specialise in a particular sector, such as biotechnology.
- Ease of administration: Even small direct-equity portfolios will consist of several shares where the individual investor must keep track of dividends received, profits and losses from share trading, etc. Tax returns can quickly become very laborious and expensive to collate. Indirect investing eases this administrative burden dramatically.
- Tax efficiency: The tax treatment of pooled funds in Ireland is now quite favourable. Indirect investing is now at least as tax-efficient as direct investing, and in some situations it may be more so.

THE INTERFACE BETWEEN THE FINANCIAL INDUSTRY AND THE RETAIL INVESTOR

Before dealing with the myriad of investment products available to retail investors, it is worth reviewing how the financial sector interacts with its retail customers. Some of the trends that we can now observe in the wider retail marketplace are evident in the financial market. For example, the concept of the 'financial supermarket' has evolved, where investment products from a wide range of suppliers are available on one platform. However, the nature of most retail financial products means that the retail financial marketplace is very different from, for example, the marketplace for cars or holidays.

In the insurance business there was a very old saying that 'insurance is sold and not bought'. In the early part of the twentieth century insurance was typically sold by door-to-door salesmen. Initially, the product range comprised very basic life insurance products only, often sold to cover funeral expenses. In time the range broadened to include more sophisticated protection and investment products. Usually this involved a 'hard sell' and the sales staff were incentivised through high upfront sales commissions. This structure was tailor-made for unscrupulous salespeople to sell unsuitable products to an unwary public. Indeed in the 1990s more vigilant and assertive regulation uncovered, and punished, some major mis-selling of pension and investment products in the UK life assurance industry.

The financial industry today is a far cry from the financial industry of only thirty years ago. Advances in technology and communications have radically altered the landscape. On the face of it, consumers are now far better informed regarding financial products, often through the internet and other media resources. However, in practice, a sales-driven ethos still dominates the way that the financial industry interacts with its customer base.

At the heart of the matter is the fundamental reality that most consumers require advice with regard to the suitability of investment products. The pharmaceutical industry provides a better analogy than the broader retail marketplace. A patient consults with a doctor, who assesses the situation and prescribes an appropriate treatment. The patient goes to the pharmacist, who supplies the prescribed medication along with advice on how to take the medication. For doctor read financial adviser, and for pharmacist read financial institution. The essential point is that there is an advisory service element involved in the provision of most financial products. Therefore, there is often an inherent conflict of interest between the selling of investment products and ensuring that the characteristics of such products are properly explained to the consumer.

Most retail investors require advice on the purchase of investment products. For the minority of investors with substantial funds it can be economical to purchase the necessary advice separately from the investment product. However, customised advice is expensive to deliver, and therefore this advice is often inextricably wrapped into the sales process. A good investment sales process should incorporate a careful assessment of the prospective investor's needs to ensure that the product is suitable.

Know Your Client and Statement of Investment Policy and Principles

Financial institutions and intermediaries typically have formal processes in place to ensure that customers are sold suitable products. In most jurisdictions these processes and procedures are driven by explicit regulatory requirements. Prospective clients will typically have to complete application forms that provide a substantial amount of financial information. Prospective clients will also be asked for information that helps to assess their risk tolerance and their investment objectives. Pertinent information regarding the prospective client should include both 'hard' data – such as income, current assets and liabilities, contingent liabilities (tax position, divorce settlement, etc.) – and 'softer' information regarding attitude to risk and investment preferences, etc. In most cases getting a full picture will require a face-to-face meeting.

Once the 'Know Your Client' (KYC) part of the process is complete, then the next step is to set out investment return targets and risk levels. Institutional funds such as pension funds will normally set out a detailed 'Statement of Investment Policy and Principles' (SIPP). For retail investors, much less formality is required. However, a good process should ensure that both the customer and the service or product provider are clear regarding:

- Investment return objectives and specific risk level/tolerance.
- Investment time horizon.
- Any specific issues such as income requirements and liquidity needs.
- Reporting frequencies and content of reports.
- Timing of formal reviews.
- Process for dealing with changed circumstances.

COLLECTIVE INVESTMENT SCHEMES (CIS)

For the retail investor there is a bewildering array of investment schemes that deliver the ability to gain exposure to the investment markets through the indirect investing route. Such investment products may be referred to as collective investment schemes. The legal and regulatory framework governing these schemes has evolved over many years in developed countries. In Ireland the legal and regulatory framework has become quite sophisticated, with changes being primarily driven by the need to implement EU-wide directives. Table 10.1 below sets out the main institutional categories of product available to Irish-based investors.

Table 10.1 Types of Investment Product

Type of Scheme	Key Characteristics
Unit-Linked Funds (Life Assurance Companies)	• Assets held by life assurance company • Company actuary creates units that match various 'pools' of assets • Units are priced at net asset value (NAV) • Units are purchased at an 'offer' price and sold or redeemed at a 'bid' price • Open-ended
With-Profits Funds (Life Assurance Companies)	• Assets held by life assurance company • Company actuary decides on an annual return and a return that is payable only at the final maturity date of a policy • Returns depend on the investment performance of the with-profits fund, but such returns are effectively 'smoothed' over the life of a product
UCITS – Undertakings for Collective Investment in Transferable Securities	• Can be either an investment company or a unit trust • Must be open-ended • Key benefit is 'EU Passport'

➡

Table 10.1 Types of Investment Product (continued)

Types of Scheme	Key Characteristics
UCITS – Open-Ended Investment Company (OEIC)	• Investment company that invests in securities • Price of shares is determined by NAV • Single price is calculated • Open-ended
UCITS – Unit Trusts	• Established under a trust deed • Trustee responsible for safeguarding and custody of the assets • Price of units is determined by NAV • 'Bid' and 'offer' prices are calculated • Open-ended
Investment Trusts	• Term 'trust' is misleading as they are companies that invest in securities, not trusts • Closed-ended • Shares normally quoted on the stock market.

The legal, tax and regulatory structures determine the precise nature of investment funds on offer in a particular country. The marketplace in Ireland is similar to that in the UK, where insurance companies and banks tend to dominate the market. There is somewhat greater diversity in the UK, where the unit trust industry is much larger than in Ireland and also there is a significant investment trust industry.

Unit-Linked Life Insurance Investment Funds

These are manufactured and marketed by life assurance companies and information on these funds is published regularly in the press. Exhibit 10.1 reproduces a sub-set of a table regularly published in the *Irish Times*, which uses data produced by MoneyMate.

Financial companies typically sell funds that include managed funds, which invest across all asset categories, as well as funds that specialise in particular geographic regions or specific asset categories. The summary information in the exhibit does not include the asset split of these funds, but this information is readily accessible from the respective companies. In fact, virtually all companies now have 'Factsheets' on every fund they sell, which provide information on the underlying investments, the performance history of the funds and a summary of the investment strategy being pursued by the fund managers.

Exhibit 10.1 Unit-Linked Funds Performance Tables

UNIT-LINKED GROSS DOMESTIC FUNDS: YEAR TO DATE

+2.54%	+0.02%	+2.89%	+1.88%	-0.23%	+0.58%
American Equity	Cash	EuroEquity	European Equity	Far East Equity	Fixed Interest

IRISH DOMESTIC FUNDS: GROSS ◆ All prices quoted in euro cent ◆

	BID PRICE CENT	YR-TO-DATE %
ABERDEEN GLOBAL		
American Equity	1139.84	3.11
Asia Pacific	5139.64	-1.02
Asian Bond	495.00	-1.31
Asian Smaller Comps	2727.31	-0.11
Australasian Equity	2030.70	-0.98
Emerging Markets	4660.14	-1.96
Euro High Yld Bond	1551.00	2.99
Euro Equity (ex UK)	875.00	0.34
European Equity	3481.00	1.13
India Equity Fund	7540.12	-7.33
Japanese Equity	212.13	1.45
Technology	262.36	2.61
UK Equity	1921.42	2.39
World Equity	1076.84	0.95
ABSOLUTE INSIGHT FUNDS PLC		
Currency B1p €	107.22	0.69
Currency B2p €	102.22	0.69
ACORN LIFE		
Cautiously Mgd 2	123.30	-0.31
Deposit Series 2	366.40	0.10
Managed Growth 2	678.30	3.07
Managed Series 2	667.30	2.41
AIB INVESTMENT MANAGERS		
Cash	161.08	0.08
Corp Bond Ex-Fin Index B	118.67	-0.73
EAFE Equity Focus Fund	96.21	1.29
Ethical Balanced Growth	219.97	0.44
Ethical Balanced Income	85.39	-0.78
Euro Bond Index B	152.93	-1.43
Euro Liquidity	100.35	0.07
Euro Prop Stocks	107.39	0.48
Euro Prop Stocks Fund PB	93.14	0.49
Eurozone Eq UK Stg Class	120.38	2.84
Eurozone Eq Index B	118.97	2.98
Eurozone Equity	112.35	2.47
EuroLongBond Index B	126.77	-1.83
Far East Eq UK Stg Class	156.10	0.19
Far East Equity	154.66	-0.17
Far East Equity Index B	774.98	0.16

	BID PRICE CENT	YR-TO-DATE %
Invest Managed B	83.78	0.96
Invest Managed A	85.49	0.98
Multimanager A	83.35	0.69
Multimanager B	81.99	0.67
MultiTrack	105.26	2.38
Target 20 Fund	60.85	2.21
UK Property Fund	72.63	1.10
Cash 2	115.32	0.00
Eurozone 2	70.84	2.35
Future	57.80	5.13
Galaxy	117.22	1.88
Global	80.15	2.48
Guaranteed 2008	100.00	0.00
Irish	50.00	1.90
Managed 1	82.89	1.92
PEP Eurozone	70.17	2.35
PEP Global	79.40	2.48
PEP Irish	58.69	1.90
PIP Managed 2	82.09	1.91
PIP MultiTrack	128.14	2.38
AVIVA LIFE & PENSIONS		
AIBIM Managed	79.98	2.32
AIBIM Managed G.	79.98	0.98
AIBIM Managed I	80.76	0.99
AIBIM Multimanager E	82.14	0.69
AIBIM Multimanager	82.14	1.68
AIBIM Multiman G.	85.22	0.70
Asian Pac High Yield	119.20	1.45
Balanced Managed	126.82	1.87
BIAM. Equity	85.00	3.66
BIAM. Managed	103.20	2.79
BlackRock Eur Ab Rtn	102.70	-2.00
BlackRock New Energy	101.30	2.12
BlackRock World Enrg	131.10	1.94
BlackRock World Gld	135.00	-7.66
BlackRock World Min	170.40	-0.35
Blue Chip Corp Bond	114.47	-0.61
Bond Fund	191.27	-0.74
Cash Fund	158.44	0.00
Equity Fund	117.57	2.87
Euro Commercial Prop	71.01	0.25
Euro Equity Fund	111.07	4.61

	BID PRICE CENT	YR-TO-DATE %
JPM Emerging Markets Eq	214.84	-3.14
JPM Global Cap Apprec	119.70	1.39
JPM Global Capital Pres	106.91	-0.24
JPM Natural Resources	135.66	-0.35
Jupiter Climate Change Sol	164.57	1.57
Jupiter Global Financials	167.59	1.35
L & G UK Property	116.92	1.88
M&G American	178.96	2.12
M&G Global Emerging Markets	110.92	1.08
M&G Global Leaders	187.67	3.05
M&G Recovery	200.85	4.84
Martin Currie Global Asia	188.19	-0.35
Martin Currie Global NA	163.75	1.61
Merrion Irish Opps	196.53	4.72
Money Dollar Fund	74.46	-0.58
Money Euro Fund	100.39	0.00
Money Sterling Fund	119.34	1.52
Neptune Global Equity	217.94	1.84
Newton BNY Mellon Glob Bon	111.77	-0.65
Schroder Euro Corp Bond	112.12	0.12
Schroder Global Prop Sec	216.31	1.35
Schroder Income Maximiser	202.27	5.55
Schroder Tokyo	165.99	0.42
Schroder UK Alpha Plus	245.72	3.36
SL Eur Inflation Linked Bd	105.45	0.41
Threadneedle Glob Select	167.44	2.35
Threadneedle Target Return	99.37	0.22
BIAM		
Equity Mutual 2	85.03	3.65
Equity Mutual 3	83.96	3.62
Euro Bond Mutual 2	142.49	-0.46
Euro Bond Mutual 3	136.89	-0.48
GRU Euro Cash	117.20	0.04
GRU Indexed Eurozone Bd	139.72	-0.38
GRU Indexed Eurozone Eq	142.07	1.30
GRU Indx Wld Ex Euro Eq	143.00	2.80
Managed Mutual 2	103.22	2.82
Managed Mutual 3	100.83	2.79
Spectrum Balanced	1381.55	1.66
Spectrum Bond Plus	1332.68	1.01
Spectrum Cash Plus	1185.44	0.04
Spectrum Growth	1440.67	2.29

The information for each fund in the data reproduced here is the bid price and year-to-date performance. In fact, most funds are now quoted on a single price basis, i.e. one price is applied for both buying and selling units to/from investors.

The principles behind the determination of unit prices are the same for all unit-linked funds:

i)   The life company ring-fences the monies that are collected from the
      sale of policies to investors.
ii)   The company's fund managers invest the assets in accordance with the
      stated investment strategy contained in the policy documents and the
      marketing literature.
iii) The market value of these assets is calculated, usually on a daily basis.
      The total value of the portfolio is divided by the total number of units
      allocated to investors to give the net asset value (NAV) per unit.
      Adjustments are made to this NAV to take account of buying costs,
      stamp duties, etc. associated with the buying of securities.
iv)   When new funds are received the actuary creates new units and allo -
      cates these to the new investors on a pro-rata basis at the quoted price.
      When investors wish to cash in their units the company redeems the
      units at the quoted price and then cancels the units. Other than in
      exceptional circumstances, investors can enter and exit the fund at the
      current NAV because of this open-ended feature of unit-linked funds.

Individual investors will normally purchase units in a unit-linked fund
through a variety of products sold by the life company. Such products fall
into two main categories:

i)   single-premium investment bonds
ii)   recurring-premium, long-term savings plans.

As the name suggests, single-premium investment bonds are appropriate
where an investor, who could be an individual or a corporate entity or a
charity, has a lump sum to invest. Usually, such bonds offer the prospective
investor the ability to allocate the investment monies amongst the life office's
suite of funds. The number of units purchased will be a function of the
amount of money invested and the price of the units on the date that units
are allocated.

Table 10.2 Investing in ABC Equity Fund – Recurring Premium

	Price of units at:	Number of units purchased
Launch	€1.00	1,000
End-year one	€0.90	1,111
End-year two	€0.95	1,053
End-year three	€1.15	870
Cumulative units		4,034
Average cost per unit		€0.99
Value of investment at end-year three	4,034 * €1.15	€4,639

The purchaser of a recurring-premium policy contracts with the life office to pay a fixed premium on a regular basis, which is usually monthly but may be quarterly or annually. After expenses the premiums are invested in the chosen fund(s). Table 10.2 illustrates what happens with a recurring-premium investment of €1,000 per annum into a notional unit-linked fund. The same annual investment of €1,000 purchases a different number of units each year, depending on the price of the fund at the time of purchase. In the illustration the price of the fund has declined in the first year, which means that at end-year one the value of the initial investment will have fallen to €900. However, the investor is now investing at a low point in the cycle and his second €1,000 investment purchases more units. Over the four years the average cost per unit works out at €0.99. In this example regular investment has worked in the investor's favour. This is referred to as pound cost averaging and is a potential benefit of regular investment in volatile markets. More units are bought at low prices than at high prices, so that the average purchase price is less than the average price of the units over the particular time period. As long as the long-term trend in equity markets is positive then investors in recurring-premium policies will eventually benefit.

With-Profits Funds

This type of life assurance policy formed the backbone of the industry in both the UK and Ireland up until the early 1980s. Throughout the 1980s and 1990s unit-linked funds and unit trusts gained in popularity as the preferred routes to gain exposure to the stock markets. Nevertheless, substantial funds continued to be invested in with-profits products up until recent years. These funds take pooling of investment return and risk to its logical extreme. Unit-linked funds allow each individual investor to 'identify' their assets on a daily basis by multiplying the number of units that they hold by the published price.

An investor holds 1,000 units in the Aberdeen Global 'European Equity Fund'. The quoted price today (Exhibit 10.1) is 3,481 (cents) and the encashment value is: 1,000 x 34.81 = €34,810.

This is not the case for a with-profits fund, as there is not a current value attributable to each policyholder. Rather, the actuary declares an annual percentage return called a bonus, which accrues to the with-profits policyholders. This is paid only when the policy matures. The actuary will also declare a terminal bonus each year that is paid out on policies maturing in that particular year. Typically the terminal bonus accounts for a very high proportion of the total return accruing to such policies. The advantage to investors of such policies is that investment returns are smoothed over time.

Their opaque structure is a major disadvantage. Many investors are not aware that the returns depend on the pool of assets within the with-profits fund and on the overall performance of the life assurance company as a business. This is because the with-profits funds of life assurance companies are used to support the ongoing development of the business. Instead of capital from shareholders, many life assurance companies rely on the capital strength of the with-profits fund. The equity bear market in the early years of the millennium and lower prospective investment returns have created major solvency issues for such funds and have resulted in much lower annual and terminal bonuses across the industry. In the UK the long-established Equitable Life was forced to drastically cut bonuses (returns) to its policy-holders in order to remain solvent. Equitable Life had problems specific to it that made its predicament far worse than most other life assurance companies. However, Equitable Life was the exception, and most companies offering with-profits-type policies have continued to do so. Two equity bear markets in the space of ten years resulted in most companies reducing pay-outs to well below investors' initial expectations.

Mutual Funds

A mutual fund is an open-ended investment company, selecting and managing a portfolio of securities. Investors buy mutual fund shares from investment companies and sell their shares back to those companies. Each company (fund) is governed by its prospectus, which is designed to describe a particular fund's objectives, policies, operations and fees. Each fund is governed by a board, which is responsible for protecting the interests of shareholders (investors). The number of shares outstanding of an open-ended investment company (mutual fund) is continually changing as new investors buy additional shares from the company and some existing shareholders cash in by selling their shares back to the company. Thus the fund's capitalisation is said to be open ended. Mutual funds are the most popular vehicle for indirect investing in the US. Approximately 50 million households in the US hold mutual funds, with total investments amounting to approximately $10 trillion.

Mutual Funds in Europe

The European mutual fund industry is also very large. The legal and regulatory framework is driven by a set of EU directives referred to as Undertakings for Collective Investment in Transferable Securities (UCITS). These aim to allow collective investment schemes to operate freely throughout the EU on the basis of a single authorisation from one member state. UCITS represent about 75% of the EU investment fund market, with assets under management amounting to approximately €6 trillion.

There have been several advances since the original UCITS Directive was adopted in 1985. New directives referred to as 'UCITS III' were adopted in 2001. UCITS III consists of two directives: a Management Directive and a Product Directive. The Management Directive seeks to give management companies a 'European Passport' to operate throughout the EU. It also introduces the concept of a simplified prospectus that sets out to provide more accessible and comprehensive information in a simplified format to assist the cross-border marketing of UCITS in Europe. The primary aim of the Product Directive is to remove barriers to the cross-border marketing of units of collective investment funds by allowing funds to invest in a wider range of financial instruments (including derivatives).

A further extension of the regulations, set to occur in 2011, is known as 'UCITS IV'. These new directives aim to strengthen the UCITS framework and to ease the path for cross-border mergers and distribution. The main developments include new rules surrounding fund mergers, new freedoms to use master/feeder funds, and revised rules on regulator to regulator co-operation. The key thrust of the draft UCITS IV Directive is that fund management firms will be able to pool and market funds more freely and easily throughout the EU, ultimately leading to cost reductions for the industry and for investors.

Open-Ended Investment Company

In Ireland, and in Europe more generally, the main form of mutual fund is an open-ended investment company (OEIC), also referred to as an ICVC or investment company with variable capital. The terms ICVC and OEIC are used interchangeably, with different investment managers favouring one over the other. ICVCs were developed to be similar to European SICAVs (*société d'investissement à capital variable*) or 'investment company with variable capital' and US mutual funds.

The key features of an ICVC are:

- It has a corporate form.
- It can have several different classes of share.
- A single price is calculated based on the net asset value of the relevant portfolio of securities.
- The ICVC has an Authorised Corporate Director (ACD), who is respon-sible for operating the company in accordance with the regulations and with the ICVC's instrument of incorporation.
- The ICVC must also have a Depositary, who is responsible for the safe keeping of the scheme's assets.
- The ACD and the Depositary must be independent of each other.

The regulations pertaining to OEICs or ICVCs require the ACD to prepare and maintain a prospectus giving information about the constitution, objectives and operation of the company. Information concerning the personnel responsible for running the ICVC must also be kept up to date and be available to investors and potential investors. The prospectus must also include a description of investment policies and the arrangements for the management of the ICVC's investments. The ACD acts as the seller and buyer of shares and it can act in either of two capacities:

i)   It can act as an agent between the ICVC and the investor; or
ii)   It may deal directly with the investor and hold the shares in what is called a 'box'. Shares will normally be held in the box for a short period of time and will either be sold to another investor or sold back to the ICVC for cancellation.

The price at which shares are sold or purchased is the single mid-market price, which is normally quoted on a daily basis.

There are three types of OEIC permitted:

• Securities companies, which invest in transferable securities.
• Warrant companies, which have powers to invest in warrants beyond the 5% limit imposed on securities funds.
• Umbrella companies, which have at least two sub-funds that permit shareholders to switch all or part of their investment from one sub-fund to another.

Markets in Financial Instruments Directive

The Markets in Financial Instruments Directive (MiFID) is an EU law that provides harmonised regulation for investment services across the thirty member states of the European Economic Area (the twenty-seven EU member states plus Iceland, Norway and Liechtenstein). The main objectives of MiFID are to increase competition and consumer protection in investment services. As of the effective date, 1 November 2007, MiFID replaced the Investment Services Directive.

MiFID covers almost all tradable financial products with the exception of certain foreign exchange trades. Some of the key aspects of MiFID include:

• Authorisation and Regulation: Firms covered by MiFID are authorised and regulated in their 'home state' (broadly, the country in which they have their registered office). Once a firm has been authorised, it will be able to use the MiFID passport to provide services to customers in other EU member states. These services will be regulated by the member state in their 'home state'.

- **Client Categorisation:** MiFID requires firms to categorise clients as 'eligible counterparties', professional clients or retail clients (these have increasing levels of protection). Clear procedures must be in place to categorise clients and assess their suitability for each type of investment product. That said, the appropriateness of any investment advice or suggested financial transaction must still be verified before being given.

Unit Trusts

Historically, unit trusts constituted a very large part of the UK market for collective investment. In Ireland unit trusts have always accounted for quite a small proportion of the market. The preferred form of legal structure for new funds in the UK is now the ICVC.

A unit trust is constituted by a trust deed. The trustee owns the assets of the trust and is therefore responsible for the custody and safe keeping of the assets held by the trust. This role is normally taken by a bank or an insurance company. As custodian of the assets the trustee maintains a register of unitholders and generally oversees the management of the trust fund. A professional investment manager will be appointed to invest the funds in securities in accordance with the investment objectives of the trust. The trustee must be independent of the investment manager. The trustee has the role of protecting the interests of the unitholders and ensuring that the manager manages the assets in line with the investment strategy stated in the trust deed. Like ICVCs, unit trusts are open-ended and therefore inflows and outflows involve the creation and cancellation of units in the trust.

When an investor contributes money to the fund he receives a number of units in the fund, with the price of the units determined by the total value of the funds under management in the trust divided by the number of units in issue.

Authorised Unit Trusts

Only unit trusts that are authorised by the Financial Regulator are permitted to advertise. Unauthorised unit trusts are legal but can be marketed only to professional investors. All authorised unit trusts are governed by a trust deed which covers the detailed running of the trust. It will include the maximum management fees that can be paid to the various service providers to the trust, including fund management fees. The precise method of calculating the price of units will be detailed as well as the provisions enabling new investors to join. The trust deed will also include some limitations on the investments made by the fund manager. For example, a maximum of 10% of the net asset value of a trust can be invested in unquoted securities.

Pricing of Unit Trust Units

The value of a unit at a particular time is determined by the net asset value (NAV) of the trust. The NAV is based on the market value of the securities held by the trust less the market value of any liabilities. If a trust has a market value of €20m, with 20 million units in existence, then the NAV per unit would be €1 (i.e. €20m divided by 20m units). If the value of assets were to double to €40m, then the NAV per unit would also double to €2 per unit, provided that there was no change in the number of units in issue. Bid and offer prices of units are quoted for a trust. Expenses such as administration costs, dealing costs, stamp duties, sales commissions, etc. have to be taken into account when calculating the price of units. These expenses are reflected in the spread between the bid and the offer price. Units in unit trusts are purchased from the managers at the offer price and sold back to the managers at the lower bid price.

Investment Trusts

As with unit trusts and ICVCs, investment trusts allow investors to pool their funds in order to benefit from economies of scale and portfolio diversification. However, the term 'trust' is in fact misleading, as they are companies rather than trusts. An investment trust is a company that is set up to invest in securities. Just like any quoted company, an investment trust sells shares to the public for cash, and this cash is then used to create investment portfolios. The flow of funds into the trust (or investment company) is limited by the number of shares sold at its initial public offer. The capital raised from this sale of shares is exactly the same as the capital raised by any company that goes for an IPO. The only difference is that the capital of the investment trust is invested in other companies (usually, but not always, other quoted companies). The board of the investment trust will appoint a fund manager, and other service providers such as a custodian, to provide fund management and related services to the trust. Post the IPO, prospective new investors can purchase shares in the trust only on the secondary market. Unlike ICVCs, investment trusts cannot create new shares to satisfy new demand. Therefore, the flow of funds into the company is limited by the number of shares that have been issued, and as such they are 'closed-ended funds' in contrast to the open-ended structure that pertains to ICVCs, unit trusts, and indeed unit-linked life assurance funds.

If investors wish to exit the investment trust they can sell their shares only on the secondary market. One consequence of being closed-ended is that the price of the shares in any investment trust is determined by the interaction of buyers and sellers at any one time. Investment trusts publish their NAV per share on a regular basis, and investors pay close attention to this figure.

Exhibit 10.2 Investment Companies Listed on the London Stock Exchange

INVESTMENT COMPANIES

	Notes	Price	Chng	2010/11 High	Low	Yld	NAV	Dis or Pm(-)
Conventional (Ex Private Equity)								
3i Infra	†120.50	·	125.30	101	4.6	112.1	-7.5	
Abf Gd Inc..	107.25	·	109	95.50	1.9	111.6	3.9	
AbnAsianIn	†155.25	+2.50	175	127.25	3.9	157.7	1.6	
Wts.......	38.25	+0.75	51	27.50	·	·	·	
AbnAllAsia.	297	·	326.25	237	0.5	342.8	13.4	
AbnAsian...	547.75	+11	670	366	1.5	616.3	11.1	
AbnLatAmin	106.25	+1.25	113	103	0.9	102.4	-3.8	
Sub.........	14	-0.25	22.25	12.75	·	·	·	
AbnNewDn .	811	+8.50	940	620.50	1.2	886.9	8.6	
AbnNewThai	241.50	+3	288.50	165	2.1	292.8	17.5	
Sub	55.50	+2	87.25	14.75	·	·	·	
Abf Sml	670	+14	699.50	490	2.8	765	12.4	
AbsoluteRet	117.50	+1.25	123.50	110	·	137.6	14.6	
AcenciADbt	83.88	+0.13	86.25	70.25	·	100.5	16.5	
Acorn	177	+0.25	177.50	108	3.2	205	13.7	
ActiveCap .	18.25	·	22.50	13.37	·	23.4	22	
AdvDvpMk.	452	-12.75	515.50	367.50	·	515.5	12.3	
Albany......	285.50	+1.50	288	234	3.5	342.7	16.7	
Alliance....	362.50	+6	381	292.80	2.2	438.2	17.3	
AltAstsOps.	51.50	·	68.50	44.50	·	79.7	35.4	
AltInvStrat .	111.50	-0.13	114	99.50	·	130.2	14.4	
Altin $......	£32.39	-0.51	£34.17	£28.77	·	£44.1	26.6	
Anglo&Ovs	†112.25	+1.50	116	85.25	2.7	118.8	5.5	
Art Alpha .	†313.50	-0.50	330	222	0.9	321.5	2.5	
Sub.........	78.50	·	89	50	·	·	·	
AshmoreG..	822.50	-7.50	845.50	650	·	968	15	
EUR €	8.08	·	·	·	·	–	·	
USD $	8.05	-0.02	·	·	·	–	·	
Athelney Tr ‡	135	·	135	112	3.5	145.9	7.4	
Atls Japan..	82	-0.25	86.25	75.75	·	·	·	
Aurora......	246.25	+1.25	281.50	158	1.4	270.5	9	
BSRT.......	99.50	+0.25	108	77	·	100.9	1.4	
BG Japan...	206	+1.25	215.50	151.50	·	226.2	8.9	
BG Shin	170	+3.25	185	114.50	·	179.9	5.5	
Bankers	417.10xd	+4	428	336.20	2.9	476.1	12.4	
BrngEmEu..	885	+9	942.50	700.50	0.3	978.4	9.5	
BH Global ..	£10.84	-0.06	£11.80	£10.52	·	£12	9.5	
EUR €	10.75	·	·	·	·	–	·	
USD $	10.80	-0.05	·	·	·	–	·	
BH Macro .	£16.84	+0.06	£18.24	£16.30	·	£17.9	5.9	
EUR €	16.45	+0.08	·	·	·	–	·	
USD $	16.54	+0.14	·	·	·	–	·	
BiotechGth.	159.25	-1.50	178	143	·	173.8	8.4	
BlckRFrnt ..	100.25	-0.25	108	99	·	·	·	
BlckRckARS	870.50	·	878	730	·	£10.1	13.7	
EUR €	8.45	-0.15	·	·	·	–	·	
USD $	8.98	·	·	·	·	–	·	
BlckRCom..	158	+1	169.75	107.78	3.5	155	-1.9	
BlckRGtEur.	200	+2.25	204	150	1.7	207.7	3.7	
Sub.........	27.75	+0.25	37	10.50	·	·	·	
BlckRHSUK.	127.75	·	127.37	96	·	125.8	-1.6	
BlckRHSCsh	99.13	·	100.75	97.75	·	100.6	1.5	
BlckRckLat	q686.50	+3	789	552.50	2.4	703.2	2.4	
Cnv Bond $.	£839.97xd	+2.14	£942.84	£741.83	0.0	·	·	
BlckRwEgy .	38.75	+0.38	49.78	36	·	46.5	16.7	
Sub.........	3.13	·	8.13	2.13	·	·	·	
BlckRSmlr..	539.75	+4.75	564	283.58	1.1	615.9	12.4	
BlckRWld..	q788.50	+18	830	490	0.8	906.2	13	
Brit Ast	137.20	+2.20	140.70	104.10	4.5	138.9	1.2	
Brit Emp....	497.50	+11.40	514	396.50	1.5	526.9	5.6	

However, unlike ICVCs, this NAV acts as a reference point for the price of the shares in an investment trust, and does not determine the price at which shares actually trade. The shares in an investment trust can trade at a discount or a premium to this NAV per share, depending on the balance of supply and demand in the secondary market at any point in time. In fact investment trusts often trade at a discount to NAV, although sometimes they can trade at a premium. Exhibit 10.2 presents some information on investment trusts (investment companies), which is published on a daily basis in the *Financial Times*.

The final column of information is the discount or premium that the company's price is trading at relative to the net asset value (NAV) per share. This is calculated by dividing the share price by the NAV. The first company listed is the venture capital company 3i, whose share price was 120.5p and whose NAV was 112.1. In this case the shares were trading at a premium of 7.5%. There is no single satisfactory explanation to explain why investment trusts usually trade at either a discount or a premium to NAV. In fact usually such companies trade at a discount, as can be seen from Exhibit 10.2. (Note that by convention a discount is a positive number and a premium is a negative number.) The incidence of tax may provide part of the explanation. Under London Stock Exchange and UK Revenue rules investment trust companies must limit their investment in any one company to 15% of total assets. As long as the trust satisfies the rules as set by the Revenue, it achieves 'approved' status. As a consequence of this, gains made by the trust are exempt from capital gains tax. However, the income of the company is subject to corporation tax, and dividends paid by the trust company to its shareholders are taxed in the hands of shareholders in the normal way. In contrast the tax treatment of ICVCs is more favourable, in that the ICVC itself pays neither capital gains tax nor income tax. Rather, the investor in an ICVC is taxed at a composite rate of tax on the total investment gains made at the point of encashment. The recent investment performance of a trust also impacts on the discount to NAV. If a trust is going through a period of underperformance, this will often manifest itself in a relatively high discount to the published NAV per share. Another issue concerns the accuracy and timeliness of the NAV figure. In the case of the premium to NAV cited above for 3i, it may be due to an NAV figure that was calculated on 'old' valuations. While investment trust companies usually trade at a discount, there are occasions when they trade at a premium. Specialist trusts in areas of keen interest may trade at a premium as the demand for shares exceeds supply. For example, trusts focusing on emerging markets have in the past traded at a premium to NAV at times when investors were scrambling to gain exposure to such markets. Direct investing in these markets is often restricted and very expensive, and specialist trusts may be the only viable way to gain investment exposure.

Exchange-Traded Funds (ETFs)

Like investment trusts, ETFs are shares in investment companies that are bought and sold on stock exchanges in exactly the same way as ordinary shares are traded. This sets them apart from mutual funds and ICVCs. The defining characteristics of ETFs are that they are open-ended funds that passively replicate the performance of a particular index, commodity or currency and are linked on a recognised stock exchange. They operate an unusual process to ensure that the shares always trade very close to the NAV of the fund. Special trading rights are granted to selected institutions by the company sponsoring the ETF. If the ETF share price is lower than the NAV per share, an ETF institutional investor can buy ETF shares and turn them in to the sponsoring company for an equivalent amount of underlying stocks, which the institution can then sell for an immediate profit. If the ETF share price is greater than the NAV per share, the process is reversed. The institutional investor sells the ETF back to the sponsoring company and buys the underlying stocks on the market for a lower aggregate price. The underlying stocks can then be delivered to the sponsoring company instead of actual shares in the ETF. This trading mechanism creates an arbitrage process that ensures that the traded price of an ETF is very close to its NAV.

The first ETF was launched in the US in 1993 and since then the market has mushroomed. Initially ETFs aimed to track an index or a market passively. ETFs therefore can be viewed as index funds and not as synthetic derivatives. They trade and settle like single shares and are typically backed by baskets of securities designed to track indices. ETFs offer diversified exposure and generally have lower expense ratios than traditional active and index mutual funds. More recently some ETF promoters have offered funds that are not strictly passive but incorporate a particular theme or provide leveraged exposure to a market or index. It is estimated that approximately $1 trillion is invested in ETFs.

Asset Classes Covered by ETFs

ETFs cover all the major asset classes, including equities, government bonds, corporate bonds, property, commodities, currencies and a variety of alternative assets such as hedge funds and private equities. Sub-classes of assets are also covered by specialist sector ETFs, and 'Style' ETFs are also available. Examples include ETFs that invest in global infrastructure, and those that adopt a 'value' or a 'growth' theme to their portfolios.

Advantages of ETFs

- Costs: The annual management charge in a typical ETF ranges from 0.15% to 0.75%. In addition, investors will pay stockbroking commissions on purchase and sale of ETFs. These vary enormously, from online execution commissions as low as 0.1% up to approximately 1% for advisory-type brokerage services.
- Administration/Transparency: Once an investor has opened a stock-broking account ETFs can be bought and sold in exactly the same way as ordinary shares. The promoter of the ETF will make publicly available the underlying holdings in an ETF on a daily basis. A price is constantly available for an ETF throughout the trading day.
- Diversification and Asset Allocation: Each individual ETF allows investors to remove the stock-specific risk that typifies many individual share portfolios. If desired, investors can focus on the asset allocation decision and implement their preferred strategy through the use of a relatively small number of ETFs.

Disadvantages of ETFs

- Tax: Depending on the jurisdiction and an investor's particular circum - stances, ETFs may not be as tax efficient as other investment vehicles. Nevertheless, in most jurisdictions the net impact of any differences in tax treatment is usually quite minor.

- Lack of Umbrella Structure Relief: In Ireland investors in UCITS funds or life company policies can transfer between funds within an umbrella structure without triggering a chargeable tax event. This does not apply to ETFs. This is a significant disadvantage for active investors; whereas the impact on investors that trade infrequently may be quite marginal. For tax-exempt investors, such as pension funds, this is not an issue.

Sponsors of ETFs and Types of ETF

The major issuers of ETFs include Blackrock, State Street Global Advisors, Vanguard, Lyxor Asset Management, Deutsche Bank and Nomura Asset Management. There are in excess of one hundred different promoters offering a total of over eight hundred different ETFs.

There are two forms of ETF. The first is the fund that uses cash to buy securities outright. It then has the flexibility to engage in stock lending to generate extra income. The second does not buy the underlying assets of the index that it is tracking, but instead buys a swap-based product (or derivative) from a third party that is designed to replicate the index returns for the fund. The key difference between the two is that the second form exposes the fund to counterparty risk.

Other structures include exchange-traded commodities (ETCs) and exchange-traded notes (ETNs). ETCs enable investors to gain exposure to commodities without trading futures or taking physical delivery. Some ETCs are fully backed by the relevant commodity. For example, many gold ETCs are securities backed by the equivalent amount of gold bullion with the bullion being deposited and stored in a bank vault. Another type of ETC is a security backed by a swap-based (derivative) contract.

Structured and Capital-Guaranteed Investment Products

In Ireland these are often generically referred to as 'tracker bonds', and the typical structure is as follows:

- The product itself is a straightforward deposit account and therefore the investor deposits funds with the financial institution.
- As with a normal deposit account the capital is guaranteed. Unlike a normal deposit account the capital is guaranteed only as long as the funds are held on deposit for a pre-specified period of time, which usually ranges from 3 years to 6 years. Early encashment will be subject to penalties.
- The investment return is not a rate of interest, but a return that depends on the performance of a particular stock-market index or a composite of indices.

- At the end of the life of the product the investor receives his original capital plus the investment return, the latter depending on stock market performance.
- Deposit interest retention tax (DIRT) applies to the return achieved in the same way as if it were normal interest on a deposit.

In order to create these products, financial institutions utilise derivative markets. A typical tracker bond consists of two underlying components:

i)   A zero-coupon bond that has a term exactly matching the term of the tracker bond;
ii)   An option that is purchased from an investment bank and that promises to pay out a return at the end of the term based on the performance of a predefined stock-market index.

These products have proved to be very popular with retail investors and the financial industry has proved to be adept at designing innovative products. There is now an almost bewildering array of such products in the marketplace.

Hedge Funds

Hedge funds have grown in popularity amongst high net worth investors over the past decade. Whilst they are still largely the preserve of the very wealthy investor, hedge fund retail products have started to move into the mainstream. Minimum investment amounts of €100,000 or higher are typical for these products, although in some markets products are available with minimum investment amounts as low as €10,000. The typical hedge fund that is available to retail investors is a 'fund of funds'. As such the manager invests only in other hedge funds, which controls the risk but of course also limits the potential upside. The investment objectives of these funds differ from those of 'long only' funds in two key respects:

- The return objective is normally an absolute return and not a relative return.
- A wide array of investment assets and investment strategies are encompassed within a typical retail hedge fund. In contrast traditional investment products usually limit their investment to a well-defined and often narrow set of assets and/or markets.

Management fees in the hedge fund universe are much higher than for traditional funds. The underlying hedge funds typically charge an annual management fee of 2% of funds under management plus a performance fee equal to 20% of returns generated. A 'fund of funds' hedge fund will have charges that vary but are typically 1% of funds under management plus a performance fee equal to 10% of returns generated. Despite the recent higher profile of hedge funds and moves by regulators to allow private investors access to such funds, for the foreseeable future the traditional collective investment schemes will continue to absorb the lion's share of retail investment monies.

INVESTMENT DECISION MAKING FOR THE PRIVATE INVESTOR

In most countries, individuals who invest directly in the stock market are a minority – the overwhelming majority of the investing public invest indirectly using some of the products described in this chapter. For the private investor the type of investment vehicle used – a unit-linked fund, an OEIC or a unit trust – is relatively unimportant, since there is now a level playing field as far as tax is concerned across the different structures. Of far greater importance

Table 10.3 Matching Products to Investor Requirements

Investment Requirements and Constraints	Investment Product Categories
Regular Income Required	Deposits Low-Risk Managed Funds Structured Products Paying Regular Income
No Tolerance for Capital Fluctuation	Deposits Capital-Guaranteed Products
Some Capital Fluctuation Acceptable	Most Collective Investment Schemes
Short Time Horizon and Premium on Marketable Investments	Deposits Money Market and Bond Funds Low-Risk Managed Funds
Medium Time Horizon and Moderate Requirement for Liquidity/Marketability	Most Collective Investment Schemes
Long Time Horizon and Capacity for Illiquid Investment	Most Collective Investment Schemes Structured Products with long investment period (up to 7 years) Hedge Fund Products

is the investment strategy being pursued, and the fund managers who are best equipped to deliver the targeted, risk-adjusted returns. Therefore the starting point for any investor is an assessment of their investment goals, investment time horizon and tolerance for risk. Once this step has been completed, the investor is then faced with a wide array of investment choices that include all the product structures already discussed. In addition, there are also deposit-based products and hybrid products that combine capital guarantees with exposure to stock markets, including absolute return-focused hedge funds. Table 10.3 illustrates in broad terms the link between an investor's particular requirements and constraints, and the categories of investment products that are capable of meeting those goals.

THE MECHANICS OF INDIRECT INVESTING

Most investors accept that direct investment in stock markets is a risky business and requires a considerable amount of skill and time to be successful. What is often not properly appreciated is that indirect investing can also involve high levels of risk, since most investment products are built upon underlying investment strategies that are exposed to market risk. Therefore, the majority of private investors require professional advice to help them choose the right products to match their specific requirements. The financial services industry, however, is geared to sell financial products, with impartial advice sometimes coming a poor second. The inherent conflict in combining advice and sales has resulted in a high proportion of investment products being sold through investment intermediaries. Such intermediaries normally sell the products of many different financial institutions and, at least in principle, are in a position to offer impartial advice. Unfortunately this hasn't always worked to the best interests of the individual investor, as intermediaries are generally rewarded through commission payments from the financial institutions. This creates a bias in the system whereby intermediaries may push those products that offer the highest rates of commission. In the UK there have been a number of high-profile investigations by the regulators into the mis-selling of investment products relating to endowment policies and personal pensions.

In Ireland the same issues arise concerning the difficulty in getting appro -priate and impartial investment advice. Nevertheless, the industry has been forced to become more consumer-friendly over the years through initiatives largely driven by pressure from regulators/legislators and consumer groups. The key areas in which changes have come about include:

- Transparency: Commission and charges must now be clearly set out before a product is sold.

- Cooling-Off Period: After signing up to a product consumers now have a cooling-off period, during which they are entitled to change their mind with no financial penalty.
- Fee-Based Advisers: Many intermediaries now offer their clients the option of paying a fee for advice and commission-free (or very low-commission) products.

The establishment of a single regulator for the financial services industry in Ireland has been a key development in improving the investment landscape, particularly from the consumer's point of view. The Irish Financial Services Regulatory Authority (IFSRA) was established in May 2003 and regulated the manufacturers of financial products (banks, insurance companies, etc.) and the distributors of such products (insurance brokers, mortgage brokers, investment advisers, etc.) until September 2010. The Central Bank Reform Act 2010 created a new single unitary body – the Central Bank of Ireland – responsible for both central banking and financial regulation. This new structure replaced the previous related entities, the Central Bank and IFSRA. The Act commenced on 1 October 2010. Despite the extensive advances achieved in the development of the Irish financial services industry, there are still many instances whereby clients of such institutions feel that the products that they were sold have not delivered the expected returns. Some of this reflects a general over-optimism that still pervades both the industry and its clients with respect to expected returns. It also reflects the inherent tension between the sales process, which must extol the virtues of a product to make the sale, and the need to set out clearly the risks associated with those expected investment returns.

RETAIL INVESTMENT PRODUCTS COMPARED

In this section we compare and contrast:

- investment companies with variable capital (ICVCs)
- unit-linked life funds
- exchange-traded funds (ETFs)
- capital-guaranteed products.

Table 10.4 provides a brief summary of the main features of each of these investment vehicles.

ICVCs, unit-linked funds and ETFs all provide investors with essentially the same pooled investment solution. The legal structure of ICVCs and ETFs is such that the underlying assets are held directly by the investment company. Investors hold shares in the company whose only asset is a

Table 10.4 Main Features of Investment Products

Investment Vehicle	Legal Structure	Investment Characteristics	Other Features
ICVCs	Open-ended investment company	Returns and risk driven by the investment strategy of the fund	Shares bought and sold directly with fund promoter
Unit-Linked Funds	Life policy	Returns and risk driven by the investment strategy of the fund	Units bought and sold directly with life company
ETFs	Open-ended investment company	Returns and risk driven by the investment strategy of the fund	Institutions deal directly with fund promoter in creation/ redemption of shares Private investors buy/sell on secondary market where shares are quoted on recognised stock exchanges
Capital-Guaranteed Products	Bank deposit	Risk bounded by bank guarantee on capital invested Returns driven by formula related to specific market indices	Two sources of counterparty risk: the bank that takes the deposit and the institution that provides the derivative contract to underpin return promises

portfolio of financial securities. The value of the shares will rise and fall in a direct linkage to the portfolio of securities. In effect there is no counterparty risk to the investor. Unit-linked funds issued by life companies provide an identical investment solution. However, the underlying assets are held on the life company's balance sheet. The investor owns units in a unit-linked fund and gets a promise from the life company that the returns on these assets will be passed on to investors in the fund. Therefore, the financial strength of the life company is an important consideration when investing in unit-linked life products.

Capital-guaranteed products are quite different and usually rely on derivative products. Counterparty risk is a very important consideration and often these products involve promises from more than one financial institution. In a typical structure an investor places funds in a fixed-term deposit (usually three to five years), where the bank guarantees to return the original capital at maturity. The 'interest' or return will be provided by a derivative security, usually a call option, on some predefined market index. Usually this will be a second financial institution. Therefore, the investor is taking counterparty risk to the bank for the capital sum invested, and to the financial institution that writes the call option for the expected return.

Management Fees/Commissions and Charges

Historically, the charging structure for retail financial products has had two layers:

i)   Initial upfront sales commissions ranging between 1% and 5% for the sum invested.
ii)   An annual fund management charge levied on the current market value of the fund, typically 1% to 1.5% of portfolio value.

Product structures evolved to operate effectively in this type of environment. Bid–offer pricing was the norm, with most spreads of the order of 5%. The bulk of this spread funded upfront sales commissions. Fund management charges were typically levied on the portfolio of assets as a cost to the fund. Therefore, unit or fund prices were net of these fees.

This market and product structure created an environment that lacked transparency and that incentivised salespeople to sell those products that paid the highest commissions, rather than the most suitable products for individual clients. Financial institutions that sold directly to the public tended to frontload their profit. The market has evolved to improve transparency and to remove the worst excesses of an upfront commission regime. Most investment products now adopt a single pricing regime. All commissions and charges have to be clearly disclosed at the point of sale, and a higher proportion of total expenses are now in the form of the annual management charge. Despite these changes the basic structure of the market has not altered. In Ireland the remuneration of salespeople for investment products continues to be mainly in the form of point-of-sale commissions. Banks and financial institutions typically structure their products to generate substantial upfront profit. Regulatory changes in the UK have, however, been more forceful and the Financial Services Authority will be enforcing a fee-only regime from 2012.

THE FUTURE FOR RETAIL INVESTMENT PRODUCTS IN IRELAND

Unlike in the US, where there is a long tradition of direct investment in the stock market by individuals, direct investment in stocks and shares by Irish individuals is still a minority activity. Indeed, even in the US investment volume through vehicles such as mutual funds has long eclipsed direct investment by individuals in the stock market. Trends in Ireland are likely to mirror those in Europe, where the bulk of stock market-related investment occurs through collective investment schemes. EU directives will continue to determine the legal and regulatory framework, and in widening consumer choice through the encouragement of cross-border competition. For the individual investor distinguishing between the array of investment and savings products on offer will remain a daunting task. The key role of investment intermediaries and product providers in properly advising clients will become even more important in the future. The 2000s was a decade of very low returns for most risk assets. Predicting the future is impossible but the 2010s has begun with low inflation and exceptionally low interest rates. A decade of nominal returns below long-run historical averages seems likely for all assets. In such an environment the pressure on product providers and intermediaries to deliver better value for money on investment products will be intense.

SUMMARY

- As an alternative to purchasing financial assets themselves, all investors can invest indirectly, which involves the purchase of shares in an invest - ment company or units in a unit trust or unit-linked life assurance fund.
- Collective investment schemes are classified as either open-end or closed-end, depending on whether the number of shares or units are fixed or constantly changing.
- In Ireland the bulk of indirect investing occurs through open-end investment vehicles such as ICVCs, unit-linked life assurance funds and unit trusts.
- The key benefits of indirect investing include:
  - diversification
  - ease of administration
  - tax efficiency.

➡

- For open-ended investment vehicles investors buy and sell shares or units at the net asset value, which is determined by the current market value of the securities held by the investment company or trust.
- Capital-guaranteed products, which combine exposure to stock markets and/or bond markets with guarantees on the original capital investment, now attract large inflows of funds from private investors.
- For the very wealthy, hedge funds offer an alternative to traditional equity and bond funds. Regulators in several jurisdictions are now moving to allow hedge fund products access to the wider retail investment market.
- For private investors, matching their specific requirements to the appropriate investment products usually requires expert financial advice.

QUESTIONS

1. Regarding fund types, which of the following is/are TRUE?

   A. An investor in a unit-linked fund receives units in proportion to his/her contributions.
   B. The investor in a unit-linked fund is exposed to the market risk associated with the underlying assets.
   C. Many large pension funds prefer to invest on a segregated fund basis, as it enables the fund managers to construct dedicated, customised portfolios.

   1. A and B only
   2. All of the above
   3. B and C only
   4. None of the above

2. In assessing the suitability of an investment strategy for a client, an investment manager will be concerned with the client's:

   A. Attitude to growth versus security
   B. Existing liabilities
   C. Investment time horizon
   D. Pattern of cash inflows and outflows
   1. A and B
   2. A, B and C
   3. All of the above
   4. B and C

➡

3. Diversification, ease of administration, tax efficiency/neutrality and value for money are the key attributes that investors look for in collective investment schemes. Set out and compare how the following vehicles score on each of these attributes:

   A. Unit-linked life assurance funds
   B. UCITS funds
   C. Unit trusts
   D. Investment trusts
   E. Funds of hedge funds

4. You are an investment adviser and a client has given you the following information regarding his investment requirements:

Time horizon:	Long
Inflation protection:	Extremely important to at least match inflation
Growth over inflation:	Some real growth but risk-averse
Income:	No requirement for immediate income
Marketability:	Personal circumstances could change in three years

   Make a list of at least four different assets (and more if you deem it appropriate) that you would recommend. For each asset, explain why you have chosen it and what investment requirements it fulfils.

Case Study Exercise

After spending several years abroad John and Christine Casey came back to Ireland and developed a successful business in the west of Ireland consisting of a restaurant, a B&B and a very successful tourist shop. Their children were not interested in running the business so they sold it once John reached the age of 65.

John has always been a risk taker and, against the advice of Christine, he invested a substantial portion of their capital in Irish bank shares. The collapse in the market has shaken him badly. Fortunately, Christine insisted that a large portion of their assets should stay on deposit. Also, Christine managed the bookkeeping side of the business and from an early stage she invested in a pension plan. On retirement this funded the purchase of an annuity (with no indexation) that will generate annual after-tax income of €25,000.

They have two children, Patrick (24) and Stephanie (26), who have both left home and are financially independent. John and Christine would like to be able to help out their children financially when they come to buying a house.

John and Christine have recently appointed you as their financial adviser, and have provided you with the following information:

Assets:

Family home	€650,000 no mortgage, recent valuation
Deposits	€775,000
Balanced managed fund	€240,000 recent valuation
Emerging markets equity fund	€102,000

Living Expenses:

They estimate that they need a net annual income of approximately €40,000.

On retirement they felt that they were financially secure and confident in their ability to meet their financial needs, and in their capacity to help their children. The economic and financial crash has shaken their confidence and they are now worried about their long-term financial security.

As their financial adviser you have told them that before making any decisions, in consultation with you, they need to establish a 'Statement of Investment Policy'. You have undertaken to produce a draft SIP.

1. **Before producing your draft SIP, what extra information would you seek from the Casey family?**
2. **Produce the draft SIP for the Caseys. This should cover issues such as the Caseys' investment objectives, tolerance for risk, investment time horizon, etc.**

Chapter eleven

Pension Fund Investment

This chapter introduces pension schemes and the legal and regulatory framework within which they operate. The role and responsibilities of pension fund trustees are outlined, particularly with regard to the fund's investments. The particular risks attaching to pension fund investment are described and investment objectives outlined. The central role of the trustees in determining investment strategy is discussed.

Learning Objectives

After reading this chapter you will be able to:

- Define the principal types of pension fund and the legal and regulatory framework within which they operate in Ireland
- Outline the role and responsibilities of pension fund trustees, particularly with regard to investment
- Describe the long-term and short-term time horizons which influence a fund's investment objectives
- List the various types of risk that are important to pension funds
- Recognise the factors that determine investment strategy and drive the selection of the fund's asset mix, benchmark and added value objective and accompanying exposure to benchmark and active risk
- Appreciate the central role of the trustees in the determination of investment strategy.

PENSION SCHEMES: AN INTRODUCTION

A pension scheme is an arrangement whereby an individual (the employee) and the employer may set aside monies dedicated to providing the employee with an income in retirement.

Monies set aside are paid into a pension fund and in turn are invested. Therefore, the pension fund is comprised both of the monies paid in and the returns – capital and income – generated on them.

It is out of these resources that pensions are paid to scheme members in retirement.

PENSION SCHEME TYPES

There are two broad categories of pension scheme.

i)   *Occupational Pension Schemes*
     Typically, in these schemes both employer and employee make contributions into the pension fund. In some 'non-contributory' schemes only the employer makes contributions.

ii) *Individual Pension Schemes*
     An employee in non-pensionable employment, or a self-employed individual with a source of taxable income from a trade or profession, may establish an individual pension scheme through a retirement annuity policy issued by a life assurance company.
     The relatively recent introduction in 2003 of Personal Retirement Savings Accounts (PRSAs) permits individuals to save for their retirements throughout their careers and to maintain these savings as they move through different employments and between employments.

Defined Benefit and Defined Contribution Schemes

Occupational schemes differ depending upon how the retirement benefits are determined and how the scheme's assets are invested and administered. They may be defined benefit schemes, defined contribution schemes or, occasionally, a combination of these.
     Individual pension schemes are invariably defined contribution schemes.

Defined Benefit ('Final Salary') Schemes

A defined benefit scheme promises the employee a pension in retirement. Generally, the pension is determined as a percentage of final salary for each year the individual member has been in service with the employer. The employer (or 'sponsor') and employee each pay contributions into a common pooled fund. The individual member does not have a specific, identifiable fund; assets of all members are commingled in the common pooled fund.
     A key feature of a defined benefit scheme is that the scheme's commitment to pay the defined percentage of final salary as pension and other benefits is underwritten by the employer. The employer undertakes to ensure that the scheme has sufficient assets to pay the promised benefits. Therefore, in defined benefit schemes, investment risk is borne by the employer.

Defined Contribution ('Money Purchase') Schemes

Under defined contribution schemes the contributions to be paid by the employee scheme member and the employer are defined, rather than the actual retirement benefits. The contributions and the investment returns they generate are accumulated to retirement age and the monies thus accumulated will be applied in purchasing the pension: hence the term 'money purchase schemes'.

In defined contribution schemes each member has a separately identifiable fund. The key feature of the defined contribution scheme is that the retirement benefit depends on the value of the individual's specific fund on retirement and on the investment conditions prevailing at that time (which determine the amount of pension or annuity that the member's fund will purchase). There is no employer guarantee. Therefore, in defined contributions schemes, it is the member who bears the investment risk.

THE REGULATORY FRAMEWORK

Occupational Pension Schemes

The Trust Structure

Occupational pension schemes are normally organised as trusts. A trust is a legal structure or vehicle that places responsibility for the management of a certain property (e.g. a pension scheme) in the hands of a third party – the board of trustees.

The trust is a legal entity in its own right and it is separate and distinct from the sponsoring company (the employer). The trust protects the beneficiaries of the scheme by requiring the trustees to act in their interest.

Legal Framework

The objectives and responsibilities of a pension trust are defined by:

i)   Its trust deed, in effect the constitution of the pension scheme, which sets out the rules and responsibilities of the trust.
ii)   Trust law, much of it long-standing case law.
iii) Specific legislation:
   • Trustee Act 1893
   • Trustee (Authorised Investments) Act 1958
   • Pensions Act 1990, incorporating regulations under the EU Pension Directive
   • Pensions Amendment Act 1996
   • Pensions Amendment Act 2002
   • Various family law, tax and social-welfare legislation.

The Pensions Act 1990 was amended from September 2005 to enable Irish pension schemes to operate on an EU cross-border basis and to permit employees in Ireland to participate in overseas EU pension schemes. This implemented an EU Pensions Directive commonly referred to as the IORPs Directive.

The Responsibilities of Trustees

General Legal Responsibilities

In discharging their responsibilities to the beneficiaries of the scheme, trustees must:

- act in good faith;
- exercise their own discretion, having made all necessary enquiries and investigations and taken advice as appropriate;
- act in the best interest of the beneficiaries.

In addition, Section 59 of the Pensions Act 1990 imposes the following general duties on pension scheme trustees:

- To ensure that the contributions payable by employer and members are received.
- To provide for the proper investment of the resources of the scheme in accordance with the rules of the scheme.
- Where appropriate, to make arrangements for the payment of the benefits as provided for under the rules of the scheme as they become due.
- To ensure that proper membership and financial records are kept.

Investment Responsibilities

The overall responsibility of trustees in relation to investment matters is set out in Section 59(b) of the Pensions Act of 1990: 'to provide for the proper investment of the resources of the scheme in accordance with the rules of the scheme'.

Clearly, the legislation is not over-prescriptive when it comes to matters of investment. The 'proper investment of the resources of the scheme' is not defined.

Trustees, therefore, rely on general trust law for guidance:

i)   Trustees are subject to a duty of care. They must invest with the care which an ordinary prudent person would take in investing for the benefit of other people for whom he or she felt normally bound to provide.

First, the duty of care implies a requirement to invest prudently, i.e. in a diversified manner. Second, the duty of care points to a requirement to obtain expert advice. The power to delegate the investment function is implied. However, responsibility cannot be delegated and remains with the trustees, who are obliged to take reasonable steps to satisfy themselves that the appointed fund manager or managers have the necessary knowledge and expertise. The trustees must continue to monitor the management of the investment function.

ii)   The trustees must have regard to the fact that the purpose of the scheme is to provide retirement benefits for the employees. As such, the best interest of all should be taken to mean the best financial interest.

iii)   The trustees must recognise also a duty to the sponsoring employer who, as a beneficiary of investment performance, has a legitimate interest in the efficient management of the scheme.

Investment Regulations: The EU Pensions Directive

Regulations under the Pensions Act 1990 have been made to implement the EU Pensions Directive (often referred to as the IORPs Directive) into Irish law.

The regulations reinforce the prudent person principle by requiring trustees to:

- Invest the assets of the scheme in a manner calculated to ensure the security, quality, liquidity and profitability of the portfolio as a whole.
- Invest the assets of the scheme predominantly on regulated markets.
- Properly diversify the assets of the scheme to avoid excessive reliance on any particular asset, issue or group of undertakings.
- Only invest in derivative instruments in so far as they –
  (a) contribute to a reduction of investment risks
  (b) or facilitate efficient portfolio management.
- Borrow monies only on a temporary basis for liquidity purposes.

The regulations also require trustees of large schemes, i.e. with 100 or more members, to prepare a Statement of Investment Policy Principles (SIP) as follows:

(a) a written statement of the principles must be prepared and maintained;
(b) the statement must be reviewed at least every three years; and
(c) be revised following any change of investment policy which is incon - sistent with the statement.

The SIP must include:

- the investment objectives of the trustees;
- the investment risk measurement methods;

- the risk management processes to be used; and
- the strategic asset allocation with respect to the nature and duration of pension liabilities.

The Liabilities of Trustees

Any act or neglect on the part of a trustee which is not authorised or excused by the terms of the trust deed, or by law, is a 'breach of trust'.

A trustee will be required to make good, from his or her own personal assets, any shortfall in trust resources arising from a breach of trust for which he or she is deemed responsible.

It is possible for trustees to limit the extent of their liability and to obtain certain indemnities both at law and under the terms of the trust. Also trustees may protect their personal positions further by effecting Trustee Indemnity Insurance Policies.

Section 3 of the Pensions Act 1990 states that where a trustee, in his capacity as trustee, contravenes a provision of the Act or a regulation thereunder, he shall be guilty of an offence. Additionally, where in any report, certificate or other document required by the act a person makes a false or misleading statement, he shall be guilty of an offence. A person guilty of an offence shall be liable on summary conviction to a fine and/or imprisonment.

Individual Pension Schemes

Personal pensions and PRSAs are essentially contracts between the individual and the pension or PRSA provider. The investment arrangements are defined explicitly in the policy documents or contracts that govern these schemes.

While there may be a choice as to the type of investment available, this choice may be exercised only within the terms outlined in the contract.

THE PENSION FUND'S REQUIREMENTS

The pension fund's requirements extend over a complex and dynamic framework of assets, liabilities and cash flows. The fund's assets generate investment returns that are uncertain and volatile. Liabilities extend into the long-term future and are subject, obviously, to inflation and also to the shifting longevity of beneficiaries. Cash flows are volatile, subject to an ever-changing mix of employer and employee contributions, pension payments and investment returns. Management of the fund is involved with potentially very large sums of money over very prolonged time horizons.

Figure 11.1 attempts to illustrate the various factors that drive fund requirements.

Figure 11.1 Pension Fund Requirements, The Funding Standard

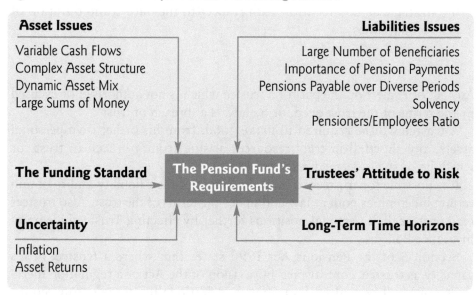

The Funding Standard

Pension fund investment, because of the nature of the fund's promise to pay pensions, is necessarily concerned with the long term. However, the scheme must also be concerned with providing security for beneficiaries on an ongoing basis.

The Pensions Act of 1990 introduced a Funding Standard, which ensures that members of defined benefit schemes can have confidence in the ongoing solvency of the scheme.

Under the Act the fund's trustees must submit to the Pensions Board an actuarial funding certificate, certifying whether or not the fund meets the Funding Standard.

A scheme shall be deemed to satisfy the Funding Standard if, in the opinion of the scheme actuary, the resources of the scheme at the effective date of the actuarial funding certificate would have been sufficient, if the scheme had been wound up at that date, to provide for the liabilities of the scheme and the estimated expenses of winding up the scheme. Liabilities will include pensions in payment, additional benefits due by way of additional voluntary contributions or rights transferred from another scheme, and benefits in respect of reckonable service.

A new actuarial funding certificate must be prepared within three years of the immediately preceding certificate. In addition, each annual report of the scheme must include a statement by the actuary that the Funding Standard continues to be met.

The Funding Standard requirement thus injects a short-term solvency dimension into the long-term nature of pension fund liabilities. The investment objective of the scheme must embrace both these long-term and short-term requirements.

Where a scheme fails to meet the Funding Standard, a funding proposal must be submitted to the Pensions Board. In certain circumstances the end date of the funding proposal may be extended beyond the date of the next Actuarial Funding Certificate, to a maximum period of ten years.

Pension Fund Investment Risk

In Chapter 6 investment risk is defined, measured, analysed and discussed.

Because of the critical importance of pensions to the lives of pensioners the pension fund must survive and prevail in the long run. The pension fund will focus in particular on avoiding permanent loss of capital and on its ability to meet essential payments.

However, even within a single pension fund, perceptions of risk may differ.

* On the one hand, the employee may be primarily concerned that the pension fund is soundly invested and will be in a strong position to pay pensions in perhaps twenty or thirty years' time.
* The sponsoring company's finance director, on the other hand, while acknowledging the long-term imperative to pay pensions, may have the additional perspective that strong shorter-term performance will reduce funding costs.
* The fund trustees will attempt to ensure that the investment returns generated by the fund's portfolio will satisfy both these perspectives, whilst maintaining a surplus of assets over liabilities so that the requirements of the Funding Standard are met.

In managing the risks surrounding the pension fund the trustees will pay particular attention to the following.

Liability Risk

This is the risk that the value of the fund's assets over time fails to keep pace with the value of its liabilities.

Historically the conventional wisdom was that equities were the asset best placed to meet pension fund liabilities, because of the linkage that exists between, on the one hand, growth in the economy, growth in profits and growth in share prices and, on the other, growth in the economy, growth in wages and growth in pensions.

However, as discussed in more detail in Chapter 12, this conventional wisdom has been questioned in recent years. The present value of the fund's liabilities is determined by a discount factor which keys off bond yields. Therefore, it is argued, bonds are a more appropriate match for liabilities.

Certainly, the difficult investment environment of the early years of the new century and the 2008 financial crash has sharpened trustee awareness of the requirement for fund assets to keep pace with fund liabilities.

Downside Volatility

The implosion of the technology bubble ignited the severe equity bear market of 2000 to 2003. Investors then received a stark reminder of the downside volatility of equity markets. The sharp fall in share prices during the banking and credit crisis of 2008/2009 delivered a further reminder of the downside volatility inherent in high equity exposures. In response, pension trustees and pension regulators have been striving to 'de-risk' their investment strategies.

The requirement to avoid unacceptable exposure to downside volatility is underlined by the need to comply with the relatively short-term requirements of the Funding Standard.

Benchmark Risk

In determining their fund's overall investment strategy trustees will often specify a 'benchmark asset mix'. This refers to an ideal portfolio mix which, if maintained over the life of the fund, will deliver the required risk and return characteristics.

Benchmark risk is the risk that the selected benchmark asset mix exposes the fund to fluctuations in asset values that differ over time from fluctuations in the value of liabilities.

Active Risk

The fund's investment manager may be mandated by the trustees to generate 'added value', i.e. returns in excess of benchmark returns. The search for 'added value' or excess return involves taking incremental risk over the risk embedded in the benchmark asset mix.

Active risk refers to the incremental risk entered into by the investment manager, on behalf of the fund, in the search for added value.

As discussed in Chapter 6, volatility is widely employed as the key measure of risk in portfolio construction. However, volatility as a measure of risk has limitations, as is illustrated in that chapter.

Therefore in assessing the overall riskiness of the fund's investment port - folio the quantitative measure of risk – volatility – is augmented by an array of qualitative measures to develop a comprehensive overview of portfolio risk and portfolio diversification.

Among the portfolio characteristics to be monitored are:

- the spread and coverage of the portfolio across asset types and across sectors;
- the concentration of the portfolio by sector and by stock;
- the portfolio's exposures to individual securities;
- the quality of the individual stocks in the portfolio;
- the volatility of the individual holdings;
- the style biases within the portfolio
  - to highly rated (growth) securities;
  - to low-rated (value) securities.

INVESTMENT OBJECTIVES

Having considered the overall legal framework within which the pension scheme operates, together with the fund's particular liabilities and characteristics and their own attitude to risk, the trustees may then proceed to define the fund's investment objectives.

Typically the trustees will have long-term and medium-term objectives for investment returns.

Long-Term Objectives

The trustees will normally express the fund's long-term return objective in terms of a required real return over the rate of inflation. As discussed earlier, pensions are linked to salaries before retirement, which in turn reflect inflation during the employee's working life. An inflation-linked objective is therefore appropriate to the fund's liabilities.

The particular real rate of return chosen will normally be that used by the actuary in the periodic valuation of the fund, e.g. typically 3% to 5% above an assumed long-term rate of inflation.

Importantly, particularly in the light of the difficulties generated by the weakness in equity markets over the past decade, the long-term objective is subject to the consideration of downside volatility discussed above.

Medium-Term Objectives

The medium-term objective's main function is to enable the trustees to monitor and control the investment management of the fund's portfolio.

Medium-term objectives may be of two kinds:

i)   *Peer-Group Objectives*
      The investment returns of the pension fund are measured and compared
      over different periods with the returns of other Irish pension funds, as
      measured and collated by an independent performance measurement
      specialist, such as Combined Performance Measurement Service (CPMS).
          The trustees may decide that the objective of the fund is:
      - to match that of the median or average fund in the survey;
      - or, more demandingly, to outperform the average return by some
        stated margin (e.g. 1% per annum) over some stated period of
        years (say 3 to 5 years);
      - or to rank within the top quartile (i.e. the top 25%) of funds in
        the survey over 3 to 5 years.

      The return objective is thus defined as to return relative to a 'peer
      group' benchmark. Where a 'peer group' benchmark is selected, the
      fund's strategic or benchmark asset mix, by definition, is the average
      asset mix of the universe of pension funds surveyed.

ii)   *Customised Objectives*
      Alternatively, the trustees may develop a strategic long-term asset
      allocation, or asset mix, for the fund which is specifically appropriate
      to its requirements and particular financial profile.
          This customised asset mix will be applied in generating a cus-
      tomised performance benchmark by applying market returns for each
      asset class to their respective allocations in the benchmark asset mix.
          The trustees will then define the fund's investment objective, either:
      - to match the return of the benchmark asset mix;
      - or to 'add value' by generating a higher return than the benchmark.
        This latter objective will require the fund to take on incremental
        risk, i.e. risk in excess of the risk embedded in the benchmark.

INVESTMENT STRATEGY

Defining Investment Strategy

It is the trustees' responsibility to identify their investment objectives and to
define the investment strategy of the fund. In particular they must weigh up and:

MATCH

The requirements of the fund –

- its long-term liabilities to pay pensions
- its short-term solvency requirement
- its tolerance for risk

AGAINST

The characteristics of the investment assets –

* their long-term returns
* their volatilities
* their ability to cope with inflation.

Investment strategy must then be crystallised into a strategic or benchmark asset mix. Trustees may take some comfort from the view that the search is not for an ideal asset mix, but for an asset mix that will be appropriate under a wide variety of circumstances.

Indeed, even if an 'ideal' asset mix could be identified the trustees might still reject it – if, for example, they felt that they would perform poorly while other funds did well. The search therefore is for an asset mix that reflects the fund's individual requirements and the trustees' tolerance for risk.

In the table below, an attempt is made to align pension fund requirements with desirable asset characteristics and with asset types.

Figure 11.2 Pension Fund Requirement/Asset Characteristics

Pension Fund Requirement	Asset Characteristics	Asset
i) Inflation Protection	Ability to cope well with inflation	Equities Property Index-Linked
ii) Growth over Inflation	Ability to generate real growth	Equities Property Index-Linked
iii) Currency Match	Euro-denominated	All euro assets
iv) Income Stream	Relatively low-yielding	Equities Index-Linked Cash
	Relatively high-yielding	Property Bonds
v) Marketability	High liquidity	Bonds Equities Index-Linked Cash

➥

Figure 11.2 Pension Fund Requirement/Asset Characteristics (continued)

Pension Fund Requirement	Asset Characteristics	Asset
vi) Matching Term	Long-term assets	Bonds Equities Property Index-Linked
	Short-term assets	Cash, Bonds Index-Linked

Because of its long-term nature and requirement to pay pensions that are linked to inflation, it is arguable that the most desirable asset characteristics of a pension fund are the ability to cope with inflation and the ability to provide returns above inflation. Historically, equities have been the asset best equipped to deliver these characteristics, and it is for this reason that equities have emerged as the dominant asset in pension fund portfolios.

Equities, however, do not offer a perfect or ideal solution. Inevitably, high returns from equity markets come at a high cost in risk or volatility terms. Equities are a high-volatility asset. Trustees must balance the potential high returns from equities against this volatility.

Diversification reduces volatility or risk, as Markowitz showed. By using his 'efficient frontier' – portfolio optimisation – a range of risk/return trade-offs may be examined and a portfolio structure appropriate to the trustee's risk appetite identified.

Equities suffer from other disadvantages:

- They are generally a low-income asset.
- Non-euro (overseas) equities do not provide a currency match for euro liabilities.
- Marketability may be restricted, especially in smaller company shares.

Although examination of the historical evidence shows that equities tend to outperform the other asset classes, there is no guarantee that this outperfor - mance will persist into the future.

Prudence therefore requires that pension funds blend into their portfolios the desirable characteristics of the other investment assets. This provides the essential diversification of assets that is key to the control of risk.

Asset/Liability Modelling

Asset/Liability Modelling is a formal, quantitative approach to the determination of appropriate investment strategy and benchmark asset mix. As discussed above, the search is not for an ideal asset mix but for one that will be suitable under a variety of circumstances. The chosen asset mix must also encompass the valid, but conflicting, objectives of trustees. For example, the requirement to generate returns that in the long term meet or exceed the actuarial hurdle rate must be balanced against the objective to ensure solvency (i.e. to ensure that the value of assets exceeds the value of liabilities). The role of the Asset/Liability Model is to help trustees to identify an efficient asset allocation strategy, which is appropriate to their objectives and risk tolerances.

The technique is an extension of the normal process of actuarial valuation. Where the actuarial valuation assumes fixed parameters, e.g. for growth in liabilities, for investment returns, etc., the Asset/Liability Model projects varying courses of inflation, asset returns and related factors into the future. Thousands of such simulations are run, probabilities are attached to certain out-turns and implied funding levels are identified. The implications of different investment strategies are thus highlighted for trustees, helping them to identify the strategy and asset mix most appropriate to their circumstances.

As always with quantitative techniques, there are important caveats. Modelling processes depend heavily on the underlying assumptions and make extensive use of historic time series. The assumptions may be unreliable and historic returns and asset correlations may be of limited use.

The Asset/Liability Model may best be seen, therefore, as a tool to help trustees to meet their risk/return objectives, augmenting the more qualitative approach discussed below.

Asset/Liability Grid

An Asset/Liability Modelling exercise is a powerful tool in informing the trustees' decision on asset allocation. Note, however, that there are important reservations around the modelling approach. The model generates results that are consistent with the assumptions and parameters fed into it. There is little consensus about these, or even about model design. Nevertheless, where trustees are comfortable with the model and parameters chosen, the Asset/Liability Model is a powerful tool in its ability to illustrate the range of options available to trustees.

A more intuitive, broader-brush approach may be adopted by incorporating the key elements into a check list: see Figure 11.3.

Figure 11.3 Asset/Liability Grid

	Bonds	Emphasise Balanced	Equities
1. Liability Profile			
pension type:			
• fixed	X		
• indexed		X	X
• final salary			X
active/retired ratio:			
• high			X
• low	X	X	
term:			
• long			X
• short	X	X	
2. Fund Solvency			
• strong		X	X
• weak	X	X	
3. Corporate Sponsor			
• strong		X	X
• weak	X	X	
4. Appetite for short-term volatility			
• high			X
• low	X		

The grid is helpful in scoping out the broad asset mix that may be appropriate for a pension fund.

Defined benefit schemes at either extreme of these characteristics will see a reasonably clear solution. The grid shows that a fund where pensions are indexed, the active/retired membership ratio is high, with a long-term perspective, with strong solvency, a substantial corporate sponsor and a high appetite for short-term volatility will opt for a high equity exposure.

Conversely, where pensions are fixed, where the active/retired membership ratio is low, with a short-term perspective, where both the fund solvency and corporate sponsor are weak and where appetite for short term volatility is low, the trustees will be drawn to a solution which incorporates a high bond content and low equity exposure.

Between these extremes the identification of the appropriate mix becomes an iterative process. In a sense the trustees must attempt to segment the liabilities into broad layers and match these against broad equity and bond characteristics.

A defined contribution scheme without the benefit of a corporate sponsor may, all things being equal, have a lower appetite for equities than a defined benefit scheme with otherwise similar characteristics.

Asset Allocation 1988–2009

Table 11.1 shows the asset allocation of Irish pension funds for selected years over the period 1988 to 2009. We can identify several significant shifts in broad asset allocation over this period:

* Reduction in the bond weighting after 1988 and a commensurate increase in the equity weighting.
* A further increase in the equity weighting after 1997, with a commensurate decline in the bond weighting

In the first decade of the new millennium, up to 2007, the equity weighting was maintained around two-thirds despite the equity bear market of 2001/2. During this period there was a small but significant increase in the property weighting from just over 6% to 9.1%. Over the entire period there was an exceptionally large increase in the equity weighting from 47.1% in 1988 to 66.3% in 2007. If we look at non-bond assets, the rise in exposure to risky assets (equities and property) is even more startling. At the end of 1988 the combined equity/property weighting stood at 52.9%, but by the end of 2007 it was at 75.4% – a rise of 22.5%. While it is true that over this period there was a general shift towards equities globally, the experience of Irish pension funds is an extreme one.

Table 11.1 Asset Mix of Irish Pension Funds 1988–2009 – Various Years (%)

	1988	1993	1997	2000	2007	2009
Equities	47.1	56.5	58.6	64.3	66.3	52.3
Property (including forestry)	5.8	5.4	6.0	6.6	9.1	8.4
Bonds(including index linked)	41.0	34.8	27.1	22.2	18.5	26.1
Cash and other	6.1	3.3	8.3	6.8	6.1	13.2

Sources: Whelan, *Irish Pension Funds: Size, Growth and Composition of Assets*, 2001; Irish Association of Pension Funds, *Asset Allocation Surveys*.

The shifts in the late 1980s and early 1990s can be at least partially explained by the lifting of exchange controls on 1 January 1989. The existence of exchange controls was a factor that forced Irish pension funds to invest in domestic equities and bonds. Following the abolition of such controls it was prudent for Irish funds to diversify out of Irish assets into overseas investments. What is curious is that this overseas asset shift was concentrated in equities rather than in bonds.

The introduction of the euro at the start of 1999 is another significant development that clearly impacted on the strategic asset allocation of Irish investors. Irish funds could now invest in a much larger 'home' (Eurozone) market without having to worry about F/X (foreign exchange) risk. Again, however, this does not explain why the increase in overseas investments was again concentrated in equities rather than bonds.

The only rational conclusion from this analysis of Irish pension funds' asset allocation strategies in the period from 1988 to 2007 is that explicit decisions were taken by trustees and their advisers to increase exposure to equities.

Asset Allocation 2007–2010

The financial crash of 2008 has had an extremely adverse impact on the asset mixes of Irish pension schemes. Relative price movements have caused a sharp fall in equity weightings and a rise in bond weightings. At end-2008, which was close to the bottom of the equity bear market, the equity weighting of Irish pension funds had fallen to 47.8%. This equates to a decline of 18.5% in just one year. Approximately two-thirds of this decline can be explained by relative price movements, with one-third due to active decisions to reduce the exposure to equities. The recovery in the markets in 2009 resulted in a rise in the equity weighting to 52.3%. However, it does seem that the era of high allocations to equities by Irish pension funds has been killed off by the financial crash. The solvency position of most defined benefit schemes has been severely weakened. Legal and regulatory pressures are forcing many schemes to 'de-risk' their investment portfolios. This is being widely interpreted as allocating a very high proportion of assets to bonds. Furthermore, even where schemes are in a strong solvency position, the tendency is to adopt a much lower risk asset allocation, involving a much lower allocation to equities than was the case up to 2007.

Variables Affecting Pension Fund Solvency

Valuing a pension fund is essentially a balance sheet exercise, where the value of the assets is compared with the value of the liabilities. Valuing the assets is usually straightforward by simply taking current market prices. The only issue is one of interpretation, particularly where the bulk of the fund is invested in volatile assets such as equities. At cyclical market bottoms this snapshot value will understate their true long-term value and vice versa at market peaks. The valuation of liabilities is much more problematic and involves many conceptual and practical difficulties. A similar snapshot valuation issue applies to the assets, with the additional complication that there are no market prices available for the present value of the future costs of the pension scheme. Complex mathematical and statistical models are required to calculate the present value of a pension scheme's liabilities. This involves making many assumptions, the two most important of which are:

- The interest rate or bond yield to use in the discount factor applied to calculating the present value of future costs.
- Assumptions regarding mortality.

The sharp deterioration in the solvency position of Irish defined benefit schemes has been driven by adverse trends in the three most important variables affecting the value of the assets and liabilities, namely:

- The poor returns from stock markets over the past ten years.
- The persistent fall in bond yields over the past twenty years.
- Clear evidence that people are living longer, leading to a requirement to alter the assumptions regarding longevity.

Benchmarks and Added Value

Whether an informal matching process or a formal Asset/Liability Modelling exercise is carried out, it is the responsibility of the trustees to identify a benchmark asset mix. This mix is the central asset allocation strategy that is most appropriate to the pension fund's requirements and liabilities.

Having selected the benchmark asset mix the trustees must go on to decide whether the fund's return objective should be to match the return on the benchmark – a 'passive' investment strategy – or to exceed benchmark return by taking on a higher degree of risk – an 'active' investment strategy.

When both the benchmark asset mix and the investment objective have been identified, risk for the fund crystallises into two distinct elements:

i)   *Benchmark Risk*
      The risk that the selected benchmark asset mix exposes the fund to fluctuations in asset values, which differ over time from fluctuations in the value of liabilities.
      Most of the risk to which the fund will be exposed is made up of benchmark risk. This underlines the importance of the decision made by trustees in selecting the appropriate benchmark asset mix.

ii)   *Active Risk*
        The active risk that the fund, because of poor investment decision making, performs poorly against the selected benchmark. Active risk is the increased risk over benchmark risk taken by trustees in an effort to generate added value – incremental return over benchmark return.

The trustees may employ a range of techniques to control active risk:

- tracking error
- risk budget
- control ranges for asset exposures.

Active risk normally accounts for only a relatively minor proportion of total risk.

DETERMINING INVESTMENT STRATEGY

Our examination of investment strategy highlights the central role played by the trustees:

- The key driver of strategy is the trustees' analysis of the particular requirements of the fund and, critically, of its attitude to risk.
- In defining investment strategy, two considerations are critical:
  - diversification controls risk
  - the higher the expected return, the higher the risk.
- Investment strategy is crystallised in Benchmark Asset Mix, an asset mix which will be appropriate over a wide variety of circumstances. Benchmark Asset Mix may be determined by matching fund requirements to asset characteristics or by employing an Asset Liability Model.
- An added-value objective may be set by actively seeking higher than benchmark return. Alternatively the trustees may decide to passively lock into benchmark return.
- Risk at that point then crystallises into two distinct elements: benchmark risk and portfolio risk. Benchmark risk will account for the bulk of risk.

THE INVESTMENT MANDATE
Designing the Investment Mandate

A key duty of the trustees is the design of the Investment Mandate under which the investment manager will carry out the responsibilities delegated to him/her by the trustees for the day-to-day management of the fund assets.

The Investment Mandate, in effect, sets out the 'riding instructions' issued by the trustees to the investment manager. It will typically include:

- investment objective, specifying value added target, if any
- the selected benchmark
- investment manager's discretion
    - the risk limits (i.e. risk budget)
    - the exposures
    - the instruments
- control procedure
    - risk limits
    - tracking error
    - exposure limits and constraints
- reporting and performance measurement standards.

The Investment Mandate has three purposes:

- It interprets for the manager the trustees' requirements and objectives.
- It defines for the manager, quantitatively, the expectations of the trustees in respect of risk and return.
- It explicitly establishes the operational parameters within which the manager will operate.

Mandate Design: The Critical Question

The critical question to be addressed by trustees in mandate design is whether or not they wish to generate 'Added Value', i.e. excess return over benchmark return. Inevitably the search for added value involves 'active risk', i.e. incremental risk over benchmark risk.

A passive investment strategy sets out to replicate benchmark returns, i.e. to generate benchmark returns whilst tightly constraining risk to benchmark risk.

An active investment strategy sets out to generate added value, excess return over benchmark return, while accepting some measure of active risk, incremental risk over benchmark risk.

Investment Constraints

In managing the inevitable trade-off between 'added value' and 'active risk' or incremental return (over benchmark return) and incremental risk (over benchmark risk) the trustees will clearly require to control the investment manager's risk exposures. This will be set out in the Investment Mandate by way of one of the following:

- *Control Parameters or Ranges*
  These specify maximum and minimum exposures to the various asset types, e.g. equity exposure might be permitted to range from 50% to 70% of total assets while within the overall equity exposure, Eurozone equity content might range from 20% to 25%.

- *Tracking Error*
  This quantifies the limit of incremental risk over benchmark risk allowed to the investment manager. For example, the investment manager might be permitted a tracking error of 3%, signifying that the funds return may deviate from benchmark return by +/– 3%. If the benchmark generates a return of 10%, the fund's expected return will be in the range 7% to 13%.

- *Risk Budget*
  The risk budget restates tracking error as an absolute quantum of incremental risk permitted to the investment manager in the search for added value. In the example above, tracking error of ± 3% is restated as a risk budget of 300 basis points. The investment manager then allocates the risk budget over the various assets types. This permits the investment manager to closely track some markets where, perhaps, potential for added value is low, thus releasing risk budget for markets where potential for added value is high.

In addition to the quantitative constraints on risk discussed above, the trustees may place additional constraints on the investment manager's discretion. These might include:

- limits on the proportion of the fund that may be invested in a single stock or in the combined issues of a single entity;
- limits on the proportion of an issue that may be owned by the fund;
- limits on exposures to derivatives;
- limits on exposures to overseas currencies and investments;
- limits on borrowings.

The Investment Mandate will also set out the trustees' requirements for high standards of corporate governance both by the investment manager itself, e.g. in avoiding conflicts of interest, and in the investment manager's discharge of its duties as the representative of the trustees as shareholders in investee companies, e.g. in the exercise of voting rights on company resolutions, in the appointment and remuneration of directors, and generally in protecting the interests of the fund as shareholder.

PENSION FUNDS IN CRISIS POST-FINANCIAL CRASH

We saw earlier how the allocation to equities (and to a lesser extent property) of Irish pension funds rose steadily from the late 1980s and throughout the 1990s. In the 2000s, up to 2007, despite the technology boom and bust, Irish pension funds maintained their very high equity exposures. Even in the period from 2003 to 2007, when equity values were rising, the solvency position of defined benefit pension schemes was under pressure due to falling bond yields and rising longevity. The market collapse of 2008, combined with further declines in bond yields, pushed much of the Irish defined benefit pension fund industry into insolvency. As a result, decisions regarding asset allocation have become heavily influenced by regulatory requirements. Below we detail these and their impact on the management of Irish pension funds.

Valuing Defined Benefit Pension Schemes

Depending on the context and objective a pension scheme may be valued on one of three bases:

- Ongoing Valuation: In normal circumstances this is the key measurement. The purpose of this measure is to compare the value of accrued liabilities with the value of scheme assets, and to recommend a contribution rate that will be sufficient over the long term to fund the benefits promised. The scheme actuary has considerable discretion in the ongoing valuation basis with regard to many of the assumptions made. However, the Society of Actuaries has laid down detailed guidelines regarding many of these assumptions.

- Minimum Funding Standard (MFS): The purpose of this method is to assess whether the scheme has enough assets to meet its liabilities on wind-up. An MFS assessment is required every year. The trustees' annual report must include an actuarial statement from the actuary stating his or her opinion regarding the MFS solvency. Where a scheme does not meet the MFS, a funding proposal has to be made to the Pensions Board.

- FRS17: The purpose of this method is to compare the value of accrued liabilities with the scheme assets on a standardised basis. A key assumption is that assets will be invested indefinitely to provide a return equal to that of AA corporate bonds.

Regulatory Requirements

An actuarial funding certificate (AFC) is required at least every three years. It includes the value of the assets, the value of the liabilities, and the percentage funding level.

If a scheme does not meet its minimum funding standard, a funding proposal must be submitted to the Pensions Board. The funding proposal is required to project forward the future MFS position. It will be affected by many variables including investment strategy, benefit changes, declining membership if the scheme is closed, and strain from retiring members. A funding proposal must be jointly agreed by the employer, trustees and actuary. A funding proposal of up to three years' duration can be simply submitted to the Pensions Board. A funding proposal of more than three years' duration must be submitted to the Pensions Board for its approval. Where a proposal is for a very long period (more than ten years) and/or where it involves a reduction on accrued benefits (commonly referred to as a Section 50 proposal), then such a proposal must involve 'de-risking'. This is normally interpreted as allocating a very high proportion of the assets, often 100%, to bonds.

SUMMARY

- Under defined benefit schemes, contributions are paid into a common pooled fund. Promised benefits are underwritten by the employer, who thus takes the investment risk.
- Under defined contribution schemes each member has a separately identifiable fund. There is no employer guarantee. The member takes the investment risk.
- Pension funds are governed by their trust deeds, trust law and specific legislation which requires funds to meet a Funding Standard.
- The trustees are responsible for 'the proper investment of the resources of the scheme'.
- The key risk for a pension fund is that the value of its assets over time might fail to keep pace with the value of its liabilities.
- The pension fund will have investment return objectives
  - in the short term, of meeting the requirements of the Funding Standard;
  - in the medium term, of generating returns which match or exceed customised or peer-group benchmarks;
  - in the long term, of generating a real rate of return over inflation.
- In determining the appropriate asset mix the trustees may informally, or formally using Asset/Liability Modelling, match the fund's requirements against the characteristics of the investment assets.

- Investment strategy is crystallised into a benchmark asset mix. Benchmark risk is the risk that the benchmark selected will not reflect the value of liabilities over time.
- The trustees may decide to generate added value over benchmark return. This exposes the fund to active risk.
- Active risk is incremental risk over benchmark risk taken on by the fund in the search for added value, incremental return over benchmark return.

QUESTIONS

Case Study Exercise 1

Alan Hughes has recently left his position at a multinational company to set up his own business. He has a defined contribution plan with his old employer (current market value €200,000). The asset mix is 85% in a global equity fund and 15% in a global bond fund. Both are actively managed. Annual management charges, including administration charges, amount to 1.5%. The adviser to the company estimates that this mix will deliver an annual long-term return of 8% net of charges.

Alan's independent financial adviser is recommending a passively managed consensus fund with the following mix:

Global equities	70%
Global bonds	24%
European property	6%

The all-in annual management charge is 0.75%. Alan's adviser estimates an annual long-term return of 6% after charges. She recommends that future contributions, planned to be €15,000 per annum from an estimated gross income of €100,000, should be invested in the new fund, and that the assets from the existing fund should also be transferred in (this can be achieved at nil cost).

1. **Set out the issues that Alan should take into account in deciding which of these two approaches to take with respect to the future management of his fund.**
2. **What is your assessment of the return expectations for each fund? Are they realistic?**
3. **On reflection Alan feels that, because his business venture is high risk, he wishes to lower the risk with his pension fund. Select a lower risk strategy for Alan and outline the long-term expected return from this strategy. Compared with the current mix of Alan's pension fund, explain why your recommended strategy will deliver a lower risk outcome.**

➡

Case Study Exercise 2

Company B is a long-established company in a sector that is declining. The average age of its 200 employees is 55 years, and there are currently 50 pensioners. The company operates a defined benefit scheme, which at December 2007 had no solvency issues. At that date the fund was valued at €110 million. In 2007 member contributions were equal to pension outgoings. Net contributions are budgeted to turn negative from the current year onwards and to have reached (€750,000) in three years. The mix of the fund at end-December was:

Irish equities	10%
International equities	55%
European property	5%
Government bonds	25%
Cash	5%

The board of the company has decided that it cannot live with the volatility inherent in the current mix, and has asked the trustees to present it with a proposal that reduces the volatility of the fund.

1. **Set out the issues that the trustees need to take into account in formulating their proposal.**
2. **If you were appointed as the consultant to this fund, what preferred solution would you offer the trustees?**

Chapter twelve

Fund Management

This chapter examines the fund management industry, its scope, recent development, role and organisational structure. The key elements of investment management firms are introduced – philosophy, process, people and performance – and investment styles and skill sets are explored. The industry's investment decision-making processes and risk-control framework are outlined.

Learning Objectives

After reading this chapter you will be able to:

- Outline the scope, recent development, role and organisation of the Irish fund management industry and discuss the challenges facing it
- Define and assess the key elements of fund management firms – philosophy, process, people and performance
- Distinguish between the various investment styles adopted by investment managers and the skill sets required to support them
- Recognise the essential difference between passive and active fund management
- Understand the different philosophies and focuses of value and growth managers
- Outline the steps in investment decision making, from analysis of client requirements to selecting individual stocks
- Review the risk-control framework normally put in place by industry participants.

THE FUND MANAGEMENT INDUSTRY

Total assets managed by the world's largest 500 fund managers grew to an estimated $62 trillion at the end of 2009, according to a Towers Watson survey. The survey also revealed that the top 20 managers' share of the total assets increased from 38.3% to 40.2%. Of the top 20 managers, 10 were bank owned, 3 were owned by insurers and 7 were independent asset managers.

Key players in the industry range at one extreme from the investment management activities of major global financial conglomerates such as UBS and Allianz Group, through the dominant managers of passive and active portfolios, such as Blackrock and State Street Global Advisors, and the large privately owned specialist fund managers such as Fidelity Investments and Capital Group, to relatively small independent specialist asset management firms at the other end of the spectrum.

In the alternative asset space, a Deutsche Bank survey estimated total global hedge fund assets of approximately $2 trillion. Funds of funds accounted for 55% of these assets.

The industry's clients include sovereign governments, pension funds, the family trusts of the wealthy, charities, corporates and private individuals. Monies managed on behalf of private individuals range from extremely large sums managed in dedicated portfolios for the mega-wealthy to quite modest amounts accumulated in a pooled fashion through collectivised investment (or savings) vehicles – mutual funds, unit trusts and life assurance policies.

The Irish fund management industry in December 2009 managed over €248bn of assets, of which €91bn was on behalf of Irish clients, according to a survey by the *Irish Association of Investment Managers*.

In the aftermath of the financial crash and the Irish banking collapse, the ownership structure of the Irish fund management industry changed radically. Irish Life Investment Managers is now by far the largest manager after its acquisition of AIBIM. Much of the industry now consists of subdivisions or branches of global insurance companies, such as Zurich or AXA, and investment management companies, such as State Street Global Advisors.

The distribution of Irish resident assets at 31 December 2009 was as follows:

Table 12.1 Assets Under Management: 31 December 2009

	%		%
Equities	48.5	Ireland	21.21
Fixed Income	31.1	Euro ex Ireland	43.41
Property	5.3	Non-euro	35.5
Cash	13.2		
Other	1.9		
	100		100

Source: AUM 2008–2009, IAIM.

An analysis of Irish residents' assets by type shows that pension funds accounted for 58.6% of the total, with life assurance company funds accounting for 26.4%.

Table 12.2 Assets of Irish Residents: 31 December 2009

Pensions	58.6%
Charities/Religious	2.3%
Life Funds	26.4%
Private Clients	2.6%
Other*	10.1%
	100

* primarily General Insurance, Corporates and Building Societies

Source: Irish Association of Investment Managers.

The Irish industry enjoyed an enormously favourable operating environment for much of the 1980s and 1990s, and up to 2007. Assets under management, the basis upon which fees are charged, benefited from strong investment returns, particularly in Ireland, during this period. The economic boom of the Celtic Tiger years, apart altogether from its impact on asset valuations, benefited the industry in two ways. Numbers in employment, and therefore in pension schemes, increased steadily and high levels of wealth creation expanded the opportunity to market investment products and services.

In recent years the operating environment has become substantially more challenging. First, there has been a significant shift of client funds from active management to lower-margin, passive management. Second, an ongoing switch from balanced mandates to specialist mandates has presented an opportunity to the major international players to win the business of Irish pension fund clients. The relatively poor market conditions, which have prevailed since the peak of the technology bubble in 2000 and were exacerbated by the 2008 crash, have curtailed the underlying growth in assets under management. Finally, the catastrophic banking crisis and sharp contraction in Irish GDP from 2009 created a harsh business environment for Irish industry for the decade beginning in 2010.

Development

The modern investment management industry developed in response to the crisis presented by the high-inflation 1970s, when investment returns were extremely poor and the industry's clients deeply dissatisfied. The industry was obliged to embrace higher standards of professionalism, sophistication and, importantly, risk management and control. Change was accelerated by the implementation of ERISA 1974 (the Employment Retirement Income Security Act 1974) in the US. ERISA refined the duties of pension fund trustees, obliging them to act not just as 'prudent men' but as 'prudent experts'. Trustees, in turn, required greater expertise of their investment managers.

In the 1980s and subsequently, the industry developed a wider and more sophisticated product range designed to deliver differentiated investment solutions appropriate to client requirements and within required risk tolerances.

The exceptional investment returns generated by markets during the disinflationary period from 1982 to 1999 boosted assets under management and these were further augmented by large inflows of new money as demographic factors shifted in the industry's favour, notably as the post-war 'baby boom' generation entered the savings phase of its lifespan. It is likely that these trends peaked in 2007 and a long period of lower returns and slower growth seems in prospect for developed economies. However, fund management firms with a global reach should benefit from rapid growth in the world's emerging economies.

Role and Organisation Structure

The role of the investment manager is to accept, safeguard, protect and invest client assets and all rights attaching thereto, to generate required returns on the assets within appropriate risk parameters, to account and report on its activities and actions, and to repay monies to the client as required.

Organisational structures vary from investment manager to investment manager, depending on the historical development of the business, its size and organisation culture. Common functions will include:

Function	Activities
Fund Management	Investment Decision Making: – strategic – tactical Portfolio Construction Transactions Treasury – deposits – foreign exchange
Research	Fundamental Economic and Company Research Stock Screening
Marketing	Marketing Strategy Business and Product Development Client Liaison

Function	Activities
Investment Accounting	Settlements Safekeeping and Custody Client Accounting Valuation and Reporting Tax Reclaims
Performance Measurement	Measurement of Risk and Return
Business Management	Strategic and Operational Management
Financial Accounting	Corporate Budgeting and Accounting Internal Audit
Compliance	Regulatory Reporting Development and Monitoring of Internal Compliance
Information Systems	Systems Development and Maintenance

Each of these activities is important in its own right. However, from the client's perspective the key differentiator in selecting an investment manager is that manager's ability to generate superior investment returns, i.e. the fund management function.

In assessing the investment organisation's fund management capability the client will focus particularly on:

i)   Investment Philosophy
     For active investment managers, investment philosophy identifies where value is available in markets and demonstrates how this insight may be applied in generating superior investment returns.
     For passive investment managers, investment philosophy is defined in the belief that the pursuit of added value is futile and that, therefore, the focus of investment management should be on the replication of market out-turns.

ii) Investment Process
     Investment process refers to the methodology whereby the investment firm's philosophy is implemented in a consistent, disciplined and systematic manner in the construction of portfolios that are designed to deliver repeatable added value.

iii)   People and Resources

The fund management activity should be staffed and led by high-quality, experienced and committed investment professionals who have the support of an effective technology platform, e.g. information systems, databases, screening tools, etc.

iv)   Performance

Investment performance should support the investment manager's claims for the effectiveness of its philosophy, process, people and resources. Historical performance should be examined to test and understand:

- Its consistency
  - with the manager's philosophy
  - with the manager's investment style.
- Its recurring nature
  - was added value generated in a consistent smooth manner or was it attributable to a small number of 'lumpy' periods of out-performance?
- Its riskiness
  - how much risk was taken in generating the returns (i.e. what tracking error?)
  - what information ratio was achieved? (i.e. the ratio of added value to tracking error).

Historical performance is not necessarily a good guide to future outcomes.

The key question is whether the outperformance achieved in the past is repeatable. Is there present in the philosophy, process, people and resources an investment engine that will consistently generate superior returns in the future?

Investment Style

An investment manager's style is defined by the investment philosophy and process that determine the manager's approach to stock selection and portfolio construction.

Active and Passive Investment

The Efficient Market Theory argues that:

- markets are efficient;
- markets do a good job in reflecting information in prices;
- adding value over market returns is not easy;
- forecasting market out-turns is difficult.

Subscribers to this theory believe that assets are fairly priced by the market and that the search for added value is futile. Investors, therefore, should adopt a passive approach to investing by seeking only to replicate market returns.

The passive investor therefore sets out to replicate market or benchmark out-turns, i.e. to construct portfolios that track, as closely as is practicable, the risk and return outcomes of the market or benchmark.

The key skills employed by the passive investment manager include:

- in-depth understanding of benchmarks and of market indices;
- portfolio construction skill to replicate the benchmark and minimise tracking error;
- efficient management of cash flows;
- timely and accurate implementation of corporate events
    - mergers and acquisitions
    - secondary and scrip issues
    - share buy-backs;
- effective management of transaction costs.

Active investors, however, reject market efficiency, believing that pricing anomalies exist in the market and that, with skill and expertise, value may be generated above market returns. Of course, the active investor acknowledges that added value (additional return over market or benchmark return) cannot be accessed without incurring active or incremental risk (additional risk over market or benchmark risk). The actively managed portfolio will have higher volatility than the market or benchmark, i.e. the tracking error of the active portfolio will be higher than that of the passive portfolio. The ratio of added value to tracking error is known as the information ratio.

The key skills employed by the active manager include:

- effective data management and information collection;
- screening skill to permit a focus on key data;
- research skills;
- portfolio construction skills;
- efficient transaction management;
- risk management.

Active management requires the creation of an investment management infrastructure, people and systems to build a database, design screens, research opportunities, construct portfolios and trade in markets. By comparison with passive investing, active management is a high-cost activity. Active investment management fees, therefore, are higher than passive fees.

Successful active management has the potential to generate returns that more than compensate for the extra fees involved.

Active returns are uncertain both in absolute terms and relative to the market or benchmark. Passive returns are also unpredictable in absolute terms, but they are predictable relative to the market or benchmark.

The development of passive investment has thrown the burden of proof firmly onto the active manager. On the one hand, the active manager must persuade the client that the manager possesses a particular insight that offers the potential for repeatable added value at a cost, both in terms of fees and incremental risk, that is acceptable to the client.

On the other hand, the client in employing an active manager makes two critical judgments:

i)   that markets are inefficient;
ii)   that the client has the ability to identify a manager who will success-fully add value in the future.

Market efficiency, and thus passive investment, relies on the active investor. If everybody believed that all publicly available information is already reflected in market prices, then nobody would do any fundamental research and the market would be denied the information it relies on to create efficiency.

The passive and active investment styles may be combined in a 'core/satellite' approach to investment. The larger 'core' portfolio is managed passively, designed to deliver returns which closely replicate benchmark outturns, i.e. it is managed with low tracking error against the benchmark. The smaller 'satellite' portfolio is actively managed, designed to generate added value over benchmark returns. The active satellite may be permitted to exhibit a relatively wide divergence from benchmark returns, i.e. to be managed with high tracking error.

The relatively low tracking error of the 'core' portfolio when combined with the relatively high tracking error of the 'satellite' portfolio results in the overall tracking error of the total portfolio being maintained within prescribed limits.

A key attraction of the core/satellite approach is that a successful active manager may be able to exploit this wide discretion to generate substantial added value.

Balanced and Specialist Investment

A balanced investment manager manages a total fund or a cross-section thereof. The balanced manager makes decisions across the full range of asset and decision levels, determining asset mix, currency mix, country mix and sector and stock allocations.

The specialist investment manager focuses on a particular decision-making level, e.g. emerging market equities or US equities. The specialist manager therefore typically manages only a portion of the total fund.

As discussed above, the recent trend in Ireland has been towards specialist managers and away from balanced managers, partly driven by a shift from peer-group to customised benchmarks.

The move to specialist mandates involves the client more intensively in the investment process. Whereas with balanced mandates the investment manager appointed determines the portfolio mix at each decision level (e.g. asset mix, country allocation, etc.), with specialist managers the client must first decide the proportion of the total fund to be allocated to each specialist mandate.

Top-Down and Bottom-Up Investment

The top-down investment manager employs his global macro-economic and cyclical overview to inform decision making in sequence at the asset allocation, currency, country, sector and stock selection decision levels.

For example, a top-down investment manager might conclude, given his overall global macro-economic view:

- that equities are the asset of choice;
- that within global equities, preference is for US equities because, perhaps, the US economy is most advanced on the path to recovery;
- within US equities, because of the particular stage of the US economic cycle, that retailers are an attractive sector;
- and within retailers, preference might be for Wal-Mart.

In direct contrast, the bottom-up manager focuses, in the first instance, on stock selection. The stock selection process in turn drives sector, country, currency and asset allocations, i.e. they are an outcome of the stock selection process.

In effect, the top-down manager is drilling downwards from his global macro-economic overview to stock selection. The bottom-up manager, though, believes that his fundamental analysis gives him a more tangible sense of value at the stock level. Stock selection drives the other decisions.

In practice, both approaches are normally implemented in a risk-controlled manner to ensure that portfolios are appropriately diversified and in compliance with mandated risk tolerances. Both top-down and bottom-up managers might conclude, from their different perspectives, that only bank stocks and oil stocks are attractive.

However, prudent portfolio construction would not permit portfolios to be comprised only of bank and oil stocks. Appropriate diversification would be built in to ensure that the portfolio exhibited and maintained the required tracking error against its benchmark.

Growth and Value Investment

The growth and value styles of investment refer to approaches to active equity investment.

The growth manager is growth-oriented and focuses on companies with relatively high growth in projected earnings. The growth manager believes that market valuations do not fully reflect the expected growth in earnings per share of growth companies. When the growth companies deliver this growth, their share prices will be adjusted upwards and will outperform the general market. In essence, the growth manager believes that growth companies are underpriced by the markets. In his/her analysis of candidate companies for inclusion in portfolios, the growth manager focuses on growth in earnings, dividends, cash flows, book values and sales.

The focus of the value manager is on stocks that are low rated relative to the market as a whole, i.e. where the price earnings ratio and price-to-book ratio are lower and the dividend yield is higher than the market average. The value manager believes that over time stock market valuations have a 'reversion to mean' tendency, i.e. that over time highly rated stocks are pulled down to average ratings, while low-valued stocks are pulled up to average ratings. In terms of valuation metrics, the focus of the active manager is on price earnings ratios, price to cash flow ratios, dividend yields and price-to-book ratios relative to the market average. Value investment rests on the belief that where stock prices fall below what might be regarded as their long-term mean or normal valuation, catalysts will emerge, whether it be shareholder pressure for change, management change or strategic change (such as disposal of non-core activities), which will drive the stocks back to normal values. The research effort of the value manager is thus devoted to the identification of these catalysts within companies.

Figure 12.1 Value Investing

Again, as with the top-down and bottom-up approaches, the construction of growth and value portfolios is typically implemented within a risk-controlled framework. Portfolios are unlikely to be comprised solely of value or growth stocks, but rather will exhibit a bias to the managers' styles.

INVESTMENT DECISION MAKING

Overview

The following chart presents an overview of the investment decision-making process.

Figure 12.2 Overview of the Investment Decision-Making Process

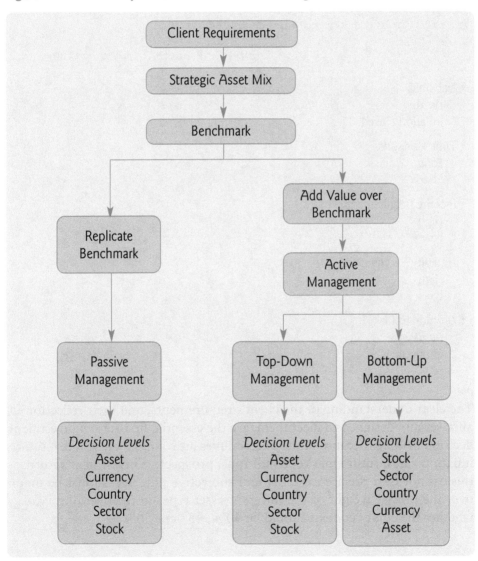

Analysis of Client Requirements

The first step in investment decision making is the analysis of client requirements. In particular the client's time horizons, short- and long-term return objectives, need for income, need for liquidity, and exposure to tax and regulatory issues are identified. A key ingredient in the analysis is the client's attitude to risk.

The process, while recognising that there is no single ideal asset, attempts to match the requirements of the client against the characteristics of the different asset classes. In Chapter 11 an asset/liability grid was illustrated to support the process for matching a pension fund's requirements against asset characteristics. Figure 12.3 adapts this idea for clients generally.

Figure 12.3 Client Requirements/Asset Characteristics Grid

	Equities	Property	Bonds	Cash
• Liabilities				
Fixed			x	
Inflation Linked	x	x		
• Time Horizons				
Long	x	x		
Short			x	x
• Income Requirement				
High		x	x	
Low	x			x
• Liquidity Requirement				
High	x		x	x
Low		x		
• Attitude to Risk				
Aggressive	x	x		
Cautious			x	x

The clear understanding of the client's requirements, and their reflection in an asset mix designed to meet them, are the essential first step in investment decision making. Because of the uncertainties attaching to the future – future inflation rates, future market conditions, prospective investment returns – this cannot be a precise exercise, and subjective judgments must be made over the precise weight of the different asset types in the overall mix, e.g. whether the equity content should be 40%, 45% or 50%.

Managed funds are a popular choice of investment vehicle for many investors, both retail and institutional. However, the investment strategy adapted varies enormously from one fund to another. Funds are typically categorised according to their risk level, with the prime determinant being the target equity weighting. Table 12.3 summarises the typical equity weighting ranges of the three common categories of managed funds.

Table 12.3 Representative Managed Fund Equity Weightings

	Cautious	Balanced	Aggressive
Equity Weighting Range	20% to 50%	50% to 75%	65% to 90%

However, these mixes are currently the subject of some controversy, because of the impact of two severe equity bear markets over the past decade. Some observers are concerned that the equity content of the balanced and aggressive mixes above overstates the risk appetite of the typical investor in these categories. In the UK, regulations are being tightened and made more specific with regard to the use of terms such as 'cautious' and 'balanced' when describing risk characteristics of funds in marketing and other literature.

Strategic Asset Mix and Benchmark

As discussed in Chapter 11, the Investment Mandate agreed between the client and the investment manager is a key document, which interprets client requirements, quantifies client expectations and establishes the operational parameters within which the manager will operate.

The Investment Mandate will define the long-term strategic asset mix best designed to deliver client expectations. This strategic asset mix sets out the normal, or central, asset mix and it is embedded in the client's benchmark.

The benchmark asset mix is the ideal portfolio mix which, if maintained over the life of the fund, will deliver the risk and return outcomes required by the client.

Replicating Benchmark Out-turns: Passive Management

When the client requirement is to replicate benchmark out-turns passive management offers a relatively low-cost solution. The benchmark, as discussed in Chapter 11, may be either a customised or peer-group benchmark. In approaching the various decision levels the passive manager must decide as follows, depending on the Investment Mandate:

Table 12.4 Passive Management: Decision-Making Alternatives

Asset Level	Bonds v Equities v Property v Cash	Peer Group or Customised
Currency Level	US v Euro v Stg£ v Yen	Peer Group or Customised
Country Level	US v Europe v UK v Japan	Peer Group or Customised or Indexed
Sector Level	Bonds: Short v Medium v Long Dated	Indexed
	Equities: Consumer v Financial v Resources	Indexed
	Property: Office v Retail v Industrial	Indexed
Stock Level	Stock Selection	Indexed

At the asset level, the mix decision is determined by the benchmark. A customised benchmark specifies the precise asset mix to be maintained. A peer-group benchmark requires the manager to replicate in the asset mix the consensus or average asset mix of the specified peer group.

At the currency level a similar approach is followed, although here there is the complication that the peer-group currency mix may not be readily available and therefore may need to be estimated. The currency mix to be maintained will be specified in the customised benchmark.

At the country level, a third possibility presents itself. Besides matching the peer-group or customised benchmark's country mixes, there is the option of matching the country mix within an appropriate index, e.g. the MSCI World Index for the equity content.

The sectoral mix of the peer group's investment portfolio is normally not available. The customised benchmark normally refers to the sectoral mixes of some appropriate indices that the passive manager will then replicate in the client portfolio. Typically, therefore, whether the benchmark follows the customised or peer-group model an indexed mix is applied at the sectoral level.

Finally, at the stock level the passive manager will normally be expected to replicate an appropriate or pre-specified index or indices. However, because of the unique nature of property investment there cannot be an available index at the stock selection level. Selection of individual properties, therefore, is always an active process.

Generating Added Value: Active Management

The role of the active manager is to generate added value over and above benchmark returns. The active manager makes active decisions at each of the decision levels. These active decisions move the portfolio away from the mixes embedded in the benchmark.

Therefore the portfolio, once it has deviated from benchmark mix, no longer replicates benchmark risk and return outcomes. Added value is the excess of the portfolio return over benchmark return. Incremental risk measures the difference between portfolio risk and benchmark risk. The information ratio, which measures the effectiveness of the manager, is the ratio of added value to incremental risk.

The degree of deviation from benchmark mix permitted to the investment manager will be set out in the client's investment mandate and will be quantified by tracking error, the extent to which the volatility of the portfolio is permitted to deviate from benchmark volatility.

The extent to which the investment manager will exercise the discretion allowed will be determined by the strength of the manager's convictions in his investment insights. The client, having permitted the manager to take higher risk in the search for higher return, is entitled to expect that the manager will, except in unusual conditions, normally exercise that discretion.

Active Management: The Top-Down Approach

As discussed above, the investment decision making of the top-down active manager is informed by his global macro-economic overview. This global overview drives decision making, in sequence, at the asset, currency, country, sector and stock levels.

The methodology followed by individual investment firms is outlined in their investment process and will vary from firm to firm. No firm has a monopoly of wisdom. Unique insights are rare.

A brief discussion of some of the approaches used at each decision level is set out below.

Top-Down Decision Making: The Asset Level

Cyclical Approach

The economic and investment cycles are examined and the relative attractions of the different asset classes identified.

Risk Premiums Approach

The relative attractions of the different assets are determined by comparing prevailing risk premiums to historical patterns.

Scenario Analysis

Risk and return projections are prepared for each asset. These projections are then optimised to produce the required mix.

Top-Down Decision Making: The Currency Level

Among many factors examined in determining the attractions of currencies are:

- relative levels of consumer prices in the different currency blocs;
- relative interest-rate differentials;
- relative projected asset returns;
- capital flows;
- trade flows;
- currency price momentum;
- long-term currency trends.

A key decision, to be embedded in the benchmark, is the required level of exposure to the client's domestic currency. This may be heavily influenced by the currency in which the client's liabilities are denominated. Other factors influencing this decision include the liquidity, depth and breadth of the domestic equity market. On the one hand US investors, whose domestic equity market exhibits these characteristics, traditionally have invested relatively minor proportions of their assets outside the US. Irish investors, on the other hand, because of the relatively small domestic equity market, have for many years invested a relatively large part of their equity portfolios overseas. Irish institutional investors since the beginning of 1999 have reduced their exposure to Irish equities, availing themselves of the opportunity presented by the introduction of the euro to further diversify their portfolios by purchasing euro-denominated equities without incurring currency risk.

Currency markets can be volatile. Currency decision making is complex. In approaching the currency mix decision the investor should emphasise

- clarity of strategic approach;
- consistency of implementation;
- strict control and risk management.

Top-Down Decision Making: The Country Level

Since the advent of the euro there is a trend amongst Irish managers to treat Europe on a euro- (e.g. France, Germany) or non-euro basis (e.g. the United Kingdom, Switzerland), rather than on a country basis.

In assessing the relative attractions of a region or country the investment manager will review:

- relative long-term economic prospects;
- relative short-term cyclical prospects;
- relative investment cycles;
- relative valuations
  - by comparison with the different regions or countries
  - by comparison with the domestic historical pattern.

The country selection decision is complicated not only by the difficulties of forecasting economic and market outcomes, but also by political and cultural differences among the various countries. Technical complications also arise on account of differences in accounting standards and variations in index composition.

Top-Down Decision Making: The Sector Level

Bonds

Bonds may be categorised by issuer (e.g. government or corporate), maturity (e.g. long-dated, medium-dated, short-dated) and by credit rating (e.g. high quality, high yield).

The relative attractions of the different categories of bond may be assessed by examining:

- anticipated cyclical patterns in economies;
- anticipated trends in inflation;
- anticipated trends in interest rates;
- anticipated trends in the yield curve, i.e. the term structure of interest rates;
- the relative attractions of bonds within individual maturity categories;
- anticipated shifts in credit ratings and credit-rating differentials.

Equities

Sector selection for equities may take place at the global, regional or country levels. Up to quite recently sector selection was country-based. The investment manager would compare the attractions of Irish banks against Irish construction companies and against Irish food companies. More recently sector selection is increasingly being approached on a European or global basis.

Methodologies employed in assessing the relative attractions of the different equity sectors include:

- fundamental analysis of the sectors' relative long-term prospects;
- projections of relative sector profitability;
- comparisons of relative valuation;
- examination of relative price momentum.

Property

Commercial property investment sectors may be categorised as office, retail and industrial. Given its fragmented structure, institutional investors rarely invest in residential property, which tends to be the preference of the 'buy-to-let' individual investor.

The examination of the relative attractions of the different sectors includes review of the following factors:

- long-term demographic and employment trends;
- short-term cyclical economic developments;
- relative sectoral valuations;
- supply and demand background within each individual sectoral category.

Top-Down Decision Making: The Stock Level

Investment portfolios, whether directly invested or invested via pooled vehicles, are comprised of individual securities. The implementation of all investment decisions requires action at the stock selection level. Every investor, therefore, has an interest in stock selection and, unsurprisingly, a myriad of approaches to decision making at the stock selection level have been developed. A general introduction to stock selection is outlined below.

Bonds

Having considered the influences on the sectoral selection decision discussed above, the top-down investor in determining the attractiveness of a particular bond will:

- compare one bond against another on the basis of credit rating, yield and sensitivity to projected changes in interest rates and the yield curve;
- compare one bond against the market as a whole on the basis of sensitivity to projected changes in interest rates and the yield curve.

Bond selection in practice ranges from the straightforward comparison of yield spreads (the difference between the yield on one bond and the yield on another) to complex quantitative modelling techniques.

Equities

All investment management firms place particular emphasis on their equity stock selection process. A wide array of different methodologies have been developed, generally based on one or more of the following approaches:

Fundamental Analysis

Fundamental analysis focuses in the first instance on the investee company itself:

- its operations
  - facilities, buildings and plant
  - products, brands, market shares
  - workforce
  - clients and customers
  - competitors
  - sensitivity to cyclical economic development.
- its management
  - development and implementation of strategy
  - operational ability
  - commitment to shareholders.
- its finances
  - generation of sales, profits and earnings growth
  - cash generation
  - dividend-paying capability
  - balance-sheet strength.
- its growth potential
  - prospects for future growth in sales, profits, earnings and dividends.

Secondly, the fundamental investor reviews the company's valuation as measured by its price earnings ratio, price to cash flow ratio, dividend yield and other measures, often by reference to peer-group and market comparisons, to determine the extent to which the company fundamentals are reflected in the share price.

Quantitative Analysis

Whereas the fundamental approach is heavily human-driven, quantitative analysis is computer-based. Financial, accounting and valuation data is collected on the universe of companies followed by the investment manager. Quantitative screens are then applied to this data to identify attractive stocks. The screens applied will vary according to the investment philosophy of the investment manager. Value managers will develop valuation-based screens, e.g. screens based on price earnings ratios, dividend yield, price-to-book ratios and others. Growth managers will develop screens based on measures of growth, e.g. short- and long-term measures of growth in sales, earnings, dividends and asset value.

Technical Analysis

Adherents of technical analysis will analyse and interpret charts of historical price data to forecast future price movements and thus identify attractive stocks. The technical analysis approach to investment rests on the belief that all available data is already reflected in the share price, so that no further fundamental analysis is required.

Property

Individual properties, unlike quoted equities and bonds, are neither continuously traded nor divisible. Large sums of money may be required for investment in an individual property, particularly for a high-quality, well-located commercial property.

For many investors, investment in property is possible only if financed to a large degree by borrowings. Banks are usually prepared to lend money secured against property. However, it is important for the investor to bear in mind that a 'geared property' (i.e. a property with associated borrowings) takes on different characteristics from that property in its ungeared state. The income attractions of property investment are diluted as the rent is offset against interest on borrowings, while the capital stream of return becomes more volatile.

Many investors, including large pension funds, carry out their property investment through pooled vehicles such as property unit trusts, limited partnerships and property syndicates.

Key considerations in property stock selection for those investors who make direct investments include:

- location
- rental yield (current rental yield and equivalent yield)
- rental growth
- risk.

Cash Deposits

In selecting a home for cash at a deposit-taking institution, the investor will take into consideration:

- the interest rate available
- the creditworthiness of the institution.

For investment managers, cash deposits are normally a temporary home for monies awaiting investment in long-term assets. At a certain cyclical point, however, cash can play an important role in investment strategy. It cushions the client portfolio from the impact of falling prices in the long-term assets and provides the wherewithal to purchase assets at lower prices after the fall.

The basic principle of diversification may be applied to cash balances. Cash is normally spread over different deposit-taking institutions and different maturities. Liquidity is a key attraction of cash balances. Investment managers normally maintain ongoing access to cash to permit them to avail of investment opportunities as they arise.

Active Management: The Bottom-Up Approach

As discussed above, the bottom-up manager focuses in the first instance on the stock selection decision level. Decisions taken at the stock selection level determine outcomes at the sector, country, currency and asset levels. In making stock selection decisions the bottom-up manager will be subject to similar considerations and influences as those outlined above for the top-down manager.

The underlying belief of the bottom-up manager is that the prospects for, and valuations of, individual companies can be assessed and predicted with a greater degree of assurance than macro-economic outcomes and their implications for countries, sectors and stocks.

Risk Control

The precise risk control framework operated by an investment management company will vary from firm to firm, depending on the firm's development, its culture, ownership and organisational structures.

Elements of the risk control framework will typically include:

i)   External Audit
      The external auditor, besides making his report to shareholders as required by company law, will also report to the firm's board on the effectiveness of the firm's risk management and risk control systems.

ii)   Internal Audit
      The internal audit function challenges, tests and reports, usually to board level, on the firm-wide risk management and internal control systems.

iii)   Compliance
       The compliance function is charged with ensuring that the firm is in
       strict adherence to regulatory and mandated requirements and to its
       own internal rule-book. The compliance function ensures that appro-
       priate and fully documented processes and procedures are in place.

iv)   Operational Risk
       The operational risk management function develops processes and
       procedures for control and management of operational risk, e.g.
       technological or systems failures, human error or disaster recovery.

v)   Investment Risk
       Typically there are three elements to control of investment risk.

       a) *Portfolio Review*
           Portfolio review subjects all client portfolios to regular monitor-
           ing and review. Portfolio review ensures that portfolios as
           constructed are aligned with the guidelines and limits as detailed
           in the relevant client mandate, for example:

           • tracking error
           • sectoral and stock exposure limits
           • portfolio distribution
           • portfolio concentration.

       A procedure for identifying and rectifying, within prescribed deadlines,
       breaches of mandate will be outlined and implemented.

       b) *Portfolio Construction*
           The first line of defence against investment risk is, of course, at
           the fund manager level. Typically the fund manager will have the
           support of technological systems that will assist in ensuring that
           portfolios are constructed in line with mandated guidelines and
           limits.

       c) *Performance Measurement*
           The performance measurement function provides detailed analysis
           of each client portfolio's risk and return characteristics. Portfolios
           are subjected to attribution analysis, peer comparisons and style
           analysis. Reports are prepared for the fund management team, for
           portfolio review and, usually, for the chief investment officer or
           investment committee.

The Efficient Market Hypothesis (EMH) and Trends in Fund Management

The Efficient Market Hypothesis (EMH)

Despite its name, the EMH is a completely different concept from Markowitz's concept of efficient portfolios and the efficient frontier. The EMH is concerned with the operation of the financial markets, and in particular with how good markets are at absorbing information into the prices of financial assets. An efficient market may be defined as one in which the prices of all securities quickly and fully reflect all available information. In an efficient market, all securities offer an expected return consistent with the level of risk. It is therefore impossible for investors to make abnormal returns in an efficient market. The current price of a financial security reflects:

- All known information, both current and past.
- Information that can be reasonably inferred. For example, if many investors believe that the European Central Bank is going to raise interest rates at its next meeting, then this will be reflected in current prices.

Market efficiency requires that the adjustment to new information occurs very quickly. It is really an empirical question as to whether a particular market is efficient or not. It is quite easy to conclude that the market for, say, the hundred largest publicly quoted global companies is more efficient than the market for mid-capitalisation Irish quoted companies.

The EMH is usually categorised into three 'forms':

- Weak Form: Historical price data should already be reflected in current prices and should be of no value in predicting future price change.
- Semi-Strong Form: Current prices reflect the historical data plus all publicly known current data. This includes data on earnings, new product developments, financing difficulties, accounting changes, etc. In a semi-strong efficient market investors cannot act on new public information after its announcement and expect to earn above-average risk-adjusted returns.
- Strong Form: This asserts that current prices reflect all information, both public and non-public. If the market is strong-form efficient, then no group of investors should be able to earn, over a reasonable period of time, abnormal rates of return by using information in a superior manner.

Since the 2008 financial crisis many of the fundamental tenets of investment theory and practice have come under microscopic scrutiny. There are probably very few investment practitioners who fully subscribe to the strong form of the EMH. Nevertheless, it is fair to say that most practitioners take the view that all of the larger markets are reasonably efficient, and indeed that many smaller markets with good technology and trading systems are also quite efficient. The economic and financial meltdown of 2008 has shaken many people's belief in the proper functioning of financial markets. Some trends that were evident before the crash are likely to persist, such as the search for better diversification. Other trends, such as the long-run shift towards passive management, could well pause and may even reverse.

Adoption of Broader Asset Allocation Strategies

The globalisation theme has been a dominant theme since as early as the 1980s. Freer capital flows and the integration of trading systems offer investors a growing array of investment choice. However, by the 2000s studies began to show that many markets were becoming more closely correlated. This created a drive to find alternative assets that were uncorrelated (or lowly correlated) with the traditional asset classes. By the time of the 2008 financial crash many investors had increased their allocations to alternative asset classes such as commodities and hedge funds. However, during the crash all risk assets fell sharply and many investors were disappointed with the outcomes of these more diversified strategies. Despite this apparent setback, the trend towards extending asset mixes beyond the traditional asset classes into alternatives remains strongly entrenched.

Active and Passive Management

From the 1980s the passive approach to fund management steadily increased its share of global funds under management. The 2008 financial crash has probably led to a pause in further gains for passive management as academics, investment analysts and investors reassess the nature and extent of market efficiency. In the short to medium term the seismic scale of the market dislocation caused by the 2008 financial panic will continue to create more opportunities for active managers. It is impossible to predict the longer-term implications. However, it may well be the case that the balance of advantage will shift back towards the active approach to fund management over the 2010s.

SUMMARY

- The implementation of ERISA 1974 raised the hurdle of investment expertise for pension fund trustees, and in turn, for investment managers.
- The role of the investment manager is to accept, safeguard, protect and invest client monies and to generate the required returns within appropriate risk parameters.
- The key elements to be addressed in assessing the capability of the investment manager are philosophy, process, people (and resources) and performance.
- Investment style refers to the philosophy and process which inform the investment manager's approach to stock selection and portfolio construction.
- Passive managers set out to replicate benchmark returns. Active managers attempt to add value over benchmark returns.
- In employing an active manager the client makes two judgments:
  - that markets are inefficient;
  - that the client can identify successful active managers.
- The passive and active approaches may be combined in a core/satellite approach.
- The top-down manager uses his global macro-economic view to inform decision making, first at the asset level and thereafter, in turn, at the currency, country, sector and stock selection levels. The bottom-up manager focuses on the stock selection level. In practice, portfolios are constructed in a risk-controlled fashion.
- Growth managers focus on measures of growth, in earnings per share, cash flows, asset values. Value managers are focused on measures of valuation.
- Understanding client requirements is the first step in the investment process and from this flow strategic asset mix, benchmark selection and added-value objectives.
- At each decision level – asset, currency, country, sector, stock – the active manager may make decisions which move the portfolio away from the benchmark.
- Added value is the excess return of the portfolio over benchmark return. Active or incremental risk is the difference between portfolio risk and benchmark risk. The information ratio, the ratio of added value to incremental risk, measures the effectiveness of the investment manager.
- The risk control framework, typically will include external audit, internal audit, the compliance function, operational risk management and investment risk management.

QUESTIONS

1. **Which of the following statements is TRUE?**

   A. Proponents of the EMH (Efficient Market Hypothesis) typically advocate an active investment strategy.

   B. Proponents of the EMH believe that only detailed fundamental analysis has the potential to generate returns above market returns.

   C. Proponents of the EMH believe that markets offer ample scope for identifying pricing anomalies.

   D. Proponents of the EMH typically advocate a passive investment strategy.

2. **Passive fund management involves the following EXCEPT:**

   A. The replication of market returns.

   B. The ability to minimise the tracking error.

   C. The skill to add value through the application of expertise in stock selection.

   D. The efficient implementation of corporate events.

3. **A key difference between an active and a passive approach to investment is that:**

   A. Active managers target an absolute return while passive managers do not.

   B. Passive management costs tend to be lower than those offered by active managers.

   C. Passive managers have higher tracking errors against a benchmark but have a better record of matching the benchmark.

   D. Passive managers use a qualitative approach whereas active managers may use either a qualitative or a quantitative approach.

4. **Which of the following statements is FALSE?**

   A. A top-down approach to fund management involves taking a global or macro view of asset allocation and country selection.

   B. In the bottom-up approach the starting point involves fundamental analysis of individual companies.

   C. Value investing focuses on stocks with very high price earnings ratios (PERs).

   D. Growth investing involves selecting stocks with potential for high growth in profits.

Chapter thirteen

The Real Economy and the Markets

This chapter identifies the central importance of growth and inflation in determining asset prices and in driving both the real economy and the financial markets. The relevance of the economic cycle in influencing the asset allocation decision is discussed. Periods of speculative excess are examined to isolate their common denominators and to identify the insight that there is a difference between price and value.

Learning Objectives

After reading this chapter you will be able to:

- Recognise the role of future cash flows and inflation in determining asset prices
- Describe the development and phases of the economic and investment cycles
- Describe the relationship, interplay and linkages between the economic and market cycles and identify their common drivers – growth and inflation
- Outline the benefits and limitations of using the economic cycle to inform asset allocation decisions
- Recognise the conditions that give rise to periods of speculative excess in markets
- Understand that there is a difference between price and value.

INTRODUCTION

Investment is a forward-looking activity. In determining the value of an asset the focus of the investor is on the cash flows that the asset will generate in the future. In assessing these flows the investor recognises that:

- In the case of certain assets, the future flows are fixed in nominal monetary terms.
- In the case of other assets, the future flows are variable depending, for example in the case of equities, on underlying company profitability or, in the case of property, on rents.
- That inflation must be taken into account when assessing the present value of these future flows.

In the case of fixed-interest securities, e.g. government or corporate bonds, the future flows are fixed, by definition, in nominal monetary terms. They are guaranteed by the issuer of the bond and their payment dates are known with precision as they are set out in the terms of the bond's issue, the prospectus.

Index-linked securities generate flows that are adjusted upwards to account for the prevailing rate of inflation. Here, although the dates of future payments are known in advance, the nominal monetary values of the flows are not as they are subject to the inflation rate. Flows are guaranteed by the issuer.

Inflation, therefore, has a very different impact on the respective values of fixed-interest and index-linked bonds. When inflation rises, on the one hand the value of fixed-interest securities falls, because the present value of the fixed (in monetary or absolute terms) future flows is eroded by rising inflation. The value of index-linked securities, on the other hand, is protected against rising inflation by the adjustment process, which increases the future flows in monetary terms to compensate the investor for higher inflation.

Future flows from cash deposits vary with the level of short-term interest rates. Clearly, investors will attempt to obtain a rate of interest that is higher than the inflation rate so as to earn a real (i.e. after inflation) return on their deposits. The rate of inflation is an important influence on short-term interest rates, and in the long run investors in cash deposits have received a real return on their monies. Nevertheless, there have been quite extended periods of negative real interest rates, i.e. when the inflation rate exceeded short-term interest rates. Clearly, there is little incentive for investors to place monies on deposit at short-term interest rates that are below the prevailing inflation rate. Here, the real value of the investment is being eroded. It would make more sense for the investor to spend his or her money now.

Future flows from investment in equities and property are intrinsically different from those arising in the bond and deposits markets in that they are not guaranteed by the issuer. Equities and property generate flows that reflect growth in profits and rents, respectively.

The flows arising on an equity investment will vary with the underlying profitability of the company. When profits are strong and rising, flows are likely to increase. Contrarily, weak and falling profitability will result in lower flows.

Similarly, rising rents boost the flows from property investment, while lower rents will result in lower flows.

Equities and property are real assets, i.e. assets that have a linkage to the performance of the economy. Over time corporate profits and property rents will reflect developments in the underlying economy. They will respond to growth in nominal gross domestic product (economic output), i.e. to real growth and inflation. Strong economic growth will drive increases in profits and rents – 'A rising tide lifts all boats.' Further, company management and landlords will attempt to protect the real value of profits and rents, respectively, against rising inflation. For example, in periods of rising inflation company management may protect profits from the higher cost of inputs, e.g. raw materials and labour, by seeking cost efficiencies or by raising product prices.

Clearly, therefore, in so far as the value of their assets is concerned – i.e. the present value of the future flows that those assets will generate – investors are deeply concerned with developments in the underlying economy and in particular with growth and inflation.

THE ECONOMIC CYCLE

The central importance of economic growth and inflation as key influences in the determination of asset valuations was discussed above.

Economic activity tends to be cyclical, marked by successive and recurring phases of expansion and contraction. This cyclical pattern tends to be reflected in the activities of businesses – the business cycle – and in developments in financial markets – the investment cycle.

An Idealised Economic Cycle

Figure 13.1 The Economic Cycle

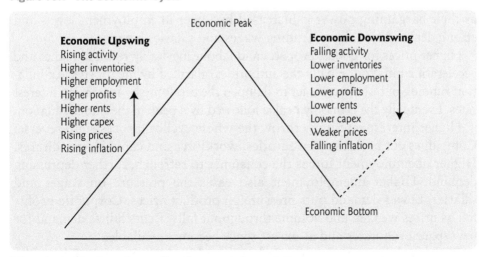

The chart depicts the path of economic activity.

In the opening phase of the cycle (bottom left-hand corner), economic activity is at a low ebb. Business and consumer confidence are low. Profits are under pressure and unemployment is high. Consumer demand and capital investment are weak. Short-term interest rates are in low ground. Earlier falls in interest rates as economic activity softened and demand for money fell have been augmented more recently by cuts in official interest rates, as the authorities attempt to revive the economy. Government expenditure is rising as the authorities compensate for the absence of business and consumer demand. Inflation is low.

Eventually, the economy begins to respond to the new environment of low interest rates and increased government spending. Some companies, encouraged by the availability of cheap money, begin to rebuild their inventory levels, which had been run down during the downturn. They increase their orders to their manufacturing suppliers. When this increased inventory is sold off they further increase their order levels.

Inventories are further rebuilt, production is expanded, workers are rehired. The workers, now back in employment, in turn spend their wages and salaries, further boosting demand. Their more secure financial situation permits them to borrow, perhaps for house purchase, boosting construction demand. Employment increases further as more companies respond to the improving background.

Corporate profitability is now strong as companies benefit from higher volume throughput. Companies also take the opportunity presented by higher demand to increase prices. Strong demand and high levels of profitability and cash flow encourage companies to invest in new production lines, new plants and new factories. Property rents rise in response to rising demand for office, industrial and retail space as companies expand. The workforce also benefits as their bargaining power is increased by lower unemployment levels and strong demand for labour, sending wages and salaries higher.

Higher prices for goods, property and labour inevitably result in higher and accelerating inflation. Finally the authorities, alarmed by the prospect of inflation running out of control, act to dampen the economy by increasing interest rates. Eventually the economy peaks, followed by a peak in the rate of inflation.

Higher interest rates now throw the whole cyclical process into reverse. Companies cut back their inventories, workforce and capital expenditures. Higher unemployment forces the consumer to retrench, further depressing demand. Higher unemployment also eases the pressure on wages and salaries. Lower demand puts pressure on product prices. Corporate profits fall as prices weaken and volume throughput falls. Rents fall as demand for new space evaporates and as excess space becomes available.

The slowdown gathers pace. Inflation and interest rates fall. Eventually the authorities act by cutting interest rates to end the slowdown and reignite the economy. The cyclical process starts over.

An Idealised Investment Cycle

Figure 13.2 below illustrates how events in the real economy are reflected in the financial markets. Again the chart depicts the path of economic activity.

Figure 13.2 The Investment Cycle

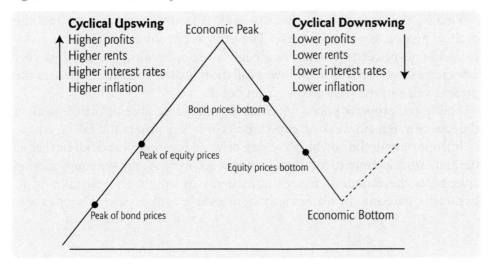

In the early part of the upswing, downward pressure on short-term interest rates ends as the authorities end the series of rate reductions and as demand for money increases. Market expectations are for higher short-term rates in the future. Meanwhile, even at this relatively early stage in the cyclical economic recovery, bond prices, which had been strong during the recession as inflation fell, reach their peak. Bond investors respond quickly, and indeed nervously, to signs of increased activity because they fear that increases in activity will be followed by increases in inflation. Bond investors, ever mindful of the damage inflicted on bond portfolios during the high-inflation 1970s and early 1980s, are extremely sensitive to any signs of emerging inflation. The mechanism driving the bond market is quite straightforward, as discussed in Chapter 3. Bond flows are fixed in monetary terms. The price of a bond is the present value of these future flows. Higher inflation erodes the present value of the future flows, thus depressing the bond price.

In sharp contrast, equity investors respond enthusiastically to evidence of increasing economic activity. They recognise that increased activity results in higher volumes, higher product prices and higher profits. Share prices rise. Property values also benefit as higher profits encourage companies to expand, take additional space and pay higher rents. Here expectations of higher profits and rents are boosting the anticipated future flows from equities and property, thus increasing equity and property values.

Eventually, however, equity and property investors recognise that higher economic activity will result in higher inflation, forcing the authorities to dampen down the economy by increasing interest rates. The equity and property markets reach their peaks. Notice that the equity market anticipates the economic peak and will peak before the peak in economic activity. Equities, in particular, are a forward-looking asset; they are concerned with anticipating economic events.

Finally, the economy reaches its peak, the downturn begins and the cyclical process goes into reverse. The prospect of lower economic activity causes bond prices to bottom and begin to rise, because the bond market associates lower activity with lower inflation. Lower inflation increases the present value of the future flows from bonds.

Equity and property prices, which have been falling since before the peak in the economy, remain weak on expectations of falling profits and falling rents.

Interest rates decline owing to falling demand for money, and fall further as the authorities attempt to foster an economic recovery. Again, the equity market anticipates the economic trough and begins to improve in advance of it. Eventually, the economy reaches its bottom and the cyclical process begins anew.

THE KEY LINKAGES

Economic activity is the driver that the real economy and the investment markets share in common. Economic activity drives growth; growth drives profits and rents. Economic activity drives inflation; inflation drives interest rates. Asset values are the outcome of the flow of future payments (e.g. profits in the case of equities, rents in the case of property), discounted back to present value by a discount factor which rests importantly on interest rates. Central to the relationship are growth and inflation. This relationship is illustrated below.

Figure 13.3 The Economy and the Markets: Key Drivers

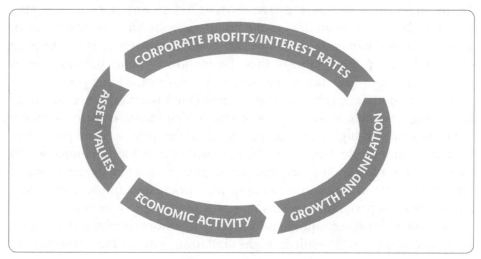

The relationship is outlined further in the figure below.

Figure 13.4 Key Linkages: Economies and Markets

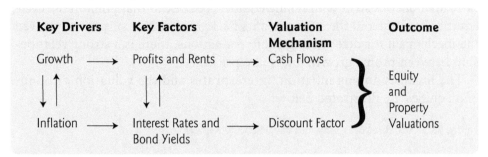

Inflation drives interest rates; interest rates drive bond yields. In fact, bond yields are long-term interest rates.

Equity valuations are derived from the interplay between corporate profits and bond yields. Growth drives the stream of corporate profits. The value of a company is the present value of that stream of future profits restated in today's money by a discount factor which rests heavily on the bond yield. The key element in the discount factor is the bond yield. The lower the bond yield, the lower the discount factor and the higher the present value of the company. The higher the bond yield, the higher the discount factor and the lower the present value of the company. In other words, low bond yields permit investors to attach high valuations to companies, i.e. high price earnings ratios. High bond yields result in low price earnings ratios.

A similar mechanism is at work in the property market. Growth in the economy drives growth in rents. The stream of future rents is discounted back to present value by employing a discount factor, which again is heavily influenced by bond yields. The lower the bond yield, the lower the discount factor, the higher the property valuation and vice versa.

The illustration above also shows that:

i) There is a trade-off between growth and inflation. For example, in the typical cycle as discussed earlier, economic growth as the cycle expands typically results in higher inflation. This causes the authorities to reduce inflationary pressures by dampening down economic activity.

ii) Higher interest rates may have a negative effect on corporate profits, because companies typically have borrowings. Higher interest rates result in higher interest charges. Nevertheless, because of the benefits arising from increased volumes of production and enhanced pricing power, corporate profits will rise strongly during the economic upturn.

When the historical data is examined we find there is a very strong linkage between falling interest rates and rising equities. However, rising interest rates are not consistent with falling equities, because at that point in the cycle equities benefit from the strong profits background. Not surprisingly, given the mechanism for determining equity valuations, there is a strong relationship between profits growth and share prices.

The linkages among inflation, interest rates and the valuation of bonds and equities are illustrated below:

Figure 13.5 The Real Economy and the Markets: Key Linkages

The price earnings ratio is a measure of the stock market's comfort with the quality and growth potential of company earnings (or profits). The higher the price earnings ratio, the higher will be the market's confidence in the company. A price earnings ratio for the stock market as a whole may be calculated by using an index of stock market prices and earnings.

The price earnings ratio is calculated by dividing the share price by annual earnings per share. The inverse of this calculation, as shown below, displays the very same relationship as an earnings yield.

Figure 13.6 The Price Earnings Ratio and the Earnings Yield

$$\text{Price Earnings Ratio} = \frac{\text{Share Price}}{\text{Earnings per Share}}$$

$$\text{Earnings Yield} = \frac{\text{Earnings per Share}}{\text{Share Price}} \times 100\%$$

By contrasting the very different investment environments of 1982 – at the beginning of the secular bull market in equities and bonds – and of 2000 – when equity markets peaked – the linkages between inflation interest rates, bond yields and equity valuations are clearly shown (see Table 13.1). High inflation led to high interest rates, high bond yields and high earnings yields (i.e. low equity market price earnings ratios) in 1982. In sharp contrast a low-inflation, low-interest-rate, low-bond-yield background in 2000 permitted equity valuation to move to high, albeit unsustainable, extremes. Prior to the 2008 bear market, valuations were not at extremely overhauled levels, as indicated by the Price Earnings Ratio of 17.00 to S&P 500 at end-2007. The catalyst for the 2008 bear market was much more about a bubble in the credit markets, rather than a bubble in the equity markets.

Table 13.1

	United States		
	1982	2000	2007
Inflation	6.0%	2.5%	2.9%
Interest Rates	16.0%	6.2%	2.0%
Bond Yields	10.0%	6.2%	4.1%
Earnings Yield	12.5%	3.5%	5.9%
(Price Earnings Ratio)	8.0	28.3	17.0

THE CYCLE AND ASSET ALLOCATION

Given the relationship between the economic and investment cycles outlined earlier in this chapter, it may be worthwhile to consider to what extent, if any, developments in the real economy might be used by investors as a basis for predicting market developments and, in particular, for determining the relative attractions of the different investment assets at a particular point in time.

However, while an idealised cycle was outlined earlier, in practice every cycle is different. The leads and lags between the various cyclical phases and events vary and the sequence of occurrences changes.

Nevertheless, by examining economic and investment cycles in the US between the Second World War and the early 1990s, it is possible to construct a 'Cyclical Clock' as follows:

Figure 13.7 The Cyclical Clock

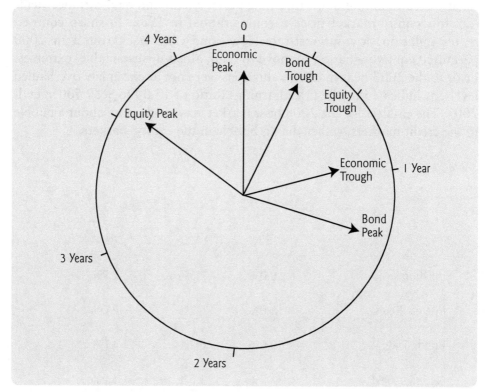

Even in the light of the limitations expressed above, the Cyclical Clock delivers some interesting evidence:

i)   The average cycle has a life of just over 4 years. Within the average cycle there is about 1 year of slowdown and over 3 years of growth. This is good news for investors in real assets, equities and property, which are predicated on growth.

ii)   The equity market does indeed perform its role as an anticipator of economic events. The peak of the equity market occurs, on average, about 1 year ahead of the peak in economic activity. The bottom of the equity market occurs, on average, some 6 months ahead of the trough of economic activity.

iii)   The sensitivity of the bond market to economic activity, which it associates with movements in inflation, is clearly shown. Shortly after the peak of economic activity, as activity slows, bond prices – which had been weak during the prolonged economic upswing – finally bottom and begin to rise. Similarly, shortly after the economy reaches its bottom and begins to improve, bond prices, which had been strong during the economic downturn, now reach their peak.

iv) The equity market cycle reflects the economic background. On average, during each cycle equity markets rise for about 3 years and fall for 1. In sharp contrast, bond markets rise for about 1 year and fall (or move sideways) for 3.

It is hardly surprising, therefore, that in the long run equities outperform bonds.

However, because of the limitations outlined earlier, the Cyclical Clock is not a precision instrument and its application is extremely limited in informing the investor as to the appropriate portfolio asset mix at any particular time. Neither is it a reliable tool for timing switches between the different asset classes, i.e. for moving from bonds to equities or equities to cash.

Nevertheless, it does pinpoint that there are two key points for investors during each cycle:

i) The Bond Market Trough

At this point in the cycle, the investor:

- should be fully invested to take advantage of the coming upswing in markets;
- should have a short-lived bias to bonds but be preparing to maximise equity exposure;
- should expect to stay fully invested for the next 2 to 3 years.

ii) The Equity Market Peak

At this point in the cycle, the investor:

- should adopt a defensive portfolio posture (i.e. cash at maximum permitted);
- should be bearish (cautious, pessimistic) on equities (i.e. equities at minimum permitted exposure);
- should be preparing to maximise bond exposure;
- should be prepared to revert to a fully invested position within 9 to 12 months.

Secondly, the Cyclical Clock does broadly indicate that there is an 'asset of choice' for the different stages of the economic cycle:

- Cash is king either side of the peak of economic activity.
- Bonds perform best during the economic downturn.
- Equities are the asset of choice during a prolonged phase of the economic upswing.

This is illustrated in the figure below:

Figure 13.8 The Cyclical Clock: Asset Strategy

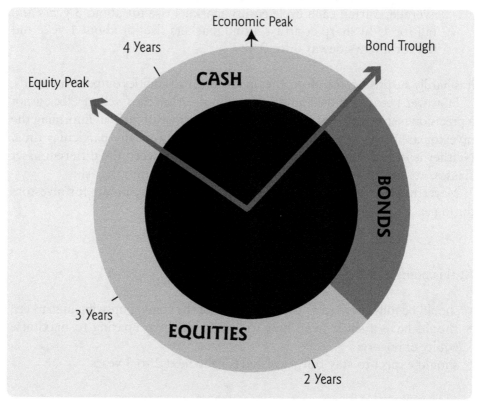

Awareness of the relationship between the economic and investment cycles, as refined by the insights available from examination of the Cyclical Clock, can help the investor to understand, track and interpret economic and financial developments. However, when predicting financial and market out-turns there is no escaping the requirement for judgment. The investor, whether he or she be the chief investment officer of a large fund management house or a private individual, must make a judgment pinpointing the precise phase of the current economic cycle, determine its implication for the investment assets in the light of the typical developments of the average cycle – as shown by the Cyclical Clock – and adjust for the unique characteristics of the current cycle. Judgment, nerve and courage are required. The position is rarely as clear in practice as it is in theory.

SPECULATION, EUPHORIA, BUBBLES, CRASHES

In Chapter 6 investors are characterised as thoughtful and rational individuals who carefully analyse their requirements and needs and tailor their investment portfolios accordingly. Investors are keenly aware that investment, a two-handed process, is about risk and return. They are focused on optimising, rather than maximising, their investment returns.

In this chapter a framework is outlined which demonstrates that the investment assets are rooted in the real world. The real economy and the investment assets share common drivers. They are linked by a series of causes and effects, actions and reactions, anticipation and outcomes. The interactions between the economy and the investment assets are sensible and logical and the sequence of developments fits comfortably into the cyclical patterns of both the economy and the markets.

Investors do indeed make informed judgments, they employ a systematic process and they act on a rational basis. This is normally the case. However, financial history shows that, periodically, investors are gripped by bouts of speculative fever that may overwhelm their normal thoughtful, rational and systematic approach to investment. During these periods, first enthusiasm and then greed and euphoria develop into a mania that can drive asset values far from the solid ground of the real world. There have been many such episodes throughout history. Some, despite the long periods which have elapsed since they occurred, are indelibly imprinted in financial folklore – notably 'Tulipmania' in Holland during the 1630s, and 'the South Sea Bubble' in Britain in 1720.

Episodes of this vintage do carry lessons and insights for us today, not least on the dangers involved in excessive borrowing. However, our focus in this chapter is on occurrences of more recent vintage: those that took place in the twentieth century.

Figure 13.9 The Dow Jones Index: 1924–1934

Wall Street: The Great Crash of 1929

Perhaps the speculative episode most firmly embedded in financial folklore is the Great Crash of 1929. Its short-term financial consequences during October 1929 were dramatic enough, but the long-term fallout in the Great Depression of the 1930s was calamitous for the world economy.

Share prices on Wall Street, which had been rising through 1924, 1925 and 1926, accelerated in 1927 and simply charged ahead in 1928 and 1929. Borrowings played a key role in the acceleration, as they invariably do during bubbles. Investors bought shares 'on margin', using money lent by their stockbrokers, while highly geared investment trusts piled borrowings on borrowings in the fashion of pyramid sales schemes.

A number of the key events during the momentous month of October 1929 are set out below to illustrate their dramatic impact at the time, but also to highlight those elements that tend to recur in bubbles.

1929

Wed. 2 October   Brokers' loans at new high of $6.8bn. Brokers' loans to investors consistently hit new highs during the run-up to the peak of the Technology Bubble in March 2000.

Wed. 23 October   Heavy selling.

Thurs. 24 October   Huge volume of forced selling. Forced selling occurs when the broker, having lent money 'on margin' for the purchase by the client of stocks that have now fallen in price, and in the absence of fresh funds from his client, liquidates the investor's position. Forced selling dramatically changes the dynamics of the market. The typical investor is sensitive to market price; he will be reluctant to sell his stock at a price that is sharply below recent levels. The broker engaged in forced selling is insensitive to price, focused only on raising cash. Forced selling hugely accentuates market downside.

A consortium of bankers, in an effort to steady investors' nerves and share prices, support the market by investing $240m.

In 1929 this operation had its desired effect but only for a few days. It failed to turn the market. However, in 1974/5 a consortium of insurance companies successfully stabilised and turned round the UK market after its huge fall of 1974.

Fri. 25 October   Market steady in large volume.

Sat. 26 October   Market steady in large volume, but weak towards close.

Mon. 28 October   Share prices routed.

Tues. 29 October   Massive forced selling in huge volume.

Wed. 30 October   Companies increase dividends. The 'Great and Good' rally round in an attempt to allay investor fears by pointing to the health of business and of the economy.

Again, in October 1987 after the large one-day fall in the US market, many of the major US corporations announced share buy-backs.

As mentioned earlier, the debacle of the Great Crash of 1929 was followed by the global suffering of the Great Depression of the 1930s. The shock suffered by the financial and economic systems from the stock market collapse was exacerbated by poor economic management.

The Crash of 1987

The foundations of the 1987 crash, in typical bubble fashion, were built on debt. The 1980s were the era of the leveraged buy out (LBO), whereby financiers or 'corporate raiders' employed highly borrowed investment

Figure 13.10 The Dow Jones Index: 1983–1993

vehicles, often financed with a significant element of high yield or 'junk' bonds, to acquire quoted companies. The period culminated in the extraordinary events of the takeover of RJR Nabisco, memorably described in the book *Barbarians at the Gate*.

At the peak of the corporate raiders' influence, no company seemed to be too large to be safe from the threat of takeover. Upon acquisition the acquired company would be 'run for cash', with the new owners focusing on EBITDA – Earnings Before Interest, Tax, Depreciation and Amortisation – rather than on the shareholders' typical focus on earnings. Asset-disposal proceeds and cash flows were applied in debt reduction, with a view to eventual relisting of the company to provide an exit for the raiders. Market valuations moved to a cash-flow basis from the normal earnings basis. The key to valuation was 'private market value' – the price a raider funded by debt could afford to pay to buy the company.

Share prices continued their strong rise into 1987, until finally a sustained rise in bond yields (i.e. long-term interest rates) forced a more sober reappraisal of valuation.

Figure 13.11 US Treasury 10-Year Bond Yield: 1985–1987

Prices collapsed, falling by 22.6% in a single trading day on 19 October 1987. The decline in prices was ratcheted downwards by derivative-based strategies, including program trades and portfolio insurance, which spewed out sell orders in an unprecedented fashion.

Thankfully, on this occasion a more robust and sophisticated financial and economic infrastructure, and timely corrective action by the monetary authorities in the US and elsewhere, helped to avoid longer-term economic repercussions.

The Technology Bubble

The technology bubble and, in particular, the mania for investment in internet and dotcom companies may be traced back to the Netscape Initial Public Offering (IPO) of August 1995. The price of Netscape shares rose by 108% on the day of the IPO, valuing the company at $2.2bn. However, it was not until late 1998 that the really explosive phase of the bubble kicked in with dramatic rises in the share prices of technology, media and telecommunications (TMT) companies.

Figure 13.12 The NASDAQ Index: 1998–2001

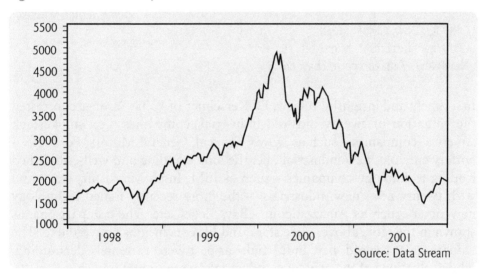

Source: Data Stream

The technology mania, like all bubbles, was based upon a real-world opportunity. In the previous decade the convergence of telecommunications and computer technology via the internet transformed, through e-mail and e-commerce, the way in which we live our business and personal lives.

However, during 1999 and into early 2000, investor enthusiasm for technology and technology-related stocks ran well ahead of any likely real-world benefits. Investors, again as in the 1920s, used margin debt and other borrowings to fuel their demand. Nor was the phenomenon restricted to private investors. Institutional investors and corporate managements also leapt on the bandwagon. Demand for stock well outstripped supply. The supply imbalance was exploited by the investment houses as they introduced ever more fragile technology stocks to the market. They curtailed supply and magnified hype by issuing to the public only a very small proportion of total stock, thus further exacerbating the supply imbalance.

At the peak of the bubble, in March 2000, TMT valuations had reached absurd levels. There was simply no way that these companies could grow at the rates implied for the lengths of time implied by their valuations.

Table 13.2 Peak Valuations: 10 March 2000

	Price/Earnings	Price/Sales
Old 'Old Industrials'	12.6	0.6
Old 'New Industrials'	69.2	7.3
New 'New Industrials'	N/A	85.7
NASDAQ	147.1	11.0
S+P 500	28.3	2.1

Source: Paine Webber

Old Old: Dow, GM, Ford, etc
Old New: Intel, IBM, Microsoft, etc
New New: Amazon.com, Ebay, etc

In a timely and insightful review, Ed Kerschner of Paine Webber contrasted the valuation of twenty old 'old industrial' companies, i.e. 'smokestack America' companies – such as Dow Chemical, General Motors, Ford, etc. – with twenty old 'new industrial', i.e. the long-standing and well-established leading technology companies – such as IBM, Intel, Microsoft, etc. – and with twenty new 'new industrials' – the more recently issued technology newcomers such as Amazon.com, eBay, Siebel, etc. The comparisons, as shown in the table above, were stark and his conclusions unavoidable. The valuations of the old 'new industrials' at best were extremely demanding, while valuations of the new 'new industrials' were simply foolish.

By coincidence, on the very day on which Kerschner's review was issued, the Nasdaq index peaked at 5048.6. Over the next two years and seven months it retraced its earlier gains, falling by 78% to its low on 9 October 2002.

The Credit Crisis

That global economic developments prior to 2007 were unsustainable and inherently unstable was well known. The threat presented by the 'global imbalances' was well recognised. It was clear that US consumers, living beyond their means and building up an enormous US balance of trade deficit, could not expect to be indefinitely funded by those countries – China, Japan, Latin American nations and OPEC members – that were recycling their US dollar export proceeds back into the US. Eventually, the 'merry-go-round' would stop and the consequences would be severe.

Figure 13.13 US Consumer Spending

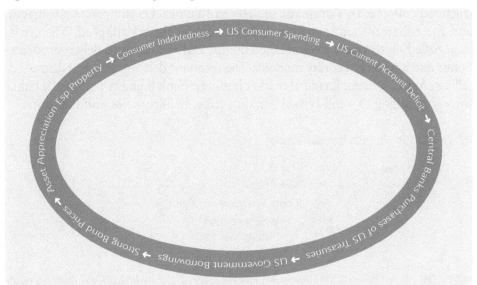

Meanwhile, whilst the game persisted, money was easy and cheap and risk was rewarded. Risk appetites grew, fuelled by banks whose lending standards first weakened and then collapsed. Leverage was rampant, often via complex, opaque, securitised instruments poorly understood by issuer and buyer alike. Driven by waves of liquidity, asset bubbles developed across a variety of asset classes but most pertinently in commercial and residential property.

Figure 13.14 Bubble Expansion Phase

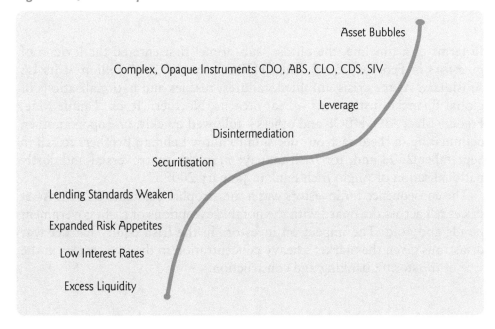

Eventually the weakness in US house prices proved to be the catalyst that triggered collapse. In a dramatic sequence of failure, US sub-prime mortgages and the collateralised instruments built around them collapsed. The crisis then rolled on through collateralised credit, real estate, bank debt, corporate bonds and into global equity markets. The resultant deleveraging and distressed selling eroded, in turn, financial market liquidity, bank liquidity and finally bank solvency, leading to a full-blown banking crisis, bankruptcies and bail-outs.

Figure 13.15 Bubble Contraction Phase

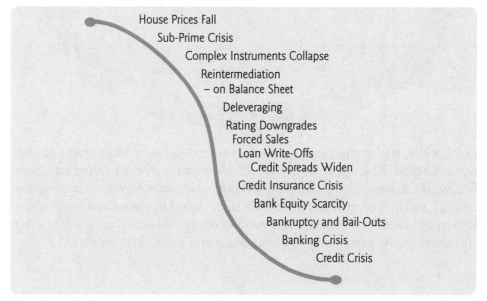

In terms of a timeline, the phrase 'sub-prime' first entered the lexicon of investors in February 2007 when HSBC wrote off $1.7 billion at its US subsidiary. As the crisis unfolded, failures, rescues and nationalisations of global financial institutions – Bear Stearns, Northern Rock, Fannie Mae, Freddie Mac, AIG, HBOS and others – followed quickly, one upon another, culminating in the disastrous decision to allow Lehman Brothers to fail in September 2008 and, for Irish taxpayers, in the controversial and costly nationalisation of Anglo Irish Bank in January 2009.

The consequence for investors was a catastrophic outcome to 2008. Asset prices fell across the board with the notable exceptions of cash, government bonds and gold. The impact on investors in the Irish equity market was disastrous given the market's heavy concentration in the two sectors in the 'eye of the storm': banking and construction.

Figure 13.16 Catastrophe 2008: Asset Classes

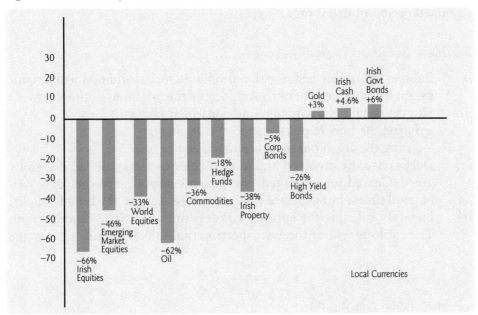

The real economy, of course, could not be immune from banking sector trauma. As market liquidity evaporated and credit contracted, business and consumer confidence collapsed. Concerted action by governments, through unprecedented fiscal and monetary stimulus, averted depression but could not prevent the global economy from plunging into its severest recession since the 1930s.

After a very sharp and steep recession, economic recovery got under way in mid-2009. Equity markets, anticipating this, rallied strongly from depressed March 2009 levels. However, this did not signal the end of the credit crisis, which, in a new iteration, extending into 2010, settled on the sovereign debt markets. A 'flight to quality' helped drive government bond yields in the large, 'core' developed economies – the US, Japan, Germany, France, the UK, Switzerland – to extraordinarily low levels. Meanwhile, corresponding yields in 'peripheral' countries, and particularly in a number of Eurozone countries – Greece, Ireland, Portugal and Spain – rose sharply relative to 'core' government yields as investors demanded high-risk premiums (measured by 'spread', or differential, between core and peripheral yields) as protection against the deterioration in public finances and higher risk of credit rating downgrades, or even defaults, of the debt-burdened peripheral countries.

The long-term implication of the credit crisis signals a period of low, subnormal growth in global developed economies as governments, the financial sector and consumers attempt to reduce the indebtedness built up during the excesses of the liquidity bubble in what is expected to be a sustained period of deleverage.

Bubbles: Common Denominators

i)   Bubbles invariably begin with a profitable real-world opportunity, for example the riches of South America or the potential of the internet.

ii)   Human nature is a common and consistent factor:
      – during the bubble phase, greed and euphoria;
      – during the crash phase, fear and anger.

iii) Debt is usually involved and in particular overborrowing, driven by greed. Geared (or leveraged) investments perform spectacularly well in good times, but generate calamitous losses when the bubble bursts.

iv)   Inevitably, during the episode business morality comes under strain. The exploitation of the unsuspecting (gullible?) investor may range

Figure 13.17 Speculation Marches On

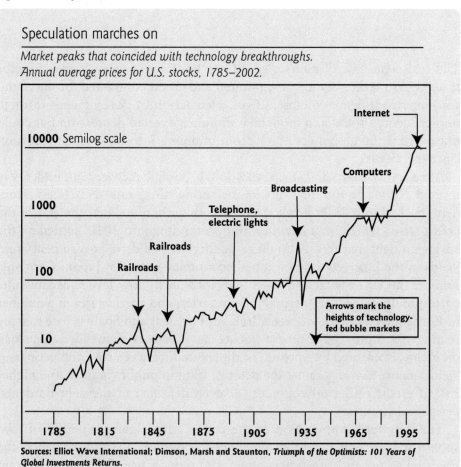

Speculation marches on

Market peaks that coincided with technology breakthroughs.
Annual average prices for U.S. stocks, 1785–2002.

Sources: Elliot Wave International; Dimson, Marsh and Staunton, *Triumph of the Optimists: 101 Years of Global Investments Returns.*

from liberal interpretation of rules and regulations to outright theft and fraud.

v) The downside, when it finally arrives, is severe and long-lasting.

vi) Finally, and unfortunately, investors' memories are short. The next generation of investor is fated to repeat the mistakes of history.

Bubbles: Key Insights

Unfortunately, the history of bubbles does not provide a reliable guide to pinpointing when the bubble might burst.

More mundane, but nevertheless telling, insights do emerge:

i) There is a difference between value and price.

As discussed earlier, the value of an investment is the present value of the stream of future earning which that investment will generate.

The price of an investment is the result of the interaction of buyers and sellers in the marketplace. When buyers outnumber sellers, the price will rise, perhaps well above the intrinsic value of the investment. The opposite will occur when sellers outnumber buyers.

During episodes of financial mania, price will diverge widely from value. However, an ongoing focus on value offers the investor the best possibility of staying on solid ground.

ii) Investment is about risk and return. The higher the expected return, the higher will be the risk. Geared (or leveraged) investment is inherently much more risky than an ungeared exposure to the same asset.

SUMMARY

- In determining the value of an asset, the focus of the investor is on future cash flows and their sensitivity to inflation.
- Investors are concerned with developments in the underlying economy, and in particular with growth and inflation.
- Economic activity tends to be cyclical, marked by successive and recurring phases of expansion and contraction. This cyclical activity is reflected in the financial markets.
- Growth and inflation are central to the relationship between the real economy and the financial markets.
- Inflation drives interest rates; interest rates drive bond yields. Growth drives profits. Equity valuations are derived from the interplay between corporate profits and bond yields.

➡

- Every cycle is different. Nevertheless, examination of cyclical economic patterns yields insights for investment management
  - the typical cycle lasts just over 4 years in the US;
  - the equity market acts as an anticipator of economic events;
  - the bond market is extremely sensitive to economic activity.
- There are two key points of time for investors in each cycle: the bond market trough and the equity market peak.
- Periods of speculative fever tend to have common characteristics, notably overborrowing, low standards of business morality and the excesses of human behaviour – greed and euphoria, fear and anger.
- There is a difference between value and price.

QUESTIONS

1. **Which of the following statements is FALSE?**

   A. At an equity market peak share prices will tend to be much higher than value estimates based on discounted present values.
   B. Analysis of the economic cycle provides a framework for determining the relative attractions of the different assets.
   C. The leads/lags vary from one cycle to the next.
   D. Debt and, in particular, over-borrowing usually play a very minor role in stock market crashes.

2. Outline the likely progress of a typical economic cycle, starting with a depressed economy suffering from high unemployment and recent high interest rates but with falling inflation.

3. In relation to the typical economic cycle you described in answer to question 2 above, trace how you would expect equity markets to react as the cycle progresses.

4. Outline how you would expect an investor to benefit from typical economic cycles.

Chapter fourteen

Performance Measurement and Style Analysis

This chapter deals with the measurement of investment returns. The calculation methodologies most commonly used are described and their suitability for comparing returns across managers discussed. Risk-adjusted return methodologies are also covered. The attribution of performance over the various sources of return is briefly outlined. The CFA Institute's Global Investment Performance Standards for the calculation and presentation of investment returns are described. The chapter concludes by discussing style analysis and manager selection.

Learning Objectives

After reading this chapter you will be able to:

- Describe the important methods of calculating returns, the time-weighted and the money-weighted rates of return, and their uses
- Explain the importance of dealing appropriately with cash inflows and outflows to and from the portfolio
- List the key principles involved in comparing returns of different managers
- Describe the measures of risk-adjusted returns
- Explain the methodology underlying performance attribution
- Describe the vision, objectives, scope and fundamentals of GIPS
- Analyse an investment manager's style, using both quantitative and qualitative approaches.
- Know the key questions to be asked in manager selection.

PERFORMANCE MEASUREMENT: KEY PRINCIPLES

Whether the investment portfolio has been directly invested by the investor or entrusted by the investor to an investment manager, the calculation of investment returns and the attribution and comparison of investment performance are critical elements in portfolio monitoring and control. The key principles of performance measurement are outlined below.

Total Returns

Measurement is of total returns, comprising both capital growth and income return.

Time-Weighted Rate of Return

The time-weighted rate of return is the compounded rate of growth of the initial portfolio market value during the evaluation period.

The overall evaluation period is divided into subperiods. A new subperiod is established whenever a cash inflow or cash outflow arises. The time-weighted rate of return for the period as a whole is calculated by compounding the returns of the subperiods.

The methodology assumes that all income arising is reinvested in the portfolio during the evaluation period. All cash inflows and outflows are assumed to occur on the first day of each subperiod.

Assume that a portfolio at market value of €1m on 1 January 2011 experienced flows and market valuation changes as follows:

Table 14.1 Portfolio Valuations and Flows €000

Cash Flow	Opening Fund	Income Arising	Portfolio Valuation @ MV	Closing Fund
	1.1.11 1,000	Jan'11 5	31.1.11 1,050	31.1.11 1,055
1.2.11 100	1.2.11 1,155	Feb'11 4	28.2.11 1,100	28.2.11 1,104
1.3.11 200	1.3.11 1,304	Mar'11 10	31.3.11 1,400	31.3.11 1,410

i) Cash inflows of €100,000 on 1 February 2011 and €200,000 on 1 March 2011 determine the beginning of new subperiods.
ii) The invested portfolio is valued at close of business on the day preceding cash inflows (or outflows).
iii) Income is assumed to arise gross of tax. Income arising of €5,000, €4,000 and €10,000 is assumed for the three subperiods.
iv) Income arising is added to the closing portfolio valuation at the end of each subperiod to give closing valuations for the fund at the end of each subperiod.

Subperiod returns are calculated as follows:

Table 14.2 Time-Weighted Returns: Subperiod Returns

$$\text{Return} = \frac{\text{Closing Fund} - \text{Opening Fund}}{\text{Opening Fund}}$$

Subperiod 1 (January): $\dfrac{1,055,000 - 1,000,000}{1,000,000}$

$$= .055$$
$$= 5.5\%$$

Subperiod 2 (February): $\dfrac{1,104,000 - 1,155,000}{1,155,000}$

$$= -.044$$
$$= -4.4\%$$

Subperiod 3 (March):

$$\frac{1,410,000 - 1,304,000}{1,304,000}$$

$$= .081$$
$$= 8.1\%$$

Subperiod returns are combined to give the time-weighted return for the total period as follows:

Table 14.3 Time-Weighted Returns: Full-Period Return

$$RT = [(1 + Rp1)(1 + Rp2)(1 + Rp3)] - 1$$

where: RT is the time-weighted return for the full evaluation period
   Rp1 is the return for subperiod 1.
   Rp2 is the return for subperiod 2.
   Rp3 is the return for subperiod 3.

$$=$$
$$[(1 + .055)(1 - .044)(1 + .081)] - 1$$
$$=$$
$$1.090 - 1$$
$$= 0.090$$
$$= 9.0\%$$

Because the time-weighted rate of return excludes the impact of cash inflows and outflows it is a good measure of the performance of the investment manager, and it permits the performance of one manager to be compared to that of another, given the conditions for fair comparisons are complied with.

The methodology does require, of course, that portfolio valuations be prepared whenever inflows or outflows take place. With modern technological systems this is no longer an onerous requirement. Indeed most large-investment managers have the capability of producing daily time-weighted returns.

Money-Weighted Rate of Return

The money-weighted rate of return is an internal rate of return over the full evaluation period. It accounts for the impact of cash inflows and outflows which are assumed to arise midway through the period, i.e. the calculation assumes the investment manager had (or had not) use of cash flows for half of the evaluation period.

Using the details of the previous example, the money-weighted rate of return emerges as follows:

Table 14.4 Money-Weighted Return: Full Period

$$\frac{\text{Closing Fund} - \text{Opening Fund} \pm \text{Net Cash Inflows}}{\text{Opening Fund} \pm \frac{1}{2}(\text{Net Cash Inflows})}$$

$$= \frac{1,410,000 - 1,000,000 - 300,000}{1,000,000 + 150,000}$$

$$= .096$$
$$= 9.6\%$$

and compares to our earlier calculation of the time-weighted return of 9.0%. Note that where there are no cash inflows or outflows, the time-weighted and money-weighted returns will be the same, e.g. subperiod 1 above.

Table 14.5 Money-Weighted Return: Subperiod 1

$$\text{Money-Weighted Return} = \frac{1,055,000 - 1,000,000 - 0}{1,000,000}$$

$$= 0.055$$
$$= 5.5\%$$

But where the inflows or outflows are large in relation to the opening valuation, significant differences will emerge, e.g. subperiod 3 above:

Table 14.6 Money-Weighted Return: Subperiod 3

$$\text{Money-Weighted Return} = \frac{1,410,000 - 1,104,000 - 200,000}{1,104,000 + 100,000}$$

$$= 0.88$$
$$= 8.8\%$$

compared to our earlier calculation of a time-weighted return for this sub-period of 8.1%.

The money-weighted rate of return does provide the client with useful information on the growth of the fund.

However, it is affected by the timing and amounts of cash inflows and outflows, which are beyond the control of the investment manager. It is therefore not a good measure of the performance of the investment manager, neither is it useful in making comparisons of different managers' performances.

The time-weighted rate of return has been adopted as the industry standard for performance measurement purposes.

Like-for-Like Comparisons

Where the returns of different funds are being compared it is important that comparisons are on a like-for-like basis, i.e. that the funds share certain key characteristics:

Investment Mandate

The investment mandate – the investment manager's riding instructions – sets out the objectives of the fund and the scope and discretion allowed the investment manager in delivering those objectives. Comparisons of the investment returns generated by different managers should be informed by the discretion allowed to them in the mandates. Obviously, the risk tolerance allowed the manager is critical in assessing returns. Risk is dealt with separately below.

Asset Class and Currency

Clearly, out-turns of funds that are invested in different asset classes or denominated in different currencies are not comparable.

Treatment of Income

It is important, particularly when measuring and comparing the returns of unit trusts and mutual funds, to ensure that treatment of income is comparable. Most funds roll income arising into the unit price. Some funds, however, distribute income to unitholders.

Treatment of Costs

Treatment of costs may vary between different types of fund. The returns of segregated funds, for example, are normally shown gross, i.e. before costs, while the returns of unit funds are normally shown net, i.e. after costs.

Tax Treatment

Tax treatment varies widely, depending on the type of investor and the type of fund. Common treatment of tax is essential in making comparisons.

Risk

The investment mandate defines the risk tolerance permitted to the investment manager in the search for investment returns. Comparisons of the manager's investment returns must be assessed in the light of the risks taken to generate them.

Volatility, as discussed in Chapter 6, is the standard measure of risk.

Among the measures commonly used in measurement of risk and return are:

i)   **The Sharpe Ratio**
      The Sharpe Ratio is a measure of the excess return over the risk-free rate of the portfolio relative to the total volatility (standard deviation) of the portfolio:

$$\frac{\text{Portfolio Return} - \text{Risk-Free Rate}}{\text{Standard Deviation of the Portfolio}}$$

ii)   **The Treynor Ratio**
      The Treynor Ratio, like the Sharpe Ratio, is a measure of excess return per unit of risk. Excess return is again defined as the difference between the portfolio's return and the risk-free rate.

      The risk measure, however, is the relative systematic risk as measured by the portfolio's beta. The portfolio's beta is regarded as an appropriate measure of risk because, with a well-diversified portfolio, the unsystematic risk is close to zero. The Treynor Ratio is calculated as follows:

$$\frac{\text{Portfolio Return} - \text{Risk-Free Rate}}{\text{Portfolio Beta}}$$

iii) **The Information Ratio**

The Information Ratio measures excess return over benchmark return against incremental risk over benchmark risk (i.e. tracking error):

$$\frac{\text{Portfolio Return} - \text{Benchmark Return}}{\text{Tracking Error}}$$

The Information Ratio recognises that excess return cannot be generated without accepting incremental risk. It measures the success of the investment manager in translating incremental risk into excess return.

All three ratios may be used to rank the returns of different investment managers.

Performance Attribution

Attribution of investment performance – the analysis and identification of sources of investment return – is an essential tool of investment management, with applications at the fund manager level for both passive and active managers; at the risk control level; and in client reporting.

Investment management firms employ sophisticated statistical tools, such as multi-factor models, for performance attribution purposes. These may be proprietary or commercially available. These models attribute performance over the various investment decision levels discussed in Chapter 12 – asset allocation, currency, country, sector and stock selection – as well as over market timing and over the factors that determine stock selection.

The following example is advanced to illustrate the principle of performance attribution in a simple fashion.

Assume that an active investment manager has constructed a portfolio that deviates from benchmark both at the asset allocation and stock selection levels. Portfolio weightings and returns compared to benchmark are set out in Table 14.7.

Table 14.7 Investment Out-turn

| | Benchmark | | Portfolio | |
	Weight	Return	Weight	Return
Equities	70	10	60	12
Bonds	30	5	40	4
Return		8.5%		8.8%

At the asset allocation level, the portfolio's exposure to equities at 60% is 10% less than benchmark exposure. The equity benchmark returned 10%. This underexposure of 10% cost 1% of return. Bond exposure in the portfolio at 40% was 10% above benchmark. The bond benchmark returned 5%. The overexposure to bonds added 0.5% to return. Overall, however, the asset allocation decision cost –0.5% of return.

At the stock selection level, the portfolio returned 12% against the benchmark's 10% on its 60% equity exposure, for a contribution of 1.2% to performance. The portfolio returned 4% against the benchmark's 5% on its 40% exposure to bonds, which cost –0.4%. Overall, the stock selection decision added +0.8% to return.

At the total fund level, therefore, outperformance of +0.3% is made up of a negative contribution from asset allocation of –0.5% and a positive contribution from stock selection of +0.8%.

This information is extremely valuable for the investment management firm. Whilst a single period's out-turn, say for a quarter or even one year, might not prompt major changes in approach, persistence of this trend might alert the fund manager to the need to sharpen or add resources to asset allocation decision making. Again, persistence of the trend might encourage the risk control function to initiate a process with the fund manager which might result in asset exposures being brought closer to benchmark. At the client reporting level, the performance attribution analysis provides useful information for updating the client on developments in the portfolio.

Table 14.8

Global Investment Performance Standards (GIPS)

The CFA Institute (formerly known as the Association for Investment Management and Research) has championed, sponsored and funded Global Investment Performance Standards, a single standard for presenting investment performance. To date over 25 countries, including Ireland, have adopted the GIPS Standards. Comprehensive details of these standards are available at www.gipsstandards.org.

The Benchmark return of 8.5% is made up as follows:

Equity Contribution	70% × 10%	7.0%
Bond Contribution	30% × 5%	1.5%
		8.5%

The Portfolio return of 8.8% is made up as follows:

Equity Contribution	60% × 12%	7.2%
Bond Contribution	40% × 4%	1.6%
		8.8%

This results in outperformance of 0.3% for the period by the investment manager. Next, the sources of this outperformance are identified:

Sources of Performance

Asset Allocation

Equities (60% – 70%) × 10%	–1.0%
Bonds (40% – 30%) × 5%	+0.5%
	–0.5%

Stock Selection

Equities (12% – 10%) × 60%	+1.2%
Bonds (4% – 5%) × 40%	–0.4%
	+0.8%
Outperformance	0.3%

Vision Statement

A global investment performance standard leads to readily accepted presen-tations of investment performance that:

i) Present performance results that are readily comparable among invest-ment management firms without regard to geographical location.

ii)   Facilitate a dialogue between investment managers and their clients about the critical issues of how the investment management firm achieved performance results and determines future investment strategies.

Objectives

i)   To obtain worldwide acceptance of a standard for the calculation and presentation of investment performance in a fair, comparable format that provides full disclosure.
ii)   To ensure accurate and consistent investment performance data for reporting, record keeping, marketing and presentations.
iii)   To promote fair, global competition among investment management firms for all markets, without creating barriers to entry for new investment management firms.
iv)   To foster the notion of industry 'self-regulation' on a global basis.

Fundamentals of Compliance: Key Requirements

Definition of the Firm

- The standards must be applied on a firm-wide basis.
- Total firm assets must be the aggregate of the market value of all discretionary and non-discretionary assets under management within the defined firm.

Document Policies and Procedures

- Firms must document, in writing, the policies and procedures they use in establishing and maintaining compliance with all the applicable requirements of the GIPS standards.

Firms' Fundamental Responsibilities

- Firms must make every reasonable effort to provide a compliant presentation to all prospective clients.

Input Data

- Portfolio valuations must be based on market values.
- For periods between 1 January 2001 and 1 January 2010 portfolios must be valued at least monthly. For periods beginning 1 January 2010 firms must value portfolios on the date of all large external cash flows.
- Accrual accounting must be used for fixed-income securities and all other assets that accrue interest income. Market values of fixed-interest securities must include accrued income.

Calculation Methodology

- Total returns must be used.
- Time-weighted rates of return that adjust for external cash flows must be used. Periodic returns must be geometrically linked.
- Composite returns must be calculated by asset weighting the individual portfolio returns using beginning-of-period value and external cash flows.
- A composite is an aggregation of individual portfolios representing a similar investment mandate, objective or strategy.
- All returns must be calculated after deduction of the actual trading expenses incurred during the period.

Composite Construction

- All actual, fee-paying, discretionary portfolios must be included in at least one composite.
- Terminated portfolios must be included in the historical returns of the appropriate composite up to the last full measurement period that the portfolio was under management.
- Carve-out segments excluding cash are not permitted to be used to represent a discretionary portfolio.
- Firms are not permitted to link simulated or model portfolios with actual performance.

Disclosures

- Firms must disclose the minimum asset level, if any, below which portfolios are not included in a composite.
- Firms must disclose the currency used to express performance.
- Returns must be disclosed as gross-of-fees or net-of-fees.
- Firms must disclose relevant details of the treatment of withholding taxes.
- Firms must disclose the fee basis appropriate to the presentation.

Presentation and Reporting

- The following items must be reported for each composite presented:

    i)   At least 5 years of performance that meets the requirements of the GIPS standards; after presenting 5 years of performance the firm must present additional annual performance up to 10 years.
    ii) Annual returns for all years.
    iii) The number of portfolios and the amount of assets in the composite.
    iv) A measure of dispersion of individual portfolio returns for each annual period.

- Returns of portfolios and composites for periods of less than 1 year are not permitted to be annualised.
- Performance track records of a past firm or affiliation must be linked to, or used to represent, the historical record of a new firm or new affiliation if:

    i)   Substantially all the investment decision makers are employed by the new firm.
    ii) The staff and decision-making process remain intact and independent within the new firm.
    iii) The new firm has records that document and support the reported performance.

- The new firm must disclose that the performance results from the past firm are linked to the performance record of the new firm.

Besides the requirements and mandatory disclosures detailed in the GIPS standards, guidelines and recommendations for reporting are also provided. These GIPS standards, which were revised in 2005 for implementation from 1 January 2006, promote the highest performance measurement and presentation practices and they eliminate the need for separate local standards.

Verification

Detailed verification procedures are also set out in the GIPS standards. Verification is the review of an investment management firm's performance measurement processes and procedures by an independent, third-party verifier.

Verification Tests

These involve:

- whether the firm has complied with all the composite construction requirements of the GIPS standards on a firm-wide basis;
- whether the firm's processes and procedures are designed to calculate and present performance results in compliance with the GIPS standards.

A single verification report is issued in respect of the whole firm; verification cannot be carried out for a single composite. Without such a report from the verifier, the firm cannot state that its claim of compliance with the GIPS standards has been verified.

Sample Presentations

Samples of GIPS-compliant presentations are available in *Global Investment Performance Standards*, CFA, 2010, which can be downloaded from www.gipsstandards.org.

STYLE ANALYSIS: GROWTH AND VALUE INVESTMENT

Introduction

As discussed in Chapter 7, an equity investment manager's style is defined by the investment philosophy and process that determine the manager's approach to stock selection and portfolio construction.

The predominant styles adopted by active equity investment managers are growth and value. Both growth and value may be further categorised into large capitalisation and small capitalisation.

Style analysis is designed:

- to help the investor understand the investment manager's approach to equity investment;
- to confirm that the investment manager has the capability to deliver, over a reasonable period of time, results which are in line with the investment style adopted;
- to confirm that the characteristics of the portfolios constructed are aligned with the style adopted.

The growth manager is focused on growth, and in particular on growth in earnings per share, and seeks stocks which will have relatively high earnings growth within the universe of stocks followed.

The value manager is focused on valuation, and in particular on stocks which are relatively low-valued within the universe of stocks followed.

The Price/Book Ratio (i.e., Market Price/Net Asset Value per share) is typically used to categorise stocks into growth or value. Growth stocks are those stocks within the stock universe that exhibit a higher Price/Book ratio than the average of the universe. Value stocks have a lower Price/Book ratio than the average.

The growth manager believes that growth in earnings per share will normally increase the Book Value per share. Assuming no change in the Price/Book ratio, the share price will grow if earnings grow.

The value manager believes that over time the Price/Book ratio of low-rated stocks will return to some normal level, i.e. will revert to mean. Therefore, even with no change in book value per share, the share prices will rise.

The major risk faced by the value manager, therefore, is that the Price/Book ratio does not increase. The growth manager faces two risks:

- that earnings growth does not occur as expected; and
- that the Price/Book ratio declines, preventing the earnings growth from being reflected in the share price.

Style Analysis: Qualitative Inputs

Analysis of the inputs of both growth and value managers focuses on the key elements of successful investment management firms discussed in Chapter 12. A qualitative examination is carried out of the investment manager's:

- philosophy
- process
- people.

Emphasis is placed in particular on:

- the key, or ideally the unique, insight which the manager brings to stock selection;
- the repeatability and consistency of the investment process in generating superior investment returns;
- the stability and expertise of the investment team;
- the competitive advantages and potential weaknesses of the investment management firm.

In particular, this process of due diligence of the capabilities of the investment manager is designed to determine the conviction which drives the manager's philosophical growth or value approach, the discipline and rigour of the investment process, and the knowledge, expertise and commitment of the investment team.

Style Analysis: Quantitative Outputs

The output of the equity investment manager – the completed portfolio – is examined quantitatively with specific measurements for value and growth portfolios.

Value Portfolios

Analysis of the value portfolio is relatively straightforward. Focus is on the valuation of the portfolio relative to the appropriate market index.
    Key measures examined include:

- Portfolio Price Earnings Ratio (PER) relative to Index PER
- Portfolio Dividend Yield (DY) relative to Index DY
- Portfolio Price-to-Book Ratio (P/B) relative to Index P/B.

A value portfolio will stand on valuations which are below market valuations. Therefore, the portfolio PER will be lower than the index PER. The portfolio

DY will be higher than the index DY, and the portfolio P/B will be lower than the index P/B.

Growth Portfolios

The measurement of the characteristics of the growth portfolio are significantly more complex and require a considerable data bank, because focus is on fundamental profit and earnings growth data.

Key measures include:

Historical Growth

Earnings per share	–	relative to index
Dividend per share	–	relative to index
Book value per share	–	relative to index
Cash flow per share	–	relative to index

Prospective Growth

Earnings per share
Short-term	–	relative to index
Long-term	–	relative to index

Shorter-term measures of earnings momentum may also be examined, e.g. incidence of rising and falling estimates of earnings per share (based on 'sell side' stockbroking analysts' estimates) and incidence of positive and negative surprises in earnings-per-share outcomes against estimates.

Performance

The ultimate measure of the investment manager's ability to construct successful value or growth portfolios is, of course, investment performance. Portfolio out-turns for risk and return are measured against index outcomes and, where available, against relevant style indices, e.g. value or growth indices.

MANAGER SELECTION: KEY QUESTIONS

The investor, or the trustees of a pension fund, in embarking upon a process designed to select a manager who is to be entrusted with the management of their investments, will consider the key elements of successful investment firms as discussed in Chapter 12, and the issues involved in performance analysis and attribution and style analysis as discussed earlier in this chapter.

In addition, the investor might usefully revert to first principles. The first step in investment is in the investor's own mind. Requirements and objectives must be clearly outlined and communicated to prospective investment managers. Secondly, no matter how detailed or sophisticated the manager selection process, eventually the manager selection decision is reduced to the investor or trustees making the judgment that Manager A is better equipped to meet the fund's requirements and objectives than Manager B. A useful, practical step in informing this judgment is a site visit to the investment manager's offices, where ideally a meeting with the investment team might also be arranged.

Key Questions

Philosophy

What is the key insight that enables the investment manager to add value over market returns?

Process

Describe how the investment process implements philosophy in a consistent and repeatable fashion. Is there a process that applies to the house as a whole or is it individual to a particular manager, team, fund or product?

Outline the investment firm's risk control framework.

Outline the following with respect to process:

- ... valuation metrics
- ... stock characteristics
- ... portfolio construction.

People

Is there a dominant individual (a 'star manager'), or is there a team-based approach? What discretion does the manager/team have? Describe the team members':

- ... background and experience
- ... responsibilities
- ... reward and incentivisation.

SUMMARY

- The time-weighted rate of return is the compounded rate of growth of the initial portfolio market value during the evaluation period.
- Because the time-weighted rate of return excludes the impact of cash inflows and outflows, it is a good measure of the performance of the investment manager and it enables the performance of one manager to be compared to that of another. The time-weighted rate of return is the industry standard.
- The money-weighted rate of return accounts for the impact of cash inflows and outflows. It provides useful information on the growth of the fund. It is not suitable for making comparisons.
- Comparisons should be made on a like-for-like basis.
- Measures of risk-adjusted return include the Sharpe Ratio, the Treynor Ratio and the Information Ratio.
- Performance attribution over the sources of return has wide application across the investment firm.
- The CFA Institute has developed standards for the calculation, disclosure and presentation of investment performance. These have been adopted in over 25 countries, including Ireland.
- Style analysis employs both qualitative and quantitative techniques. The investment manager's inputs – philosophy, process, people and resources – are examined qualitatively. Quantitative analysis of the portfolio and its constituent stocks employs an array of ratios which vary according to the manager's growth or value style.

Chapter fifteen

Investment Returns: History and Prospects

This chapter presents extensive data on the historical returns achieved by the various asset categories for the major markets. Investment returns for Irish assets are also examined in detail. The more recent experience of low equity returns since 2000 is contrasted with the era of high returns in the 1980s and 1990s. The chapter concludes with the authors' assessment of some of the key issues that are likely to dominate investment thinking and practice over the medium term.

Learning Objectives

After reading this chapter you will:
- Be familiar with long-term historical investment returns
- Be aware of the unusually high returns delivered by both bonds and equities during the 1980s and 1990s
- Be able to identify the problems created for pension funds due to the combination of low equity returns and low long-term government bond yields.

In Chapter 13 the linkages between the real economy and the financial markets are explored and two common drivers – growth and inflation – identified.

Inflation is important for its effect on interest rates and bond yields. Growth is important for its positive effect on the future cash flows generated by the real assets: equities and property. The price of the real assets, the present value of those future cash flows, is determined by applying a discount factor which keys off bond yields.

The Irish economy and financial markets in recent decades offer a powerful illustration of the influence of growth and inflation.

Table 15.1 The Irish Economy, % p.a.

	Real GNP Growth	Inflation
1960s	4.0	5.4
1970s	3.5	14.8
1980s	2.1	6.0
1990s	6.7	2.7
2000s	2.8	3.1

(Source: Dept of Finance)

Table 15.2 Real Returns on Irish Assets, % p.a.

	Bonds	Equities	Cash	Property
1960–1969	(2.1)	11.1	1.4	N/A
1970–1979	(5.2)	0.5	(3.1)	(2.6)
1980–1989	9.5	14.0	4.1	1.5
1990–1999	8.1	11.8	5.4	12.5
2000–2009	2.4	(5.8)	0.1	0.9

(Source: © 2005 E. Dimson, P. Marsh, M. Staunton, IPUT, IPD); Authors

In the 1960s real growth in GNP was an impressive 4.0% per annum, as Irish economic development belatedly accelerated after the stagnation of the 1950s. Inflation gradually picked up during the decade, averaging a relatively high 5.4% per annum for the full period. As shown in Table 15.2, Irish equities responded well to the good growth background, generating real returns of 11.1% per annum. Bonds suffered, generating negative returns in real terms because of their inability to cope with rising inflation. Cash deposits generated real returns as deposit rates responded to higher inflation.

The high-inflation 1970s proved an especially traumatic decade for investors as inflation surged following two oil shocks and inappropriate government responses both in Ireland and in our main trading partners. Bonds, cash and property real returns were heavily negative for the full decade. The dynamic characteristic of equities, the ability of companies to respond to a changing environment, enabled equities, despite some dramatic capital declines particularly in 1974, to generate a marginally positive real return of 0.5% per annum over the decade. Growth in GNP in the 1970s, despite the very difficult inflationary background, was respectable at 3.5% per annum and supported equity returns.

Inflation in Ireland peaked in 1981 at 20.4%. The long downward journey in inflation was a key influence in the dramatically good returns generated by all asset classes in the 1980s and 1990s. Equity performance in the 1980s was particularly noteworthy, as it was achieved against a relatively poor growth background. Clearly, in the 1980s the impact of the significantly lower discount factor was the more important influence in determining equity prices.

The 1990s' combination of high growth and low inflation generated high returns across all four asset classes.

Ireland, of course, as a small, open economy is sensitive to international developments. Ireland benefited from two particular global trends of the 1980s and 1990s: disinflation and globalisation. Globalisation was important in that trade liberalisation benefited Ireland's important export business, while liberalisation of capital flows helped Ireland to attract substantial volumes of foreign direct investment. Important domestic factors in Ireland's economic transformation included a sustained improvement in the national finances, wage moderation resulting from social partnership, a three-way contract between labour, employers and the State, and a young, productive and growing labour force. Meanwhile, Ireland's participation in the euro in January 1999 resulted in full convergence, give or take some basis points, between Irish and German interest rates. The low-inflation environment discussed earlier, of course, would of itself have resulted in significant reductions in interest rates and bond yields from those prevailing during the 1980s. However, membership of the Eurozone eliminated the premium (for market size, liquidity and risk) which had historically attached to Irish rates.

The transformation of the Irish interest rate structure during the 1990s was dramatic. At year-end 1992, during the currency crisis of that winter, Irish three-month money market rates stood at just under 17%, while ten-year bond yields were at 9.5%. By the end of 1999, money market rates had fallen to 3.33% and bond yields to 5.55%.

The combination of a favourable international background and a transformed domestic economy permitted Irish financial assets to generate returns in the 1990s that compared with the very best of those generated by our major trading partners:

Table 15.3 Real Returns on Bonds, % p.a.

1990–1999			
Ireland	8.1	Germany	5.6
US	5.7	UK	9.3

(Source: © 2005 E. Dimson, P. Marsh, M. Staunton)

Table 15.4 Real Returns on Equities, % p.a.

1990–1999	
Ireland	11.8
US	14.2
Germany	9.9
UK	11.2

(Source: © 2005 E. Dimson, P. Marsh, M. Staunton)

The significant outperformance of Irish equities by US equities during the 1990s was a function of the US equity market's greater exposure to the technology bubble and, as we go on to see, was reversed after the bubble imploded.

The uniquely favourable background of the 1990s first faded and then reversed as the following decade progressed. The implosion of the technology bubble after its peak in March 2000 and the Twin Towers terrorist attack of 11 September 2001 slowed global growth. This inevitably affected Irish economic activity at the beginning of the 2000s. However, Irish growth reaccelerated during the period from 2003 to 2007 as the building and construction sector boomed on the back of soaring property prices, which were driven in turn by reckless lending by an inadequately regulated banking sector. The buoyancy of revenues from property and construction undermined the fiscal discipline of the exchequer. The government deficit in 2008 rose sharply when revenues from these sources collapsed. The crisis in the government finances was greatly exacerbated by the costs of rescuing the Irish banking sector. By 2009 the government deficit had expanded to an estimated 32% of GDP. Meanwhile, the global credit crisis had pushed the world economy into the most serious recession since the 1930s. Economic activity in Ireland fell sharply. GNP fell by 3.5% in 2008 and by a further 10.7% in 2009.

Table 15.5 The Irish Economy, % p.a.

	Real GNP Growth	Inflation (HICP)
2000–2007 Boom	6.3	4.0
2008–2009 Bust	(7.2)	0.7
2000s	2.8	2.9

(Source: Dept of Finance)

Not surprisingly, as shown in Table 15.2, the returns generated by Irish assets were significantly lower during the 2000s than those prevailing in the halcyon decade of the 1990s. However, the comparison in Table 15.2, though dramatic, does not fully capture the extent of the attrition suffered in Irish assets at the latter end of the decade.

Clearly, the adverse global background of crisis in the credit, banking and sovereign debt markets, together with the severe global recession that they precipitated, played important roles in the poor Irish out-turns, but negative domestic influences were equally powerful.

As discussed in Chapter 13, the consequences of the credit crisis for investors in 2008 were catastrophic, resulting in dramatic falls in asset classes across the board with the notable exceptions of government bonds and cash. Irish government bonds generated positive real returns of 2.1% in 2008. However, as the credit crisis, in a new iteration in 2009/10, alighted on the sovereign debt markets, government bond yields in the 'core' developed economies – the US, Japan, Germany, France, the UK, Switzerland – were driven lower by a flight to quality. Meanwhile, in the 'peripheral' countries of the Eurozone, yield spreads over German yields rose sharply as the extent of the deterioration in the public finances of Greece, Ireland, Portugal and Spain became apparent and as the cost of banking bail-outs, particularly in Ireland, escalated. Spreads between Irish and German ten-year government bond yields, which had been almost fully aligned as recently as 2007, had widened to over 6% by late 2010.

Irish consumer price inflation in 2009 was negative at 4.5%, transforming low nominal returns, from cash and bonds, into relatively strong real returns.

Table 15.6 Real Returns from Bonds 2008–2009, % p.a.

	2008	2009	Annualised
Ireland	2.1	6.5	4.3
UK	11.8	(3.3)	4.0
US	24.6	(15.5)	2.6

(Source: Barclays Capital; Authors)

Commercial property values fell sharply in 2008 and 2009 from grossly overextended levels in a dysfunctional and highly illiquid market as investors, developers and banks attempted to reduce their over-indebted positions. Distressed selling pushed the market further downwards.

Table 15.7 Real Returns from Property 2008–2009, % p.a.

	2008	2009	Annualised
Ireland	(37.1)	(19.7)	(28.9)
UK	(23.2)	(0.2)	(12.5

(Source: IPD)

Irish equities suffered dramatic falls in 2007 in advance of the global bear market and in 2008 when the market generated a negative return in nominal terms of 66%. These heavy falls were, of course, attributable to the dramatic deterioration in Ireland's economic circumstances, but they also reflected the highly concentrated nature of a market that, close to its peak, was composed of banking and building and construction sectors which accounted for some two-thirds of total market capitalisation.

Table 15.8 Real Returns from Equities 2007–2009, % p.a.

	2007	2008	2009	Annualised
Ireland	(28.0)	(67.3)	35.6	(31.7)
UK	1.0	(30.4)	25.9	(4.0)
US	3.2	(38.9)	28.7	(6.7)

(Source: Barclays Capital; Authors)

Clearly, these poor outcomes for the Irish long-term assets reflect the very sharp deterioration in the Irish economy relative to its developed world peers; this is illustrated in Table 15.9. However, the relatively heavy falls in Irish assets were just as attributable to the overheated valuations of Irish assets at the peak of the boom and to the concentrated and illiquid nature of the markets themselves.

Table 15.9 The Real Economy 2008–2009, % p.a.

	Real GDP	Inflation (HICP)
Ireland	(7.2)	0.7
Germany	(1.9)	1.5
Eurozone	(1.8)	1.8
UK	(2.5)	2.9
US	(1.1)	1.7

(Source: Dept of Finance)

Nominal returns from cash fell sharply in 2009 as central banks reacted to the severity of the recession with unprecedented easing of monetary policy. Short-term interest rates in nominal terms fell to extraordinarily low, crisis levels. These low rates were sustained into 2010. However, deflation in Ireland, where the Consumer Price Index fell by 4.5% in 2009 and the comparable EU Harmonised Index of Consumer Prices fell by 1.7%, kept Irish cash returns in 2009 in positive real ground. Irish retail deposit rates remained above official European rates. The deeply troubled Irish banks were obliged to pay high rates to attract and maintain deposits, even though their deposits were subject to a government guarantee, which had been introduced in September 2008.

Table 15.10 Real Returns on Cash, % p.a.

	2008	2009	Annualised
Ireland	(0.6)	6.3	2.8
UK	4.2	(1.7)	1.2
US	1.4	(2.6)	(0.6)

(Source: Barclays Capital; Authors)

The consequences of the 2008 catastrophe for investors, particularly for those with significant exposure to Irish long-term assets, were severe. Individuals, charities, pension funds and other investors suffered substantial losses. Irish defined benefit pension schemes were doubly hit by very poor investment returns and by the effect of low discount rates, which key off German bond yields, on the valuation of their liabilities. By 2010 the majority of Irish pension schemes were unable to meet the minimum funding standard.

Many investors undertook a root and branch review of investment strategy in an attempt to avoid similar difficulties in the future. The lessons of the period were bitter but, frustratingly, they were not new. Adherence to investment fundamentals, which had been widely disregarded during the bubble phase, would have protected investors against the worst of the problems. We might classify these key fundamentals as the 'known knowns', perhaps to ensure that we remain aware of them when next we enter a bubble period.

The Known Knowns

The Importance of Diversification

The Irish equity market experience during 2007 and 2008 underlines the danger of over-concentration. The widespread falls across the spectrum of assets in 2008, including assets that had been selected for their low correlation with equities, highlight the requirement that assets 'do what they say on the tin', i.e. that they exhibit low correlations with equities not in the long term but in times of stress.

Liquidity

The credit crisis highlighted the importance of reliable counterparties. The steep falls in Irish property values demonstrate the dangers when illiquid assets are subject to distressed selling. The illiquidity of assets significantly reduced investors' flexibility. US endowments were subject to significant difficulties when they found that their critically important cash balances had been pre-committed to private equity investments.

Realistic Return Expectations

The markets are rooted in the real world, which is an uncertain and competitive environment. Profits are hard earned. Investors should adopt realistic expectations for returns. The solid ground is in the long-term numbers discussed in this chapter. Short-term returns are a function of the particular investment environment prevailing at the time. Long-term returns comprise periods of high and low growth, high and low inflation and indeed periods of war and peace.

Income is the dominant component of long-term returns, underlying the importance of yield. Income is recurring, quite predictable and never negative. Capital gain or loss, in sharp contrast, is volatile and unpredictable, and, as we saw in 2008, it may be heavily negative.

It is noteworthy that even the relatively modest returns that the long-term history tells us to expect will not be available to investors who overpay for their initial investment.

Equity Market Volatility

Again, the long-term history indicates that equities are the high-return asset. However, these high returns come at the cost of high volatility. Many investors were shocked by the extent of the downside in equities in 2008. They should not have been. There were many similar episodes in history.

Leverage

Leverage (or gearing) exaggerates the upswings and the downswings. The success in the good times of highly leveraged investors is often attributed to their genius. It is simply arithmetic. It works in similar fashion on the way down.

PROSPECTIVE RETURNS

Index-Linked Bonds

The long-term investor seeking maximum certainty of future returns will opt for index-linked bonds for their guarantee of a real return over the rate of inflation. At end-October 2010, real returns on long-dated, index-linked issues compared to historical real returns on conventional fixed-interest bonds are shown in Table 15.11.

Table 15.11 Real Returns on Index-Linked Bonds, % p.a.

	Historical Bond Returns		
	Market Yield October 2010 Index-Linked Bonds	Real Return 50 Years to 2010 Fixed-Interest Bonds	Real Return Long Term
US	1.2	2.9	2.4*
UK	0.8	2.5	1.2**

(Source: Barclays Capital)

* 85 years
** 111 years

Real yields are currently in low ground, based on the above comparisons. However, the real yields currently available in the US are not dramatically lower than the very long-run historical levels. The current perception that they are extraordinarily low is due to the folk memory of high real returns generated by bonds during the 1980s and 1990s. Nevertheless, it cannot be denied that the investor buying long-term, index-linked bonds at today's values is locking into relatively low returns.

Fixed-Interest Bonds

Whilst the investor in fixed-interest government bonds receives returns that are guaranteed in nominal terms, these returns may be eroded by inflation.

Table 15.12 Nominal Returns on Fixed-Interest Bonds, % p.a.

	Historical Bond Returns		
	Market Yield October 2010	Nominal Return 50 Years to 2009	Nominal Return Long Term
US	4.0	7.0	5.5*
UK	4.1	8.5	5.1**

(Source: Barclays Capital)

* 85 years
** 111 years

The contrast between the yields currently available and historical long-run returns is rather more demanding in the case of conventional government fixed-interest bonds, particularly in comparison with the post-war experience.

Today's buyer of fixed interest bonds is locking into returns that compare unfavourably with the long-term historical returns, and even more unfavourably with the returns generated since the 1950s.

A crude estimation of the bond market's view of future inflation may be calculated by subtracting the current real yield from the current fixed-interest yield – although strictly the nominal fixed-interest yield includes an inflation risk premium that rewards the fixed-interest investor for the risk he takes on inflation.

Table 15.13 *Inflation Expectations v. Historical Levels, % p.a.*

	'Forecast' Inflation	Inflation 1959–2009	Inflation Long Term
US	2.8	4.0	3.0*
UK	3.3	5.9	3.9**

(Source: Barclays Capital)

* 84 years
** 110 years

'Forecast' inflation in the US is actually extremely close to the long-term level, but substantially lower than the level of the fifty years to 2009: 4.0%. This average level was bounded by extremes of 7.4% p.a. for the ten years to end-1979, and 2.4% p.a. for the ten years to end-2006. On the face of it, the US fixed-interest investor is currently allowing little margin for error on inflation.

The UK bond investor is more adventurous still. The market expectation of 3.3% is well below the long-term number and just over half the average of the past fifty years. In the UK this average was bounded by an extreme of 13.1% per annum for the ten years to end 1971, with the lower boundary being 2.6% p.a. for the ten years to end-2005. Warren Buffet argues that investors, instead of looking forward, look into the rear-view mirror at recent experience, and that is rarely a reliable guide to the long-term future. There appears to be a clear risk that UK investors are overweighting the recent experience.

The two components of nominal bond yields are the real yield and expected inflation. Clearly, bond yields at end-2010 were built upon low numbers for both. Bond investors saw a low-inflation, low-risk world.

There is no escaping the conclusion that bond-market returns going forward will be low.

Equities

The government guarantees the real return of the index-linked bond investor and the nominal return of the fixed-interest bond investor. The equity investor receives no such guarantee. The equity investor takes more risk than the bond investor and therefore is entitled to expect a higher return. This reward for taking higher risk is known as the Equity Risk Premium (ERP). Long-term equity returns, in nominal terms, are made up of the yield on fixed-interest bonds plus the Equity Risk Premium.

An examination of long-term bond and equity returns shows that over the long run the equity investor does indeed receive an Equity Risk Premium. Of course, if he did not then investors would no longer take equity risk and the capitalist system would collapse.

Table 15.14 The Equity Risk Premium: Long Term, % p.a.

	Long Term	1960–2010
US	4.3*	2.6
UK	3.9**	2.9
		(Source: Barclays Capital)

* 85 years
** 111 years

Table 15.14 above indicates a reasonably consistent ERP across the markets over the long run. However, over shorter-run, ten-year periods the ERP has displayed dramatic volatility.

Table 15.15 The Equity Risk Premium: Shorter Term, % p.a.

	1950s	1960s	1970s	1980s	1990s	2000s
US	18.4	6.9	0.7	4.0	8.9	(3.4)
UK	16.1	6.3	1.8	8.7	2.4	(1.8)
					(Source: Barclays Capital)	

In the unusual conditions of recent years of strong bond markets but with equities enduring two bear markets in the 2000s, the ERP has been heavily negative in these important markets.

Table 15.16 Equity Risk Premium: 25 Years to End-2009, % p.a.

	1984–2009	Long Term
US	1.1	4.3*
UK	1.1	3.9**
		(Source: Barclays Capital)

* 85 years
** 111 years

These negative rewards for equity risk taking may be partly explained as a reaction to the very handsome excess returns enjoyed by equity investors in the 1980s and 1990s and may be portrayed as part of the process of reversion to mean. However, the violence of the reaction has resulted in a significant overshoot on the downside, with the results that:

i)   Over the twenty-five years to end-2009 the ERP was well below the long-term historical average.

ii)   Over the fifteen years to end-2009 the ERP was negative.

Table 15.17 Equity Risk Premium: 15 Years to End-2009, % p.a.

	1994–2009	Long Term
US	(0.4)	4.3*
UK	(0.6)	3.9**
		(Source: Barclays Capital)
* 85 years		
** 111 years		

That equity investors have been underrewarded, or indeed penalised, for taking risk for such a sustained period underlines the unique conditions created by the severity of the 2000–2003 and 2007–2009 equity bear markets and the prolonged fall in bond yields.

Pessimists might consider these numbers to indicate a permanently lower level of equity risk premium (and therefore equity returns) going forward. The more optimistic, pointing to the violence of the recent undershoot, might expect a higher ERP in the short to medium term as the pendulum swings back.

The usefulness of the ERP in facilitating forecasts of equity returns is thus quite constrained. Reversion to mean points to a premium of perhaps 4%. The sobering impact of the more recent periods argues for a lower number, perhaps 3% to $3^{1}/_{2}$%, say $3^{1}/_{4}$%. Applying these outcomes to end-2010 bond yields points to long-term equity returns as follows:

Table 15.18 Projected Long-Term Equity Returns, % p.a.

	Bond Yield	ERP	Expected Equity Market Return
US	4.00	3.00–3.50	7.00–7.50
UK	4.16	3.00–3.50	7.16–7.66

By deducting our earlier calculation for 'Forecast' Inflation from these returns we get a picture of how projected long-term equity returns at end-2010 stack up against the long-term history.

Table 15.19 Projected Real Returns from Equities, % p.a.

	Nominal Return	Forecast Inflation	Real Return	Historical Return
US	7.00–7.50	2.8	4.20–4.70	6.6*
UK	7.16–7.66	3.3	3.86–4.36	5.0**

(Source: Barclays Capital)

* 84 years
** 110 years

Projected long-term equity returns on this basis compare relatively poorly with the long-term historical experience.

Whatever the constraints around using the ERP for forecasting long-term returns, the volatility exhibited over shorter-run periods makes it quite unsuitable for forecasting short-term outcomes.

An alternative approach to the calculation of equity market returns is to assume that, in the long run, the equity investor's return is comprised of the opening dividend yield on his investment together with the growth in that dividend over the long term. For a market as a whole, dividend growth may be assumed to be made up of expected inflation and real growth in the economy (i.e. that profits and dividends will grow in line with nominal growth in the economy).

Table 15.20 Projected Equity Returns, % p.a.

	US	UK
Opening Dividend Yield	2.4	3.2
Forecast Inflation	2.8	3.3
Forecast Growth	2.0	2.0
Projected Return		
– Nominal	7.2	8.5
– Real	4.4	5.2

'Forecast inflation' is the forecast for inflation derived earlier by subtracting real yields on index-linked bonds from nominal fixed-interest yields. 'Forecast growth' is based on assumed long-term growth trends in the two

economies. The trend number assumed compares to 2000–2009 experience
as follows:

Table 15.21 Assumed Trend Growth, % p.a.

	Trend Growth	2000–2009	2000–2004
US	2.0	1.8	2.4
UK	2.0	1.7	2.9

Growth rates for the period from 2000 to 2009 were heavily impacted by the
severity of the 2008/9 recession. Trend growth is forecast to be relatively
sluggish.

Equity returns projected on this 'dividend plus dividend growth' basis
compare with those generated earlier using the Equity Risk Premium, and
with long-term historical returns, as follows. The comparison is based on
real returns; 'forecast inflation' as calculated earlier is excluded.

Table 15.22 Real Returns on Equities, % p.a.

	Projected ERP Basis	Projected Dividend Basis	Historical Returns 1959–2009	Long Term
US	4.20–4.70	4.4	5.5	6.6*
UK	3.86–4.36	5.2	5.2	5.0**

(Source: Barclays Capital)

* 84 years
** 110 years

Many observers agree that prospective equity returns are unlikely to match
the exceptional levels generated over the period 1980 to 1999. These returns
are clearly a significant influence on the out-turn for the period 1959 to
2009. This latter period also included, however, the very difficult decade of
the 1970s. Current market levels indicate that prospective returns for equities
will be lower than those generated in the fifty years to 2009.

Taking a point roughly between the midpoint of the ERP range, the
dividend-based return and the long-term historical return gives the following
expectation for prospective long-term equity returns:

Table 15.23 Projected Real Equity Returns, % p.a.

US	5.2
UK	4.8

At end-2010, the markets appear to be telling us to expect low returns relative to history, with perhaps the US experience likely to be most disappointing when compared to the long-term historical number.

Property

As discussed in Chapter 13, equities and property share common drivers in growth and inflation. Over the long run, therefore, property and equity returns might be expected to be broadly similar. They will diverge over short-run periods, as they are influenced by developments specific to each asset class.

Unfortunately, reliable long-term property returns are not as readily available as those for the other investment assets. Returns are available for Ireland back to 1970, based on the Jones Long Wootton Irish Property Index for 1971, returns from the Irish Pension Fund Property Unit Trust from 1971 to 1982 inclusive and from the Investment Property Databank (IPD) thereafter. IPD have calculated returns on UK property from 1971.

Over the forty-year period to end-2009, real returns on property compare to real returns on equities in Ireland as follows:

Table 15.24 Real Returns: Ireland, % p.a.

	Irish Property	Irish Equities
1970–1979	(2.6)	0.5
1980–1989	1.5	14.0
1990–1999	12.5	11.8
2000–2009	0.9	(5.8)
40 years to end-2009	2.9	4.8

(Source: Property as above; © 2005 E. Dimson, P. Marsh, M. Staunton; Authors)

Over the full forty-year period, Irish equities have significantly outperformed Irish property. Much of this outperformance is attributable to the dramatically better out-turn for equities from 1980 to 1989, when despite a relatively poor background for economic growth Irish equities performed dramatically well, generating real returns of 14.0% per annum. As discussed earlier, the Irish investment assets benefited from falling inflation and interest rates in the 1980s. An important feature of the Irish equity market in the period was sustained activity in overseas investment and acquisitions by the leading Irish companies. This had the effect not only of reducing exposure to the difficult Irish economy, but of attracting inflows of institutional monies as the domestic institutions, constrained by stringent exchange controls, built their overseas exposure via purchases of Irish equities. Meanwhile, property returns were subdued at 1.5% per annum in real terms, despite the benefits of lower interest rates. Here, a crisis in the public finances caused the Irish government, the largest occupier of office space, to effectively withdraw from new lettings for a period.

The 1990s saw both property and equities perform extremely well and broadly in line with real returns of 12.5% and 11.8% respectively.

The decade to end-2009 saw low property returns but these were still well ahead of equity returns, which suffered from the implosion of the technology bubble in 2000–2003 and the collapse of 2008. However, post-2009 Irish property fund values continued to fall sharply and even into 2011 the Irish property market remained mired in a deep bear market.

The outcome over the full forty-year period clearly illustrates the importance of factors that are specific to one asset or the other.

Interestingly, real returns on UK property and equities, while extremely divergent on a decade-by-decade basis, are much more aligned than in Ireland over the thirty-nine-year period for which returns are available.

Table 15.25 Real Returns: UK, % p.a.

	UK Property	UK Equities
1971–1980	2.3	(5.0)
1981–1990	5.0	11.7
1991–2000	6.1	12.1
2001–2009	2.8	(0.1)
39 Years to end-2009	4.0	5.9

(Source: UBS; Authors)

In forecasting long-term property returns the obvious reference point is the forecast for equity returns. In terms of volatility, property is less volatile and therefore less risky than equities. Property returns might be expected, therefore, to be lower than those available from equities. However, property's lower volatility is at least partly attributable to its valuation basis, whereas equities employ a market-based pricing mechanism. It is arguable that property's illiquidity makes it a riskier asset than equities.

On balance, despite the divergent returns generated in Ireland by property and equities over the forty years for which figures are available, but encouraged by the more even outcome in the UK, prospective long-term property returns in line with those calculated earlier for equities are assumed.

Cash

Cash is normally regarded by the investor as a temporary home for monies awaiting investment. However, there is a phase in each investment cycle when cash becomes an important investment asset in its own right. When the prices of the other assets are falling, cash cushions the fund against the full impact of market weakness and also provides the wherewithal to purchase assets at lower prices after the fall.

Long-term returns from cash are unpredictable. Unlike bonds, it is not possible to lock into fixed, long-term returns. Cash returns fluctuate with economic activity, with inflation and with changing monetary policy.

Long-run cash returns in real terms emerge at 0.7%p.a. for the period 1900 to 2004, and at 1.2% p.a. for the period 1950 to 2004. As Table 15.2 shows, cash returns ranged from a negative 3.1% p.a. in the period 1970–1979 to a positive 5.4% p.a. in the period 1990–1999.

Levels of interest rates in 2010, given our 'forecast inflation' numbers calculated earlier, would generate long-term real returns as follows if nominal money-market rates remained constant:

Table 15.26 Real Returns on Cash, % p.a.

	3 Month Money*	Forecast Inflation	Real Return
US	0.3	2.8	(2.5)
UK	0.7	3.3	(2.6)

* rates in November 2010

Nominal money market rates will not remain constant, of course; therefore these numbers cannot be regarded as a reliable guide to prospective real returns on cash. In the absence of any reliable guide from the market, we revert to considering long-term, historical real returns:

Table 15.27 Historical Real Returns from Cash, % p.a.

	2000–2009	1990–2009	Long Term
US	0.2	1.0	0.6*
UK	1.8	3.1	1.0**
Ireland	0.1	6.2	N/A

(Source: Barclays Capital)

* 84 years
** 110 years

A prospective real return on cash of the order of 1% per annum would appear to strike a reasonable balance between the historical long-term outcome and the disparate returns of the more recent periods.

PROJECTED RETURNS

Pulling together the projections outlined above produces the matrix of projected long-term real returns shown in Table 15.28.

Table 15.28 Real Returns from Investment Assets, % p.a.

	Bonds		Equities		Property	Cash	
	Proj.	Hist.	Proj.	Hist.	Proj.	Proj.	Hist.
US	1.5	1.9	5.5	6.6	5.5	1.0	1.0
UK	1.4	1.3	5.5	5.4	5.5	1.0	1.0
Germany	1.3	(1.9)	4.5	2.9	4.5	1.0	(0.4)
Ireland	1.3	1.1	5.6	4.7	5.6	1.0	0.7

The precise projections here are relatively unimportant, given the broad assumptions employed in their calculation. What is important is the general level of long-term returns they indicate going forward. Prospective bond returns will be lower than the long-term norm, and therefore well below the relatively high returns seen in the post-war period and particularly since the 1980s. Equity returns also will be lower than the long-term experience, with US equity returns likely to be well below the long-term historical numbers. Investment returns going forward are likely to be lower than experienced over most of the post-World War II period.

Portfolio Returns

By applying expected representative return numbers to the asset mixes of various categories of managed funds, an overview may be formed of the likely returns available to investors in diversified managed funds:

Table 15.29 Projected Real Returns from Managed Funds, % p.a.

	Cautious			Balanced			Aggressive		
	Mix	Return	Portfolio Return	Mix	Return	Portfolio Return	Mix	Return	Portfolio Return
Bonds	30	1.4	0.42	16	1.4	0.22	6	1.4	0.08
Equities	14	5.4	0.76	73	5.4	3.94	88	5.4	4.75
Property	11	5.4	0.59	8	5.4	0.43	3	5.4	0.16
Cash	45	1.0	0.45	3	1.0	0.03	3	1.0	0.03
			2.22			4.62			4.92

Projected real returns range from 2.0% p.a. for the Cautious Managed Fund, through 4.0% p.a. for the Balanced Managed Fund, to 4.36% p.a. for the Aggressive Managed Fund at the high-risk end of the spectrum.

However, there is some controversy attaching to the exposure to real assets, and particularly to equities, in the asset mixes of the balanced and aggressive managed funds. There is a concern that the appetite for risk of the typical retail Irish investor in managed funds is overstated by equity exposures of 73% and 84% for the balanced and aggressive managed funds, respectively.

However, to the extent that equity contents are reined back, expected returns fall accordingly.

Similar concerns surround the equity exposures of Irish pension funds generally. Here, too, the concern is that high equity exposures overstate the appetite of trustees for the downside risk associated with equity investment, as seen so vividly during the period 2000 to 2003 and again in 2007 to 2009.

In response to these concerns a number of Irish investment institutions have launched new ranges of truly balanced and more broadly diversified funds in recent years. Typically, these new funds are notably less biased to equities and carry meaningful exposure to alternative assets. This new generation of funds is designed to deliver to investors a smoother, less volatile investment journey without foregoing much of the expected long-term returns.

This initiative, though belated in our view, is to be welcomed. Unfortunately, as relatively new funds, the total monies invested in them to date is still quite modest. The previous generation of aggressive and balanced managed funds, in which clients are heavily invested, continue to exhibit an extremely strong bias to equities. We continue to see a strategic mismatch between these equity exposures and the risk appetite of the typical Irish investor. We find it surprising that, despite two severe equity bear markets in the 2000s, the Irish investment institutions have not been more innovative in addressing the issue for their existing clients.

CONCLUDING COMMENTS

The credit crisis and its aftermath were discussed in Chapter 13 and again earlier in this chapter. The devastation caused by the crisis, across virtually the full spectrum of investment assets, has shaken investment market participants. This is especially true in Ireland, where a particularly virulent iteration of the crisis, exacerbated by domestic mismanagement, has undermined the economy and government finances, brought the banking system to collapse and triggered dramatic falls in government bonds and equity and property markets.

The investment world, in Ireland and abroad, finds itself obliged to revisit and question many of its cherished long-standing beliefs. The following list cannot be regarded as exhaustive.

- Can we really regard as efficient markets that exhibit such dramatic short-term volatility?
- Do market returns really adopt the shape of normal distributions given the regularity with which extreme events recur?
- If they do not, why do we place such weight and balance on volatility as a measure of risk?
- Is sovereign debt risk-free? Indeed, we now know it is not. What then is the risk-free rate, the key building block of all asset valuations?
- Will equity markets generate an equity risk premium? Clearly, as we showed earlier in this chapter, they have done so in the very long term. However, the equity risk premium has been, at best, well below expectations or, at worst, negative in many major markets over periods extending now to over forty years. Given this persistence of underperformance, what grounds are there for the belief that the ERP will reassert itself in the future?
- Confidence in counterparties (whether governments, banks, insurance companies, corporates or intermediaries) has been shaken. The credit-rating agencies have been shown to be unreliable and perhaps conflicted. The task of due diligence falls on the investor. How can the individual investor cope with this?
- The liquidity of markets cannot be taken as read. In the post-Lehman period liquidity contracted in many markets and evaporated altogether in some. The Irish property market was still dysfunctional a full two years after Lehman's collapse. What reliance can the investor place on asset liquidity at times of stress? What does this imply for the investor's ongoing exposure to truly liquid assets?
- Finally, why do we focus so heavily on historical correlations between assets when what is critical is how these correlations act at times of stress? We saw in 2008 how, under stress, expected correlations did not exhibit themselves and many assets fell sharply along with equities.

Clearly, the credit crisis and, in particular, the catastrophe of 2008 will generate much argument and debate in the investment world in the years ahead.

For the moment, we believe, the solid ground is in the 'known knowns' that we set out earlier in this chapter. Key among these are efficient diversification and 'know your asset'. Your asset must do 'what it says on the tin' in normal times and also, most importantly, at times of stress.

The particular fascination of the investment markets is that they are always evolving and constantly changing. At times the pace of change will confound and perplex even those rare beings who consider themselves experts. We urge readers to beware the advice of experts. We hope this book will help readers to think for themselves.

SUMMARY

- The high-inflation 1970s proved to be an especially traumatic decade for investors, as inflation surged following two oil shocks and inappropriate government responses, both in Ireland and in our main trading partners.
- Equity performance in the 1980s was particularly noteworthy, as it was achieved against a relatively poor growth background.
- The combination of a favourable international background and a transformed domestic economy permitted the Irish financial assets to generate returns in the 1990s that compared with the very best of those generated by our major trading partners.
- The returns generated by Irish equities were significantly lower during 2000 to 2009 than those prevailing in the halcyon decade of the 1990s.
- Property was outstandingly the investment asset of choice in Ireland during 2000 to 2007.
- The equity investor takes more risk than the bond investor and therefore is entitled to expect a higher return, which is known as the Equity Risk Premium (ERP).
- Many observers agree that prospective equity returns are unlikely to match the exceptional levels generated over the period 1980–2007.

Glossary

Active Manager   An investment manager who seeks to add value (outperform) over benchmark or index returns.

Active Risk   The incremental risk an active manager will accept in the effort to add value.

Alternative Investments   Non-'mainstream' assets, i.e. anything other than equities, bonds or cash (or sometimes property), for example, hedge funds, private equity (venture capital), commodities.

Asset Allocation   The split of a fund over the various asset types (classes): bonds, equities, property, cash, alternatives.

Balanced Fund   A fund invested (spread) over the various asset types.

Balanced Manager   An investment manager who manages balanced funds.

Bell Curve   A normal distribution, representing the chances of different outcomes, is shown in graphical form by a bell-shaped curve.

Benchmark   The ideal portfolio mix, which if maintained over the life of the fund, is expected to deliver the required risk and return characteristics.

Benchmark Risk   The risk or volatility inherent in the benchmark, i.e. the extent that benchmark returns will vary around the expected returns.

Beta   The sensitivity of the returns of an asset or a portfolio to a benchmark (for example, an index).

Consensus Approach   The adoption of a benchmark designed to be the average asset allocation of the manager's competitors (peer group).

Core/Satellite   Normally, an asset allocation strategy where the core, or major part, is passively invested and the remainder is managed in smaller active segments or satellites.

Corporate Activity   Corporate events such as acquisitions, fundraising, share buy-backs. These will cause a passive manager to rebalance the portfolio.

Correlation   The extent to which the prices of two assets tend to move (rise and fall) together in a straight line.

Coupon   The regular (usually fixed) recurring payments on a bond.

Credit Risk   Exposure to potential loss due to counterparty default (for example, Russian default on bond payments in 1998) or credit downgrades.

Derivative   A financial instrument, for example, future, option, whose payoff depends on (derives from) the value of another (underlying) security or instrument.

Dividend   The annual (or more frequent) distribution paid by a company out of its profits to its shareholders. Normally expressed in cents per share.

Dividend Yield   Annual dividend per share divided by the price per share.

Earnings Per Share Annual profits attributable to shareholders divided by the number of shares in issue.

Earnings Yield The earnings per share divided by the price per share.

Efficient Frontier A curve showing the highest average reward obtainable for each level of risk.

Efficient Portfolios Portfolios that produce the highest expected return for any given level of risk, or the lowest level of risk for any expected return.

Equity Risk Premium The excess return over bond returns expected from equities because of their higher risk.

Excess Return Return relative to the risk-free return. If an asset return is 10% and the risk-free return is 4%, excess return is 6%.

Fixed Income Bonds and related securities, which pay a fixed, annual (or more frequent) interest rate (coupon) and offer full repayment of principal on redemption. The interest can be zero.

Future An agreement to receive/deliver a commodity, instrument or security at a specified delivery date at an agreed price.

Growth Investment An investment style that attempts to generate added value by investing in stocks displaying above average growth.

Hedge An instrument or strategy designed to protect against risk by opening an exposure to a risk factor opposite to another such exposure.

Hedge Fund An investment fund with a high degree of investment flexibility, often with high financial gearing (leverage), and which focuses on a particular source or sources of excess return.

Hurdle Rate A target rate of return, which expected returns must, at a minimum, match or exceed.

Information Ratio The ratio of the incremental return (over benchmark return) generated by an investment manager to tracking error, i.e. the incremental risk associated with investments that are different from the benchmark.

Indexation Managing a portfolio to match the performance of a stock market or other index.

Index-Linked Bonds Bonds whose annual (or more frequent) interest payments and final repayment of capital are linked to a rate of inflation.

Investment Institution An investor, such as a pension fund, insurance company or investment management house.

Investment Mandate The working brief given by the client to an investment manager setting out investment discretion, constraints, expected added value and expected risk.

Investment Philosophy The core beliefs that underline an institution's approach to investment – where value lies in markets and how this translates into an ability to generate optimal returns.

Investment Process The consistent operating methodology that enables an active manager to carry out investment in a repeatable fashion.

Liquidity The marketability of an asset, i.e. the extent to which it can be bought and sold quickly and cheaply.

Mainstream Assets   The conventional asset classes: bonds, equities, property and cash.

Market Risk   The exposure to loss due to potential market moves.

Maturity   The time at which the principal (capital value) of a bond is repaid.

Modern Portfolio Theory   The body of theories that support the scientific approach to investment management.

Momentum Investment   An investment style that attempts to add value over benchmark returns by investing in stocks that have exhibited rising trends.

Monetary Assets   Assets denominated in financial nominal terms (for example, bonds, cash).

Normal Distribution   A bell-shaped curve that represents the probabilities of different outcomes, the most probable being at or close to the mean, and the least probable being most different from the mean.

Operational Risk   Risk arising out of the ongoing activities of an investment business, for example, regulatory risk, technological risk, risk of human error or fraud.

Optimiser   Software that generates an efficient frontier, given particular assumptions for inputs.

Option   The right to buy/sell a specified quantity of a commodity, instrument or security at a fixed price up to or on a specified date.

Passive Manager   A manager who seeks to match index or benchmark performance as closely as possible.

Performance Quartiles   A segregation of investment managers by performance into four separate quarters from best to worst.

Pooled Vehicle   A collective investment instrument in which funds belonging to many investors are gathered together and managed as a single fund.

Price Earnings Ratio   Price per share divided by earnings per share.

RFP   Request for Proposal. The questionnaire to be completed by investment managers when they pitch for the business of a prospective client.

Real Assets   Assets with linkage to economic performance, thereby capable of providing protection against unanticipated inflation (for example, equities, property).

Real Return   Investment return expressed in terms of purchasing power, i.e. nominal returns adjusted for inflation.

Redemption Yield   The rate of return on a bond if held to maturity with re-investment of all interest payments at the same rate.

Residual Risk   That part of the risk (variability) of a security's return that is not given by the security's correlation with the market (beta) and which, therefore, can be diversified. Also called non-systematic risk, company-specific risk, non-market risk and security-related risk.

Risk   Often taken to mean variability of returns as measured by standard deviation, but also consists of any source of variability of returns – especially downside – or of security, and any failure to meet a return, security target or expectation.

Risk Budget   The allocation of risk or tracking error across asset classes or across managers of different portions of a portfolio.

Risk-Free Rate (Of Return)   The return achievable with absolute certainty in a given period, for example, the return on short-dated US Treasury Bills (for a dollar investor).

Risk Premium   The additional expected return required from an asset to compensate for its risk.

Running Yield   For a bond, the annual interest rate (coupon) divided by price.

Sharpe Ratio   The ratio of annualised excess returns to total risk (standard deviation).

Specialist Manager   An investment manager restricted by his mandate to a specific asset class, style, market, sector or region.

Specific Return   That part of a security's excess return that is not explained by or correlated with the market return.

Specific Risk   Same as residual risk.

Standard Deviation   A measure of the dispersion of a set of data from its mean. The square root of the variance.

Strategic Asset Allocation   The ideal long-term portfolio mix, which will deliver required return and risk and which is embedded in the benchmark.

Tactical Asset Allocation   The adoption of an asset allocation different from the benchmark in order to enhance return.

Total Return   Income on an asset plus capital appreciation.

Tracking Error   The incremental risk of a portfolio arising from the differences between the portfolio and the benchmark. It is incurred by an active manager in the expectation of generating added value.

Value at Risk   A probabilistic estimate of the amount of loss a portfolio is likely to deliver with a given frequency.

Value Investment   An investment style that attempts to add value over benchmark returns by investing in securities with sub-normal valuation.

Volatility   A measure of risk: the annualised standard deviation of return.

Yield   See dividend yield, earnings yield, running yield and redemption yield.

Yield Curve   A graph showing the time to maturity and redemption yields of an array of bonds.

Zero-Coupon Bond   A bond with no annual coupon (interest payments).

Index